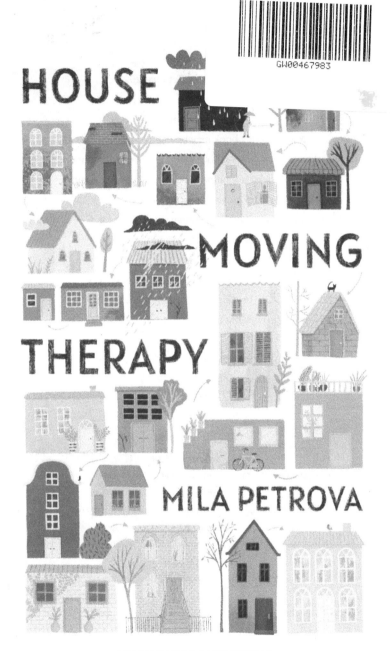

HOUSE MOVING THERAPY

MILA PETROVA

KNOWMORE PUBLISHING
Cornwall, UK

FIRST EDITION
A CIP catalogue record for this book
is available from the British Library.

ISBN paper book: 978-1-7391377-5-5
ISBN e-book: 978-1-7391377-7-9

DEVELOPMENTAL EDITING
Ameesha Green, ameesha@thebookshelf.ltd, *thebookshelf.ltd*

COPY EDITING
Jessica Powers, jlpowers@evaporites.com, *jlpowers.net*

COVER DESIGN
Karen Vermeulen, hello@karenvermeulen.com, *karenvermeulen.com*

DESIGN OF THE INTERIORS
Kathy McInnis, kathy@ivyleafdesigns.net

PROOFREADING
Karen Hamilton, info@karen-hamilton.co.uk, *karen-hamilton.co.uk*

AUTHOR PHOTO
Thom Axon, thomaxon@gmail.com, *thomaxon.com*

"All sickness is home sickness"
DIANNE M. CONNELLY

To Arthur—not quite the name,
but you'll know it's you!
Thank you for the times your arms
have been my home and for the challenge
to find a home that stands even at skyfall.

HOUSE MOVING THERAPY

MILA PETROVA

2022

TABLE OF CONTENTS

— x —

I am a book which loves moving houses.
If you've read me, please pass me on.
If you've truly read me, you won't need me.
You'll live me.

INTRODUCTION

LIFE ON THE FLOOR

Have you had your life crash and spill all over the floor, fragments leaking dark red blood and thick black terror, a small puddle for a start but spreading,

spreading
SPREADING?
What is it that got wrecked, disfigured, ripped apart, burnt
to the ground?
LOVE? Family? Home?
The humming, sweet routines of the life you've long
known?
Your vision? Mission? Job?
Health? The time you (vaguely) counted to have left?
MEANING? Purpose?
Truth? TRUST? The stability of the earth's crust?
The certain answers to the WHO ARE YOU?, what you can and
shall and would or would never ever do?

How badly did you break?

Are you whole again, or for the first time ever? The extraordinary gift of some descents into darkness, a gift claimed by so few, yet always there if you refuse to leave without it but refuse to dwell in darkness too? Or, when you undress and touch the seams of truth, are you, rather, superglued?

Have you ever had your life dumped on the floor, this time literally? Drawers pulled out, wardrobe doors flung open
    piles of clothes
    misshapen hangers
    slanting books
    scattered papers
    bike pump
    hammer
    smiling sheep
    sponges
    brushes
    cream clean Cif
    tangled cables
    seaside mug
    wrapping paper
    filthy rug –
    all tripping, slipping hazards,
    calling out to you,
    calendar declaring your move-out day is tomorrow,
    realism demanding it be a week away?
Have you ever felt total disbelief at the amount of possessions you've accumulated?

Started sorting from one pile or cupboard only to decide it's too difficult or undefinable, picked the next, then next, then next, until you returned to the first?

Have you spoken to yourself coolly, rationally that it will all be fine; motivationally, passionately that you wield magic powers and expansive time, while pushing, pushing, pushing back the flood of panic rising in the holes between the words?

Have you made dozens of donation and recycling trips, yet still tied a tight knot around a black bin bag of perfectly usable things?

What did you do with the flowerpots?

The sheets you slept in on your last night?

Oh, you didn't sleep? You thought you'd be finished by 4 p.m., then midnight, then 3 a.m., then you met the end at sunrise, mopping floors, red capillaries refusing to return home to the white sclera, bed never slept in one last time, a feeling strangely resembling that of separating from a lover without having made love one last time?

I hope you still noticed that that was the most beautiful sunrise you've seen in this house. I hope your coffee machine or kettle was not packed, or belonged to the house, and you could have a farewell drink. I hope you laughed (hysterically?) that never-ending night and blazing morning, even if you cried too.

Whether you've had your life on the floor one way or the other, or both, welcome.

DOES THIS BOOK BELONG TO YOUR LIBRARY?

This is a book about using the need to sort through physical baggage so as to shift emotional baggage. It is about tolerating material and psychological mess for longer than comfortable so as to move on feeling lighter. It digs deep into my possessions and soul in the hope of showing you new ways to dig deep into yours.

It's a book for those who want to leave with the rucksack on their back only or need a truck for their possessions. I write of both. I've tried both.

It's a book about house moves which are responsible to the environment, objects and the makers of objects; considerate of the less fortunate; adventurous and cost-efficient. It is about trips to charity shops, recycling facilities and outside of your comfort zone. It is about the lives and happiness of things, our planet and the less well-off. Those make house moving far more difficult than throwing away everything you no longer need. Yet there is nothing easier than living in accordance with your values.

It's a book about house moves which light up the inner power-house of energy. That don't tire you. That let you sleep all you want to sleep and keep your holidays for holidays.

It's a book which will help you, at moving in, open boxes as if you were decades younger, inner child rummaging through his or her treasures. "Yeeeeey, I've been waiting for you to turn up!" "I'd forgotten I had you!"

It is a book about house moves which you begin to miss.

It will give you a lot. It will ask for a lot.

It will ask you to feel what you feel and think what you think about the objects you own. Ideally, every single one of them. This takes time. Focus. Honesty. Sometimes it hurts.

It will ask you to listen to me and completely ignore me, no matter how mad or persuasive I sound. My possessions, life and inner chaos may be both unrecognisably similar to and very different from yours. It takes mental flexibility, being attuned to yourself and courage to know what's needed.

It will deprive you of the drama and sympathy around "I'm

moving house, you know how it is!" No, I don't. I no longer know how stressful, painful, time-devouring, exhausting, every-room-big-bang-exploding it is. I used to. I turned it on its head. I want to show you my ways so that you can invent yours.

If this is a book that sounds right for you, please make yourself at home. I would love you to read it. If not, thank you for stopping over. Wind in your sails too for your next journey home.

TWENTY-ONE (OR THIRTY-THREE) TIMES, NINETEEN YEARS AND COUNTING

I've moved between twenty-one and thirty-three times in the past nineteen years. Twenty-one is for 'proper' moves, in which I've packed my life in one place and took it over to another, not expecting to return and make home again in the former and expecting to stay for the foreseeable future in the latter. Thirty-three includes moves out of places where I intended to stay and did stay only temporarily. I was still looking for my 'permanent' home, waiting for it to be vacated, or hanging in space while my future took a clearer shape. On some of those occasions, I was also 'home home'. 'Home home'—I use the phrase often—is the flat where I grew up, left at nineteen, where my mum still lives and where I still 'return'.

I don't include the times I've moved until I came to England, my most radical house move of all. Most of the decisions and tasks in those times weren't mine. I was either moved by my parents (only twice actually, aged four and five) or had the broader family and family friends holding my hand (such as an uncle 'appearing' in his car when I was moving out of the student residences). If I count that, I will have moved somewhere between twenty-eight and forty times. House moving statistics, like all statistics, is fickle. It shifts up and down depending on one's assumptions and definitions.

I've moved in and out of four countries and nineteen towns, cities, villages and middle-of-nowheres. The biggest city I've lived in is London. The smallest place is either a tiny village at the foot of Sierra Nevada in Spain or Dawlish Warren on the coast of Devon, England.

The most impressive accommodation I've rented was an eighteen-room manor house, first built in the seventeenth century, still having its original front door and Dutch tiles decoration. I was taking wrong turns in it for weeks. As my only housemate was the owner's daughter, who had the family home to return to, I was often the sole Queen of the Palace. In my maid-like version, I've had a room which could hardly fit an ironing board in the space left by the bed, wardrobe, desk, chair and clothes dryer.

I've had sea views from my windows in three houses and from the street right up in another one. In one of the former, on a clear day you could see (or imagine seeing) Africa in the distance. I've lived in places overlooking a river, a mountain and a pond. But I've also had a room facing the neighbourhood rubbish bins. There are times in life when the very best you can afford, in the timeframe you've got to search for it, stinks.

I've lived by myself in eight of those places and with a boyfriend in one. The rest I've shared with thirty-seven housemates, with some significant margin for memory error (this is the count for a shared kitchen, it's twenty-nine for a shared bathroom). If you shudder at the thought of so many strangers, which all were originally, the norm in the times I'm not writing of was to have roommates. Including the ever-present boyfriends, the standard level of night-time occupancy was five persons in a three-by-three metres room. Living in shared spaces is a topic for another book. It's not mine to write.

I've lost, moved and created many homes. Until move No 16, I found it hard.

I've never wanted to move that much. My studies or work needed it. I've been quick to respond to a fluctuating budget, both in its ups and downs. I've moved for love. I've moved because of love lost. On several occasions, I sought more mental space somewhere far away and secluded. Occasionally, owners needed their properties earlier than I wished to leave. One way or another, I didn't start my house moving 'career' enthusiastically. I connect to things, places and people deeply, often slowly. It took me time to learn to leave with light suitcases. It took fifteen years longer to learn to leave with a light heart.

Most of my house moves are from the times when I was a student or a young academic recovering from a PhD. This meant on a minimal budget.

I've never had a car, so they had to be light (though I've rented vans too). They grew to be aware. When you carry all your possessions on your back, you are CERTAIN something is worth keeping.

Crucially, they were masterpieces in how not to need, not to ask for, and not to accept any help. My greatest fear in life used to be being a burden.

I hope that none of the above constraints defines your move without an alternative. They no longer define mine, but this book will be extra useful if you are counting every penny, your legs and public services are your only means of transport, and you are a hardy mule who 'does it' herself or himself (hello, sister/ brother!).

Apart from having a career in moving, I have a career in

analysing. I'm an academic researcher in the health sciences. I have studied psychology, philosophy and literature. I demand rigorous evidence, water-tight argumentation and psychological plausibility. I also talk about death and dying more—and more bluntly—than most people, as much of my recent research has been in palliative and end of life care.

This is not an academic book though. There is no explicit theory in it. There is hardly any research evidence other than that of my own life. When I create an argument, it first needs to persuade the most ignorant, stupid, sceptical and disinterested fragments of me. As I have many ignorant, stupid, sceptical and disinterested fragments, my arguments are as simple as possible, but not simpler. I will still ask you to think hard. I will ask you to admit what you don't want to admit. It may be more of a hard nut than popcorn of a book.

My experience doesn't make me a house moving expert. It makes me a house moving expert, an absolute ninja in fact, in my own life. But since our lives, houses, possessions and attachments can be incredibly, even incomprehensibly, different, the direct advice I am willing to offer is minimal. You'll have to derive most of it yourself. Only then you'll know it will withstand the storms of your life and inner chaos like nothing I'll be able to teach you.

WHAT THIS BOOK IS NOT ABOUT

This book is not about rules. I won't be telling you that if you have not worn something for the last year, or if it belonged to your ex-boyfriend/ ex-girlfriend, or if it has a hole between the legs, you should throw it out (or donate, sell, etc.). I will not prescribe an order in which to pack your possessions. I will not tell you the rough or precise number of things to keep.

I do not ridicule such rules. They simplify decision making. There is clarity and sureness about them. But they don't work for me. I have to *feel* that something is good and right to do. This requires adding too much nuance, individual idiosyncrasy and complexity to any rule I could have come up with.

Instead, I tell you about the chaos of my possessions and soul and what I do about them. I share reference points, principles, arguments and examples of making decisions. These can be emotional, pragmatic, ethical, green, psychological, philosophical.... Sometimes they will match your needs, sometimes not. But even if they don't, they can serve as food for thought. I would be just as happy if your decisions are the exact opposite to mine as long as something I wrote helped you make them.

This is not a book about the sweetness of home either. That sweetness is, of course, the goal and the background. It trickles through. It doesn't flow.

There is pain, struggle, fear, tears, loneliness, sadness, loss, blood in this book apart from the safety, order, clarity, laugher, certainty, adventure, freedom, lightness....I believe the former are unavoidable in finding our true home. By now, I've found mine and am there often (though being home is an ever in-and-out and evolving experience). But it is still a book that is more about the rocky road than the blissful destination.

This is also not a book about every sort of possession I could think of. For instance, I don't have chapters about kids' 'things', gardening or music, while these may be defining of your life. In some cases, this is because they've not been part of my life yet, like kids or gardening. In other cases, it is because I've never moved the bulk of my collection, for instance of music—my violins, LPs, cassettes, CDs and the rest have remained home home.

Yet many of the ideas I share transcend possessions. You may find the solutions for your music in the books chapter, for instance. To help you with this, the table of contents points, for each chapter after the introductory ones, to its core physical chaos topic (the material possessions a chapter is about) and its core psychological chaos topic (the psychological mess it addresses and which, for you, may be associated with the same or other types of possessions).

This is also not a book which develops an argument or a story in a way that expects you to read 'everything' or in order. If a section begins to feel as having too much unnecessary detail and/or 'overthinking it', you might be better off moving to a different chapter. The experience most likely means that a particular type of possession doesn't matter to you; that it is something you have a healthy relationship with and you know why you have what you have; or if it is in the context of a type of psychological mess, that you've long outgrown or never been troubled by it. More rarely, resistance to detail may mean avoiding to face something painful or unpleasant, whether about the house moving work awaiting you or about yourself.

WHAT THIS BOOK IS ABOUT
WITHOUT BEING ABOUT IT

I sincerely hope to be able to help you with the practicalities of your move, but I don't care much if I do.

There are at least five other things I want to talk with you about while we ponder over moving houses.

The first is adventure in the everyday. It's so typical for a house move to become about stress, dust, chaos, clutter, boxes, dry hands, exhaustion....It is also so typical to seek adventure in extreme or daring ways – going on a safari, skydiving, volunteering in an orphanage in Nepal....Yet if you put your mind to it, you will find extraordinary amounts of exploration, creativity, ridiculousness, chance encounters, insight, awe, magic and so much more while moving house. Conjuring adventure in ordinary or frustrating days is pure alchemy. A house move can be your cauldron.

The second thing this book is about without being about it is the courage to show yourself. So many of our possessions, including the homes we choose to live in, hide us. They are faceless. They make us invisible. Or they are right in everybody's face while showing none of our truth. It takes courage to show that truth, both in its shadows and its light, including through what we own.

The third thing I often write about in the background is care with integrity. So many of us care deeply for the environment and the less fortunate and act on that care. We do it sincerely. We do it systematically. But we do it sincerely and systematically until it becomes inconvenient; until it crosses a certain threshold of 'our part' or 'reasonable'; until we must refuse to eat at the place where food is served in plastic containers; until we have to cycle uphill with glass bottles and empty tins clinking in our backpack; until we have to talk to the homeless with the dead left eye. House moves are extreme tests for how far we are walking the talk we are talking.

In the same stroke, they stretch our capacity for self-care. They show us if we care as wise light souls or self-torturing self-righteous martyrs. They distil our ability to balance care and self-care.

The fourth thing this book is about without being about it is freedom. It is not about the freedom of moving from one place to another, although this can be a grand way to feel free. It is about the freedom of thousands of social pressures, myths, clichés and straightforward lies around 'home'. When you've fought for your way of thinking about something as fundamental as 'home', it will be easier to do it about other big things where we are ruled, against our best interests and the longings of our soul, by social convention and 'normal life'.

But what I write the most about without writing directly about it is that which may help you feel less lonely, less anxious and less homeless in the gaping hole that sometimes opens when moving houses. I want you to feel less scared and inadequate because of the shit inside of you (and that's irrespective of whether you are moving it from house to house or sitting on it in the same house for years). I want you to know that no matter how extreme, stinking and deep running that shit is, it is never greater than the opportunities to contain it. It's the same as the mess in a house you are moving from—it may feel overwhelming and infinite, but there are always ways to sort and contain it.

There is always a house you can move into—a physical house of enough space or an emotional house of safety, love and wisdom— that can embrace, contain and transform all the mess you bring in.

If you haven't yet found it,

let's build it.

PART I
BEGINNINGS

Chapters 1 to 4 discuss **the reasons why house moving is the time-consuming, exhausting and soul-destroying experience** it typically is. These include:

- The sheer number of decisions involved and their cognitive load. We are almost **doomed to underestimate** how much we own (*Chapter 1*).
- Four types of **'microprojects'** that a house move presents us with (*Chapter 2*).
- The **subversive and energy-draining** emotions that get triggered while we are sorting through our possessions. Unexpectedly, these are rarely the deep, dramatic sentiments most of us fear (*Chapter 3*).
- The **defaults of principles and values** we approach house moving with, while we can tame the beast only if we switch on both our defaults and their opposites (*Chapter 4*).

Chapter 5 discusses **two things you can do early on, without lifting a finger,** to make your move radically easier.

Chapters 6 and *7* are about two experiences you can hardly avoid. You can, however, prepare for:

- The **pain of disconnecting** from yet another place, which wouldn't be that important or interesting if it weren't standing for numerous other forms of unprocessed pain (*Chapter 6*).
- **Proper cleaning**, which is a perfect example of how the likes of 'I'm used to', 'I always do' (cleaning, avoiding cleaning, paying somebody to clean for me) stop us from making a genuine choice *(Chapter 7)*.

Chapters 3 [illegible]

- [illegible] [illegible] [illegible] typically [illegible]
- The [illegible] involved and their [illegible] to make [illegible]
- [illegible] aspects that are [illegible] (Chapter 2).
- The [illegible] and [illegible] that [illegible] while we are [illegible] Usually [illegible] these are [illegible] and [illegible] (Chapter 3).
- The defaults of principles and values we [illegible] with, which can [illegible] the [illegible] and [illegible] (Chapter 4).

Chapter 5 [illegible] two things you can do [illegible] without lifting a finger, to make your move radically easier.

Chapters 6 and 7 are about two experiences you can hardly avoid. You can, however, prepare for:

- The pain of disconnecting from [illegible] another place which we [illegible] and [illegible] understand.
- [illegible] standing [illegible] numerous other [illegible] (Chapter 6).
- Proper cleaning, which is a perfect example of how the [illegible] of [illegible] always [illegible] [illegible] [illegible] making a [illegible] (Chapter 7).

CHAPTER 1

WHAT MAKES HOUSE MOVING DIFFICULT (1): AN EXPLOSION OF DECISIONS, OR HOW THE POSSESSIONS OF A TWO-BEDROOM FLAT CAN TAKE UP THE SEATS OF FORTY-SIX BOEINGS

There are between 7,198 and 16,698 items in my mum's two-bedroom, eighty-square-metre flat. (I counted her possessions rather than mine, as her household will give you a far more accurate idea of the battle awaiting you. I've fought mine twenty-one times.)

The lower limit of 7,000+ treats all objects in a set or all elements within a container as one thing. A set of six forks is one thing. A folder with seventy-six documents is another. The upper limit, verging on 17,000, assumes that most of my mum's possessions will need an individual decision. For instance, while the twelve plates of her purple earthenware set are identical, some are cracked and chipped. She may want to inspect each plate before taking it to her new house. The upper limit is still within sensible boundaries. I counted, for instance, packs of napkins and 'handfuls' of paperwork, not all napkins in a pack or individual documents.

CALL IN THE AIRLINE FLEET!

If my mum decides to move, her task will be somewhere in between. The more considerate she decides to be—of the environment, objects and the makers of objects; those less fortunate than her; her own past, etc.—the closer she will be to handling around 17,000 objects. If each of these takes a passenger's seat, you will need a fleet of forty-six Boeing 747 planes. A responsible house mover will check in all the passengers with the right credentials and make arrangements for the onwards journey of all others.

If you think this doesn't apply to you because you are not a hoarder, my mum is not one either. Or, rather, she is a hoarder in the selective way most of us are—there are only some types of things we cannot let go of. On a continuum of 'bare' to 'cluttered', her flat leans strongly towards 'bare'. The three exceptions are the laundry room, which is also my brother's tool shed (still small, he has several); the clothes room; and, temporarily, the living room floor, where thirty-nine boxes of books await the next stage of a library clear-out. Most cupboards and drawers in the flat have empty spaces. I would say that no more than 10% are stuffed (no official data collected though).

Whether we know we have 'a lot' or believe 'it's not that much' (since 'it's been just six months', 'it's only a room', 'I decluttered in spring'), we are almost doomed to underestimation. Too many objects of daily life disappear from acute awareness. They become part of the flow of numerous (semi-)automatic activities. The elements of these fuse into chunky wholes in our thoughts and perceptions. Then, on the day before we leave, we finally SEE the pillows under the duvet cover and 'oh, no, please, no!' they TOO are too big to carry, too mundane to sell, generally not accepted in charity containers, and don't fit in any of the clean bags we've got left. We remember it's not only the damp clothes we need to find space for in our luggage, but the drying rack that holds them too.

We also tend to focus on items which pose logistical challenges. We are aware of the task presented by the heavy oak table. The sofa that's too big for the door. The forty-two pairs of shoes. Yet anything which was not in when we first came, even if as immaterial as four unused stamps from our trip to the U.S., a lonely sock or our faithful but unremarkable purple lunch box, calls for a decision or a set of decisions.

FOUR CORNERSTONE DECISIONS

7,198 to 16,698 possessions mean A LOT of DECISIONS. Moreover, most of those decisions will have layers.

The primary decision in a house move is **I want to keep or I don't want to keep (*Decision A*).**

This may be a *split-second decision* whereby the inner calculator spits out the result of:

like it, even love it /	don't like it, even hate it
use it lots /	haven't touched it for years
in good order /	it last smelled of burnt motor
am attached to it /	don't have much of an attitude to it
good to have it /	with or without it, won't notice
owning it is easy /	maintaining it is such a pain

and any other criteria we've used, unconsciously or half-consciously, in our judgement around 'worth keeping'.

Often enough, however, our decisions are not automatic, quick and simple. Our brain chokes.

It chokes on boundary cases. We often hit them when our (semi-)conscious criteria and values come up with conflicting answers.

For instance, I am attached to our thirty-five-year-old aluminium bread plate and use it daily when I am home home. But it looks like a concentration camp exhibit—grey, bent, scratched; joyless, yet comfortingly inert and reliable. Importantly, I am 'attached' to it is not the same as I 'love' it. I can't decide if I love it but I'll find it hard to separate from it. Moreover, if I decide to throw it away, it's possible that my mum or brother will 'save' it from the recycling bag and raise hell that I'm throwing out perfectly usable things again. I don't want to bypass domestic democracy. I don't want to argue. Yet I may not need to. It's just as likely that they are grateful I've made a decision they didn't want to make.

Apart from *thinking* about boundary cases, we may need *to do* things to inform our thinking. We try on a pair of trousers. We leaf through a book we can't remember reading. We treat, once again, the stubborn muddy raindrops on the pale pink rucksack.

Other people may need to be involved too. You go to the jewellery shop to have a stone tested. You ask your boyfriend for his opinion of a dress. The family makes a democratic decision about the aluminium bread plate. The input of others doesn't always help though. Even worse, the molehill of an unhelpful contribution to a minor house moving decision may turn into

a relationship mountain under stress, of which there is plenty
in a house move (boyfriend's "ummm, yeah, it's ok" comment
about the dress, for instance).

The primary decision of *I want to keep–I don't want to keep* is
sometimes clearly separate from, sometimes intermingled with:
I can take with me or I can't take with me (*Decision B*).

Decision B may be an 'absolute' decision—for this object
independent of any other object. This often happens when things
are at the extremes of weight and size. Think a wall-wide book-
case or a pair of tulle knickers. Absolute decisions are typically,
though not necessarily, made once.

I can take it–I cannot take it is, however, often a 'relative'
decision. *If I leave out those two shoe boxes, I can squeeze in the
juicer. Or I can have the juicer and the shoes without the shoe boxes,
but then give up on the hammock and the shoe brushes which were
in the shoe boxes.* Whether we take something depends on what
else we want to take with us.

Each alternative makes a different sacrifice. The more
constrained you are by Not Enough Room or Not Enough Money
arguments (whether to ship or buy something anew), the more
Decision B determines the contents of your luggage. You are also
more likely to be revisiting and reversing, and thus multiplying,
decisions. Your original trade-offs won't be, consistently, the best
you can make. You'll be changing your mind, time and time again.

For anything you don't want and/or can't take with you, you then
need to decide: **Let it be or let it die, and how (*Decision C*)**.

In one of its simplest forms, this is about deciding whether to
give away objects you are not taking with you (letting them be);

whether to throw them out (letting them die); or whether to recycle them (putting an end to one life and hoping for a resurrection). This process may, again, be a distinct stage or an argument in one's *keep–do not keep* decisions. For instance, if you know you can neither sell, nor donate, nor recycle your costume jewellery or CDs, you may decide to keep them after all. It's not that you want them. It's that you can't throw them out.

For many of us, the alternatives above branch out further, once again increasing the number of decisions. My own scale of handling objects I won't be moving runs from one to ten. *See* **Box 1** *at the end of this chapter.*

Finally, some objects may need to be packed or shipped at a well-chosen moment and, perhaps, replaced with a temporary solution. We need to decide **to time or not to time (*Decision D*)**.

If you want to keep your duck feather duvet but are travelling with a single suitcase, you may need a sleeping bag for the last night. If you've donated your towels, you'd better buy some kitchen roll (unless you are happy wiping your hands in your jeans). If you need to be shipping a printer, you'd better print its shipping label before you pack it....You get the idea.

HOW LONG WILL IT TAKE YOU?

Let's go back to the 7,198 to 16,698 objects in my show flat and use the midpoint of the two estimates (11,948). Let's focus on the primary house moving decision—to keep or not to keep—assuming that the flat's inhabitant (which is no longer my mum, nor me, nor you; we need some distance from this being our life!) has no constraints on what she can take with her and will throw away everything else. Let's make a set of assumptions:

For 60% of her 11,948 possessions (which is 7,169 items) she can make a split-second decision of whether to keep or throw out and has a rubbish bin right next to her. Let's give her five seconds to pick an object, make a decision about it, and either throw it out or set it aside. On many occasions, a second will be enough, but some items will be harder to retrieve, and one won't be able to sustain a robot's speed:
7,169 x 5s = 35,845s

For 30% (3,548 items) she wonders internally, but doesn't overthink, or at least not beyond thirty seconds on average:
3,584 x 30s = 107,520s

For 5% of her possessions (597 items) she wonders and wonders and wonders and goes to pee and checks the messages on her phone but doesn't start messaging back, otherwise she'll need more than the five minutes on average we are giving her here:
597 x 5 min = 2,985 min

For 4% (478 items) she wonders and either takes some relatively brief action herself or asks somebody else for advice:
478 x 6 min = 2,868 min

For 1% of her possessions (119 items) she goes through a long chain of sub-decisions and sub-actions. A bike needs repair before being sold. Muddy shoes need washing. A door needs to be taken off its hinges to remove a sofa. How about an hour on average?
119 x 1h = 119h

Now add 15% for distractions, loss of steam and the need to re-attempt decisions for objects she first made a pass on. Convert into hours, add up,

TA-DAAAAM!
295 HOURS OR 37 EIGHT-HOUR DAYS.

This is the weekends of almost half a year (twenty-four-and-a-half weekends, to be precise), if our imaginary character is sorting her possessions for eight hours on a Saturday and four hours on a Sunday. Alternatively, it is all your annual leave entitlement and all the public holidays of a year (and that's if you are lucky).

Remember that this is an estimate for a two-bedroom relatively uncluttered flat. It has human inefficiency built in but, I'd say, that of an organised person. It assumes unlimited space, finances and manpower to transport everything; total neglect for the environment, life of objects, the work of their creators, and the less fortunate (all not taken is to be thrown out); and no change in any decision once taken. It is also singularly about handling possessions (more on the 'microprojects' associated with a house move *in the next chapter*). As such, it is a conservative estimate.

It is based, however, on consciously reviewing most of your possessions. If that requires almost half of a year's weekends, you can see why after the initial enthusiasm has waned, so many of us are either packing or throwing away everything we touch, or why we bulldoze heaps of things rather than handle individual objects.

By far the most demanding house moving task is that of making decisions.

A house move is a mental marathon.

I'm training you to pack in under four hours.

BOX 1

MY LADDER OF CARE TO OBJECTS IN A HOUSE MOVE

1. **Sell**—well preserved and high value items. (I don't advise against selling lower value possessions. I've done it for years. I no longer feel the minor returns justify the time investment.)

2. **Give to friends and family**—only if they truly like and need what I no longer need. I take extra care not to latch onto the hoarders, saviours and guilt-prone subpersonalities within them.

3. **'Freecycle' or donate to a stranger in another personal way.** If 1. or 2. fail, I still want to find an ace owner for possessions I care about.

   I've mostly used Freecycle (*freecycle.org*), one of the oldest platforms for local gifting. It's available in over 5,300 towns and has over 10 million members as of August 2022. There are, however, countless current opportunities for giving away locally through apps and social media.

4. **Donate, intermediate personal.** I select a charity shop, a church, an event, etc. and give the bag to the person on duty. This is usually for old but well-preserved items I've loved or new(ish) ones I don't have much of an attitude towards.

5. **'Forget'.** This is a personal concept with at least three variants. It's also a game. I often play it when I can't bear to throw out an accessory I've loved, such as a scarf, water bottle or umbrella, yet it looks so tatty that it's a shame to be seen with it. I can't donate it either. Nobody in their right mind will want it. I then label the thing for 'forgetting'.

   This means I go about my life happily using and appreciating it, which also entails that, occasionally, I absentmindedly leave it behind. But when I remember, I don't go back to fetch it, unless it's within an easy walking distance. Then the rule of the game is to have it back, though I also cheat.

My most memorable experience of 'forgetting' is of my cousin's red umbrella, which I ultimately 'forgot' on the Isle of Skye after having tried to do it for over a year in three different countries. Maybe it wasn't me who 'forgot' it either, but the red umbrella choosing its home.

I won't be describing the other variants of 'forgetting'. You don't need to adopt my concepts and play my games. You'll lighten up your move if you are regularly inventing yours.

6. **Donate, impersonal.** This is when I drop donations in a charity container (the big charity bins which you often find in supermarket car parks, at least in the UK). The items are identical to those in point 4. I am different. I'm rushed off my feet and miserable and I don't want to talk to anyone.

7. **Recycle, go the extra mile.** Items like bras, electrics, umbrellas, old coins can be recycled, but the associated task usually becomes a microproject, as the relevant recycling facilities are limited.

8. **Recycle, standard.** This is for glass, paper, plastic, cardboard, etc.—anything that is part of normal local recycling.

9. **Abandon and hope for the best.** This is only in exceptional circumstances, a last resort for things that are TOO GOOD to be thrown away, but I've run out of time to redistribute. It's often for reasons outside of my control, for instance when a buyer pulls out of a deal last minute. I leave such items out 'to a good home', fearing it won't be one or that they won't be claimed at all.

10. **Throw away.**

CHAPTER 2

WHAT MAKES HOUSE MOVING DIFFICULT (2): 'MICROPROJECTS' ON ROOTS TO UPROOT, HARM TO REVERSE, GOOD TO ATTEMPT AND BULLETS TO BITE

I'm talking on my mobile, so it must be the twenty-first century. But it's not, it's a spacetime curve between the Middle Ages, *Kafka's Trial* and the present.

I've called to discontinue my Internet contract. It's rolling month-by-month by now. It should be a four-minute formality. But it's not.

The guy from the call centre in some happy faraway land is as upbeat as a Coca Cola ad. But something's off. Maybe if he loses me as a customer, when the lights go out, he'll have a finger joint smashed. Because I ask and I listen and I explain more clearly and I listen and I repeat and I listen, and half an hour has passed, and I'm in tears and my voice is shaking and I plead, "I just want it disconnected, I don't want a better offer, I can't take it to my next address, just...please...discontinued..."

Another spacetime curve butts in.

It's three years later. I'm in the same flat. My skin is pale, and my arms have no muscle. My smile is soft and my dark eyes have no sparkle. I am under house arrest. But I am alive. And I have unlimited-extra-superfast-broadband for-your-freedom-a-month.

We often think of a house move as the sorting through, packing and transportation of the things we have. We lose sight of the secondary tasks around it which can become (micro)projects—and (micro)nightmares—in their own right.

These microprojects come from four directions: 1) roots to uproot, 2) harm to reverse, 3) good to attempt, and 4) bullets to bite.

ROOTS TO UPROOT

First, no matter how briefly we've lived in a place, if we are good average citizens and consumers (even reluctant ones), we will have grown roots of contracts, memberships and delivery arrangements. For a start, think of your Internet provider, utility companies, and all the other companies you are paying to provide services at this address. In some cases, you will be able to transfer the arrangements. If you can't or don't want to, prepare to be charged for most early contract terminations or, on some occasions, to make all remaining payments in full. Remember to make arrangements with your healthcare providers too, particularly if you have a chronic condition or one under current investigation. The data sharing practices across the health service are often last-century. For some of us, our 'satellite homes'—e.g. an office space—are also a major source of microprojects. *See Box 2 at the end of this chapter for a list of prompts.*

HARM TO REVERSE

Second, even the most careful of us will break or damage things around a house. We also reorganise places to serve us better. Then, on preparing to leave, we'll usually find that we've damaged and shuffled around more things than we remember to have done.

I also suspect that there is a house-moving law of "Serious destruction shall occur right before you leave a place". On the day before leaving the first flat I'd rented by myself, a wall-mounted bookshelf fell off, digging a crater in the living room wall. To add insult to injury, I couldn't reassemble a rickety stack of shelves I'd taken apart on moving in. More recently, when I was giving the final clean to the only studio I've ever rented—ironically, my first lockdown accommodation—my toothbrush holder glass fell into the bathroom sink, smashing a perfect keyhole-shaped hole in it: *Enter me on leaving me.*

I used to squirm, like a 7-year-old or your average adult, before admitting to some of the damage I'd done to rented spaces. Now I relish in the honesty. I choose to behave like a grown-up. It's rare. This makes it advantageous.

In the first story, I wrote to the agency to apologise. I explained that the living room shelf was a last-minute disaster. I explained that the other 'structure' I had *chosen* not to reassemble in case the new tenants found it as ugly as I did. (Back then, I was good at not lying but still wobbly in my practice of avoiding truth sparing—namely, the addition that I didn't have brains enough to handle the midnight test in spatial thinking.) I was charged, and rather minimally, only for the living room shelf.

In the second story, I made an initial money transfer for the value of the sink, wrote to my landlord to apologise, and promised to pay the rest when the work was done. He wrote to thank me. He said the money was enough. *You have been "a exelent tenant", don't hesitate to ask for references for your new accommodation.*

In contrast, truths of the 'it wasn't me' kind don't matter unless you have good evidence. Some of the damage we do to rented houses comes from things being on their last leg by the time we've moved in. Yes, it's unfair to pay it all since you've only added the last straw. Yes, you will pay it all nonetheless. *See **Box 3** at the end on how to avoid it in the future and for "More on harm to reverse".*

GOOD TO ATTEMPT
Doing good is hard work

I recently wanted to donate our excess of books to a poor village library by a (filthy) rich monastery. It had 300 registered readers, 'including men', as the lady I spoke to announced proudly. They had little new literature, subjects with minimal holdings, and readers who've read it 'all'. But she still asked for a bibliography or a gallery of images of the book covers. They had no storage space. They'd had boxes of books donated previously, with the gift creating far more work of redistribution and disposal than bringing in value. I had every respect for the cautious way in which she welcomed gifts. It mirrors mine in giving them. I ultimately chose to donate my books elsewhere. Romance was their most sought-after genre. What a disappointment I would be.

You may expect your generosity to be met with open arms in places of serious need, no questions asked. You may even feel that it's part of the social contract of giving that the recipient handles what is of no value to either of you, as a small way of returning the big favour. Sometimes that's how it works. But sometimes your beneficiaries will be cautious about what they accept.

You too will be throwing spanners in the works, simply by having standards for the recipients of your gifts.

I don't give my things to anyone who ignores *le bon ton* or capital letters. *can i hv it pls?* means *no, you can't*. I suspect generalised carelessness when most punctuation is missing.

I am not giving away things to anyone who inhabits a melodrama either. One of our local Big Issue vendors has a birthday almost every time I talk to him, and his 'missus' has left him that same morning, and he hasn't sold a single copy today.

I know the need of many people in a melodrama is painfully real. I know their deprivation is likely to be greater than that of somebody who can write a polite sentence or avoid lying. But I've loved most of my things. I want a good new home for them. I also know that helping in such cases can be the most heartfelt and feel-good response, yet the surest way to support helplessness. I try to decide as best as I can in helping. It doesn't mean I do. It's always a work in progress.

One of the downsides of choosing your beneficiaries carefully is that the other person (people) may end up wanting more of the human connection rather than focusing on the 'task', as you might have envisaged the interaction. Years ago, I invited a young woman, with as many bags as she could carry, to the home I was leaving. I didn't know her well. I liked her for being brave. She'd just taken out a significant loan to start her own business.

She took five bags. She stayed nine hours. I didn't sleep the night after. I was packing. I had misjudged the time I needed by about eight and a half hours.

There is no such thing as selling

It is not only gifting which goes with unaccounted for work at house moving. So does good business. Think of selling. One can almost say there's no such thing. There is:

choosing amongst platforms

creating a profile if it's a new platform or retrieving the

password you'd forgotten

exploring prices for comparable items

reading on pricing strategies

taking photos

taking better photos

taking even better photos now the sun has appeared

writing ads

revising the ads

checking page views

resisting checking page views eight minutes later

responding to buyer queries

expressing (insincere) regret to latecomers that you've

already sold what you've sold

packing to post to the buyer

no, first buying some packaging

printing labels

waiting at the post office...

It's not a big deal for five or so items. But if you've been dreaming of cashing in on your wonderful but unused possessions, you didn't have just five in mind. It was at least twenty-five.

BULLETS TO BITE

A house move also creates microprojects which stretch our skills beyond what we are willing to embrace. If it's not our skills, it will be our budgets. Then we are back and forth in our decision to bite the bullet.

I love Christopher, and before that Kaloyan (though I loved him less), even if both have made me suffer at least as much as they've had me fly with the wind. I would bubble-wrap the incumbent (bike, that is) as a perfect mummy every time I was moving, but

had no idea how to box it, the far safer approach in shipping bikes.
I was abandoning attempts to learn as soon as I'd start them.
Even beginners' videos on YouTube assume you understand the
fundamentals of mechanics. I don't. I cry, defeated by them. I've
been planning to post an ad for a 'bike boxing teacher' for years
(up to £100 per lesson) but would conveniently forget until the
heat of a move. Then a lesson in bike boxing would be the last
thing I'd want added to the fire.

Years ago, shipping a bubble-wrapped bike was quite all right.
Now it's close to impossible. During a recent move, I wrote half a
dozen polite and friendly damage-will-be-my-responsibility emails
to shipping companies, all of which were requiring bikes to be
boxed. It made no difference. Nobody even bothered to answer.

I paid to have Christopher boxed in a bike shop. It cost as much
as a pair of decent sandals. I didn't mind it. Crying less is a top
reason to spend my money. Yet by the time I added the taxi fare
to take the box home (which I first carried, as the taxi couldn't
stop by the bike shop, and then carried again, as it couldn't stop
right where I lived), I had paid about a tenth of the cost of my bike,
lost half a day, was goaded by good manners to speak to the taxi
driver when I didn't want to speak to anyone, had scratched my
hand and it bled, and I stank.

No more excuses. I went on a basic bike maintenance course.
The man I was dating gave me bolt-by-bolt instructions and hex
keys a week or so before the move. I called my brother in the
process. I still ended up taking the corpus to a bike shop, as I
didn't have a 15-mm wrench for the pedals. But it was me who
did the rest. It took less than ten minutes, including the missteps.
It was EASY. I considered crying only for a fraction of a second.

I've half-forgotten how to do it by now. I still don't have a 15-mm wrench (in fact, there was a second time I didn't have one and my neighbour 'unscrewed' the pedals in the wrong direction, tightening them further. I shouldered the corpus and carried it to a bike shop once again). I'm not done with the learning and securing of equipment. Since I'll continue to be shipping bikes at house moves, I'll bite the bullet again. One day I'll chew and swallow it for good.

What are *your* bullets to bite? Can you, for instance, disconnect and set up your computer with all the peripherals by yourself, rather than seeking an IT-competent victim friend once again? Have you got paperwork you've been putting off reviewing for a few moves by now? If you drive a car, can you dare drive a rented van instead of paying five times more for a man and a van?

One move enough is enough.

It doesn't need to be a predictable, repetitive task you've been avoiding learning the skills for. It may be a one-off big and painful task created by:

- a pet you cannot take with you and need to find a good home for;
- original art or musical instruments you don't want to carry back and forth across country boundaries;
- monumental items that need special arrangements for their removal.

The more microprojects you fail to show respect for, the more nightmarish your move will be. The more mental space and time you open for these, the more adventures you'll create.

The best part? It doesn't matter.

When you've moved, a spacetime curve butts in. The nightmares become adventures.

BOX 2

Your consumer/ citizen roots AND YOUR SATELLITE HOMES

Discontinuing contracts, memberships and use of services

- Internet
- Utility companies
- City council (for local taxes and voting arrangements)
- Home insurance?
- Sports centre membership?
- Vegetable box delivery?
- Healthcare providers—in the UK at least, your new GP (General Practitioner) practice will request your patient record from your old practice, but keep in mind that the process can be slow. If the practices are using different IT systems, it may still mean having hundreds of printed pages sent over and a medical secretary summarising them on the receiving end. If you are a frequent user of healthcare services, don't leave it to formal processes only.

  For any discontinuation before the end of a contract, you owe penalties. You'll also be making a range of final payments. The sums can be non-trivial. They will accumulate across contracts. Try to accept such payments as expected items in a house moving budget. Otherwise it hurts.

Making the best of loyalty schemes

- You may partly offset the above by using the vouchers, points and rewards for the local services you've been frequenting—cafés, restaurants, hairdresser's...

ARRANGING FOR THE REDIRECTION OF MAIL

- You can do it formally through the post office. In the UK at least, it's quick, easy and affordable (unless you want your mail sent abroad).

- You may leave prepaid, self-addressed envelopes to the kind person who's agreed to manage your post.

- At some point, you'll need to inform the key organisations that use your address (bank, tax office, employer, the charities you are supporting...). The hassle of redirection is a further reason to opt out of paper mail as much as possible.

- I sympathise for the Catch-22 of situations when you can remove an old address from a system or set up a redirection only if you have a new address, yet you have no idea where you'll be living!

CLEARING 'SATELLITE HOMES'

- If you are changing jobs, you'll also need to clear your workspace (one of the rare occasions when not having a private office is a blessing).

- Think of random possessions you've scattered. Maybe you've lent books you don't want to leave behind? Do you store your yoga mat at the studio?

- In turn, your home may be serving as storage space for other people's possessions. It's time to mobilise their owners (who, by now, will not give a damn for 80%-100% of what you've kept for years).

BOX 3

MORE ON HARM TO REVERSE

- Some typical harms-to-reverse tasks **around a house**:
  - repairing or replacing broken items
  - returning furniture to its original arrangement
  - reassembling the disassembled
  - changing lightbulbs which have died
  - replacing broken curtain hooks...

- You may also want to clean, wash, repair, dismantle... **the things you are taking with you or selling/donating**. I regularly clean the mud off my walking boots on moving out. I also take clothes for alterations and shoes for repairs. It's silly. There are better times to do that. But it's even sillier to carry onwards what may not have another life in it.

- If you've damaged things around the place, you can, of course, choose to do nothing and have the **costs deducted out of your deposit**. Accepting to lose (some of) it can be the **best stress reduction strategy**.

- Some of the damage we do to rented houses comes from **things being on their last leg by the time we've moved in**. It is unfair to pay it all since you've only added the last straw, yet such experiences teach you to **inspect your next place meticulously**.

  If you are provided with an inventory of what's in it, annotate things you believe 'vulnerable'. Take photos. Whenever I've done that at moving in and referred to my annotations at moving out, I've not been charged if those things did, indeed, break.

MONEY ON HAND [illegible] EXPENSE

[illegible]

[illegible] placing broken curtain hooks.

- [illegible] the time you are living with your [illegible] frequently clean the mud off the [illegible] there are [illegible] every other [illegible] may not have [illegible]

- If you've damaged things around the place, you can [illegible] [illegible] to do nothing and have the costs [illegible] out of your deposit. Accepting [illegible] lose some of it can be the best stress reduction strategy.

- Some of the damage we're [illegible] comes from things being on the [illegible] by the time we've moved [illegible] since you've only [illegible] the last [illegible] teach you to inspect your [illegible] immediately.

- If you are [illegible] [illegible] [illegible] [illegible]

CHAPTER 3

WHAT MAKES HOUSE MOVING DIFFICULT (3): SUBVERSIVE EMOTIONS, BUT RARELY THE ONES YOU FEARED

Unless a house move is triggered by a death or a relationship breakdown, where the energy of the person we've lost infuses most of what we own; unless we are leaving a house that's been ours for decades, a backdrop to many and long periods of life having richness, ecstasy and beauty it's now lost, then extreme emotions awoken by objects will be one of our lesser troubles. We expect them. Constructively or dysfunctionally, we'll have prepared.

What few of us will prepare for, however, are the subconscious emotional components in our reasons to own, buy and keep things. Many of those emotional components are ugly. The little monsters are more disappointing than scary, attacking our ego rather than our essence, but generally well hidden. They'll rarely surface without conscious effort to dig them out. But they'll affect us. They'll cast a shadow.

The shadow will feel like doubt and uncertainty. If we hesitate for far too long what to do with an item; if we are uncertain how to apply the criteria we are supposed to be applying; if we feel a vague sense of dissatisfaction once we've made a decision, as if we've done something wrong or forgotten to consider something important, it is usually because hidden emotional fragments are battling our conscious criteria. Our conscious criteria can, of course, concern emotions too, such as whether we love an object or whether it brings us joy. This is not a point about the emotional v. the rational. It is about the invisible v. the visible, where the invisible is blocked out as dangerous or disappointing.

Somewhere deep and true, we always KNOW if we love an object or if we don't; if it feels good to have it or if we taste the dregs of the original compromise; if it is a true expression and extension of our self; if it enriches or simplifies our life meaningfully; if it stirs and carries home-like feelings. But apart from for the most clear-cut cases, this place of knowing isn't easy to reach. We need to peel layers of emotional clingfilm to get to it.

There are six examples of emotional clingfilm below (the list is not exhaustive). See if any of them envelop your possessions. Remember that the better the clingfilm sticks, the less likely you are to see it.

OBJECTS WITH A HUMAN SOUL

Most likely, your first association for difficult emotions embodied by objects has hovered over people you've loved and lost.

My mum keeps a rack of spice jars she hasn't used for almost twenty years. A basic wooden frame holds ten jars of a glass base, filthy plastic stoppers and, in some cases, decades-old spices, faint memory traces of once heady aromas. It was a present from my aunt, my mum's sister. She died at least thirty years before 'her time'. The spice jars are at the back row on the top shelf of the

most difficult to access kitchen cupboard—not to be used,
not to be seen, not to be let go of, only to be kept, holding my
aunt's spirit. As if the latter would stay in a jar.

We conflate objects and the people they came through;
the handling of objects and the handling of the complexities
of a relationship or its loss. Some of us hold onto possessions we
don't use, may not even like, as if they are physical carriers of our
relationships; as if by throwing them out, we are throwing people
and love out of our lives; as if by using them, the wound will
gape open again. We explain the attachment with passion, pain
and tears in our eyes, silencing, freezing the person who dared
question it. Others amongst us, in contrast, clear the space of any
such reminder, as if, in itself, passing on or throwing out 'their
things', 'from-them things' can take the pain away.

We discuss this topic in a chapter of its own (**Chapter 20**).
It needs focused attention. Yet anthropomorphised objects and
the excess of emotion they seem to carry rarely complicate a move
as much as we fear they would do.

ELUSIVE FEELINGS

More typically, our greatest challenges of separating from objects
come from not being able to feel deep enough rather than from
feeling too much of our buried pain.

We own and keep what we believe makes us be, feel and
appear a certain (good, better) way, whether it's more attractive,
safe, peaceful, comfortable, warm, powerful, happy, confident,
youthful. We also get rid of things for the same reason.

That's how it is meant to be. The problem is that we often
think or believe something about how we feel rather than *feel*
and *explore* how we feel. Often enough, we misjudge our feelings,

following first impressions and appearances. We don't do what it takes to sink deep into a feeling and reach its crux as a bodily experience; as a final response from our Being rather than a first-line fragmentary reaction; as a river with a name and direction under an overgrowth of vagueness, complexity, confusion and emotional rocky ground.

The more adapted to a particular society/ social group we are, or the harder we are trying to fit in, the more likely we are to own things because we've had positive feelings about them *induced* in us. It's cool, in-vogue, class- and status-hinting-demonstrating, healthy, green, fitting, ethical, flattering for your shape, age-appropriate, age-defying, endorsed by your heroes, the cycling pros, the yogis who can lift their leg past their ear, by all those radiant, grown-up, nailed-the-perfect-lifestyle people (or free-spirited charismatic rebels, for that matter), some of whom your family and friends...If you have it, you'll be a step closer to being as confident, hot, successful, strong, healthy, fit, clear-skinned, loved as them.

That's, of course, the *raison d'être* of profit-chasing marketing and advertising, but the effect can arise in far more pure-hearted ways, through somebody's infectious enthusiasm, the thorough-going belief in their life's work or magnetising photography, for instance. Whatever the source of the influence, we've allowed external images, stories and words to create temporary impressions of a feeling or sharpen a semi-feeling, as opposed to really feeling what is there for us to feel around an object.

Even with all my refined judgements about the objects I keep, it recently took me four months to accept that my eyes didn't agree with the recommendation of 500+ independent opticians for a reading lamp, a wonder using the technology of museums and galleries such as Guggenheim's and Van Gogh's, made-to-order for me, only the 898th such object in Cornwall. *Of course the images are clearer. If I can't feel it, I am not cued into what I need to feel or simply need a few more weeks to discover a new way of seeing.* Cued in or not, I am not feeling it. I will not be moving the lamp I bought for a lifetime.

We also *deduce* our well-being in possession of an object. We assume it on the grounds of past experience: *I loved my Roka rucksack, the new colours are so cool, I need one again!* We derive it from matter-of-fact beliefs we hold, often as part of a lifestyle we endorse: "Sateen sheets create the best sleeping environment." "Black dresses give you effortless style." We also 'carry over' experiences of well-being from others, expecting what they experience in relation to an object to be directly replicated for us: *She's glowing from this face cream! I'll have that too!*

All the above *are* valid ways to be led towards things that make us feel good. The bug in the system is that we often forget to do the feeling work or test how deep running or lasting a feeling is.

When, for whatever reason, *we begin to feel, remember to feel,* we realise that many of the things we own and which were supposed to make us be or feel a certain way don't do that. Or it's short-lived. Less intense than we were promised. Fickle – sometimes coming, sometimes not. Never quite complete because of some small irritating detail.

Each of our possessions (or gaping holes amongst them) can call up a theatre performance in our head. If we listen closely, many of us will find our body and our Being only as supporting cast in it, even extras without a line.

We own somebody else's things. We own somebody else's restraint.

BACKWARD JUSTIFICATIONS

We can also be deceiving ourselves about planning to use something; about needing or liking it; about it fitting or matching as a way of avoiding the conclusions and consequences of admitting the opposite.

I've carried on so many occasions, from one house to another to another (and then again and again), expensive hardly worn and uncomfortable shoes. I've 'intended' to start wearing them. They 'really' only needed a few more days of walking to loosen them. If I didn't 'intend' as I did, I would have been forced to admit before I was ready to admit that I didn't want to donate them. I would have figured out that I held onto money far more tightly than I knew; that my poor younger self or even those of my parents, for whom £100 was a fortune, still controlled me; that I detested having my hard work, money or generosity taken advantage of because I already felt taken advantage of.

You, in turn, may be carrying onwards clothes which have been too small for you for a decade. To let them go is to admit that this is and will be your body, at least until you continue to do or not do what you've been doing or not doing for that decade.

Backward justifications don't need to involve wounds to fragile egos. They can simply serve to avoid boring or complex tasks. We have some silver-plated cutlery from one of my aunts. It hasn't been used for at least fifteen years. It doesn't look vintage old. It's crude and primitive old. It may take time to find a good new home for it. We can bite the bullet and deal with the hassle or stay sentimental, forks and knives melting our hearts, even if we've never, not even once, put them on the table.

NOT BEING GOOD ENOUGH

If we summon the courage, many of us will see that our not-good-enough, not-deserving-enough and, ultimately, not-loved-enough beliefs have leaked over our possessions far more visibly than we ever thought possible.

If you are one of those people whose turn for something special comes after you've bought all the presents for all the birthdays, all the new houses, all the newborns, new degrees and broken hearts that come with this month's salary;

if, in daily life, you hear the murmur of *I'm not good enough... see her...can't ask for that...if only I were loved like that...too expensive... too much...shouldn't, can't buy it....or I can, but later...when I've achieved goal W...when, after I've become...*

then your move will have you sorting piles of mediocre, impersonal and half-loved things. You don't have it in you to be generous with yourself. It shows in what you own.

The "You're not good enough" demon can, however, appear as its exact opposite too, as almost any fiendish, dysfunctional fragment of our psyche does. It does so, for instance, when a ruby-red-lipped enchantress whispers "you're worth it" (now buy it to affirm it); when glamorous, exceptional, top-notch things trigger sweet spots, touch raw nerves, prop you up in inner eye performances, suspend thinking, hand out your card (don't things buy themselves when you HAVE TO have them?). Then when Move Day comes, it finds you sorting through a mountain of luxuries, leaving your heart cold and having no story to tell. The 'worth it' whisper is usually only the daylight rendition of the 'not good enough' one.

Often, if we are ready to see, we will find our 'not good enough' struggles externalised in both forms amongst our possessions— the less than we wanted and the more than we needed, without the saving grace of truly loving what we didn't need. While feeling undeserving is not the only explanation for such a pattern of ownership, it's one of the most frequent ones.

INACTION INERTIA

Most of us will also be passing, repeatedly, through a strange fog obscuring what we own. We'll catch a glimpse of certain objects, then move on. It's as if our thoughts and feelings are behind an opaque screen, or in a tangled ball without a clear thread to start from. With some objects, this can reach the level of a phenomenon called 'inaction inertia'.

Inaction inertia controls us when we have, time and time again, refrained from a certain type of action, as a result of which we continue not to do something (or anything). It is not because we have good reasons not to do it, or any clear reasons at all, but because that's what we've always done — make a pass. It may be about a box of paperwork we've been meaning to sort out for five moves (or the holidays of five years) but once again left it for 'next time'. It may be something calling for far less effort — a beautiful but imperfectly fitting bra we can't decide what to do with and, as a result, keep until we can.

At some point, there was a reason not to act, including not to think through the details of how to act. Now the strongest reason to decide nothing and do nothing is that the not-deciding and the not-doing have accumulated a life of their own.

EMOTIONAL FLOTSAM AND JETSAM

Finally, no matter how well-honed our decision-making criteria are, we will be carried away by emotionally charged memories, associations and actions. Unfortunately, we can't separate neatly the emotional components that enable decisions, connect the dots towards an insight, or simply add colour to our move from the flotsam and jetsam leading us down mental rabbit holes or procrastination:

My ebony salt and pepper shakers. He gave them to me on my fortieth birthday, saying I am like the spice of life and he's like salt to wounds...[heart prick] [mind drifts] [and drifts] [and drifts] [back to sorting].

This nutmeg was packed in East Germany!!! It's older than my brother! And has outlived a country! There was so much promise for the world when the Wall fell...[mind drifts] [back to it].

I look terrible in this dress, can count my bones! Worst, have lost my muscles! Where's the body I thought I had?! Must check how my bum cheeks look! [fetch mirror] *WHAT'S THAT?! IT CAN'T BE! I still exercise?! Am I getting old? Let me check again*...[and again, and again, and from this angle too, even if the mirror doesn't show anything different].

There is much more emotional clingfilm wrapping the objects we've got and keep. The chapters in the second, third and fourth part of this book are, in many ways, detailed illustrations of these and other types of emotional clingfilm and how I am peeling them off me.

I'll be ugly, weak, bloated, scared, small while doing that. If you dare to follow, so will you.

Until, one easy morning, we
stretch our soul and
find the wrapping gone.
Nothing clings to us.
Nor do we.

WHAT MAKES HOUSE MOVING DIFFICULT (4): DEFAULTS THAT ARE FAT SLICES OF OUR PHILOSOPHY OF LIFE

Sometimes you don't want to move. Your landlady is selling her house—*Your Castle*—in her divorce arrangements. It's become your divorce, too.

Sometimes it's killing you to stay. This is the house where your wife died. It used to be the house of your love and your laugher. *Your*, singular, has no meaning next to *house, love* and *laughter*. These are meant to be plural. At least in this house. You must find it singular elsewhere.

Sometimes you leapt high above yourself. It took all your courage. Now you want to turn back time, return to a small you and its small home, stay low forever. If only you hadn't burnt your ships.

Sometimes it's your home that's burnt to the ground. You are not moving. You are running for your life. If there is a humanitarian crisis of our time we all know about, it's that of refugees.

There are many more of these 'sometimes', which make house moving excruciating. They can make us lose the ground beneath our feet. But they can also give us otherworldly clarity about what to take and what to leave.

When push comes to shove, you can leave everything. All of it mattered because of the emotions, relationships, experiences, and ways of life behind it. There are thousands, millions of ways to have those emotions, relationships, experiences, and ways of life and thousands, millions of objects that can replace the ones you've left behind.

Nothing that matters is lost for long, unless you stamp your feet, insisting it existed solely in the form you've lost.

OVER-DETERMINED BY CIRCUMSTANCES OR DEFAULTS

Most of the house moves we will experience will have none of that back-against-the-wall, now-or-never, knickers-on-your-bum quality (unless you are the sort of person who seeks and creates drama as a way of life). And while that's mostly a blessing, it's also one of the greatest sources of house moving trouble.

In extreme circumstances such as the above, our decisions are over-determined by 1) said circumstances and 2) our most salient needs and limitations. The rules are harsh and clear. You don't contemplate on degrees of object love or the reality of a need. You act from the clock ticking, suitcase filling, and a skin or soul needing saving. Life can be at its easiest when it's most difficult.

When, in contrast, life is (relatively) normal, our move is over-determined by house moving rules and defaults. We all have them. It doesn't matter if you've moved twenty-one times, haven't moved for thirty-nine-and-a-half years or if you are "just getting it done", no system, no awareness, come what may and whichever way it happens. There is no house move without first principles.

Some of those principles filter down from broader life. If you typically optimise costs (that is, worry about money), you will instinctively be drawing and re-drawing money saving scenarios, checking cost comparison websites, and adding up the earnings from glorious eBay sales. If you typically worry about the environment and the underprivileged in society, you'll be, once again, on a quest for donation opportunities and recycling sites.

Your guiding principles may be house moving-specific, too. Maybe you are drawn to the lightness, clean slate and legend-weaving power of leaving with a single suitcase. That single suitcase will channel all your house moving decisions. Maybe you have a high-flying job, a toddler, a baby on the way and a husband floating a start-up on midnight oil. It MUST be as easy and simple as possible. Somebody else has to pack and clean and ship and unpack and all. You PAY.

If we care to give an account of what matters to us in a move/ this move, we will identify most of our principles, rules and defaults. What we'll rarely identify is how deep they reach and how broadly they branch out. More often than not, they are a fat slice of our philosophy of life, a full-bodied expression of our values system.

IN THE MATHS OF THERAPEUTIC MOVING, 1 > 8

One of my guiding principles in house moves is REDISTRIBUTE. That is, I do my best to find a new home for any of the things I am not taking with me and also recycle/ dispose responsibly of what has finished its current life cycle. When I dug deeper, I found out that I redistribute for eight main reasons:

1. I have ten fish and ten birds I am trying to save from choking on plastic bags. I haven't seen them. I've not given them

names. I haven't adopted them through a charity to which I donate monthly. But I think of them whenever it feels as if another plastic bag or plastic cup is neither here nor there for the planet. I am responsible for my ten birds and ten fish and how I live makes no meaningful difference to the Earth, but it means whether they live or die, how they live and die.

2. I redistribute because I hated the mountains of rubbish throughout Kathmandu. I wanted to wave hands like a windmill and shout to the clouds over Everest that rubbish collection is one of the greatest achievements of civilisation and that for the first time in my life I am CERTAIN that civilisation is a good thing and I want to belong to it. And I was so angry with that airhostess, a friend of a friend's sister, who had recommended Kathmandu as one of the top three destinations in the world. Maybe from the air you only see the mountains of the Himalayas, not those of wrappings, bottles and single use objects on the streets and river of Kathmandu.

   On rarer occasions, I don't believe we've got time left to save the planet. But I've never not done what I believed was right only because it was pointless. The pointless right never achieves anything now. It's often ridiculous. You are ridiculous attempting it. Then one day, hoping nothing, expecting nothing, you see a mountain moved. It's your pointless right that did it.

3. I redistribute because I was once a student who bought her summer dresses in charity shops. There is now a time machine in each donations box, and I pass on clothes to my younger self through it, and I see her beam in her 'new' dress when she meets that tall silly boy she was in love with at the time. I redistribute because in those winters when the Cold War was

over, it was even colder. I could see my breath even at home. I redistribute because I am me me but I am also me him— young, shy and long haired, with a guitar and a dog, begging in central Cambridge. Me me earns above the average for the country, has six degrees, has faith in life, and feels so well, oh, SO WELL most of the time! Me him, well, *he* will soon die of drugs and despair. He looked so unfittingly homeless when he first came, a temporary glitch in fate to be soon rectified. He didn't always have sleeves on, but his good, innocent, defenceless heart was always on them. Now, five or six years later, it's a scared, bleeding, mean heart. Now street life becomes him. When I remember I am him and those like him, I can't throw things out.

4. I redistribute because in the ninth century I was a merchant in Canada (although I challenged my twelve-year-old classmate who was consulting a book on former lives that Canada didn't exist then). I get a thrill from selling. I would happily man a stall at the market.

5. I redistribute because I need to feel I am better than I am. I am not one of those who buy the best striped top ever only to be bored with it within a week, then buy a new one, and again. Easy fish in the nets of marketing and advertising and good psychologists of shop assistants; diggers in the graveyards of 'things of yesterday'.

6. I redistribute because forgotten, unused things suffer, weep and are slowly dying. Things are happy when they can serve you. This is what my brother and I thought as kids. We still know what the other means by saying that a thing was crying and dying and they had to do something about it. One of my landladies, a most refined woman, once told me that I looked

to her like a Shintoist ("Have you heard of them, dear, they believe that things have a soul?") every time she saw me polishing my leather boots. (Her Armanis and Chanels taught me that no shoes are self-polishing or immune to wear and tear.) Incidentally, she's the only landlord who's ever made me cry, saying that I was taking the rubbish out and offloading the dishwasher less than my fair share and should be helping out more. But the point was the soul of things, not of people, and that in caring for the souls of things you can be wise, not only childish.

7. I redistribute because I love the jolts of joy when a person and a thing meet, the feeling of "that's exactly what I needed!" I am a matchmaker in moving. And I set things free, just as I do with lovers, to find a grander love. I redistribute because of the brief encounters. Because of that sparkly blue-eyed just-turned-mum to whom I passed on a tray and a blender, but we mostly exchanged a sense of wonder—lives having taken routes we'd never charted; logic and destinations once intended kicked off the map; us being all the more jittery-thrilled, grateful and clueless for it. I redistribute because of that junior doctor who came for cleaning spray and cushions and left with my rainbow-curved lamp, hammer, hex keys and all else I wanted a good family to have. Because of that warm-hearted middle-aged white man, his much younger wife and baby in a basket, all beaming next to one another, who now sleep in my bed and eat from my table. Because of so many luminous men and women throughout the years.

8. I redistribute because once you take it seriously, it becomes obsessive. It doesn't let you off. You are on fire and you leave with half a bag of rubbish, a sense of duty completed, a bagful

of stories, and three spring onions and two scraped carrots for the flight. Even if it costs you a sprained ankle and fifty-one sleepless hours, which then make your flight neighbour shout at you and shake you, as no polite requests can reach you for an hour and she really needs to pee, PEE, please...NOW! I said 'obsessive'.

I don't redistribute for one single reason.

1. Somewhere along the way, I woke up to find that apart from the soul of things, the lives of others and the health of our planet, there are my soul, life and health. I not only need to seek a good balance, a golden mean. I need to check if the direction of care may need to be reversed. When you are obsessively caring for the planet, too compassionate of your less fortunate brothers and sisters, too committed to respect the soul of things and the labour of those who've made them, you may be giving the planet, the people suffering, the things in danger of being abandoned the love, care, backing and commitment you yourself are lacking. You need to redistribute the care, starting with yourself.

In the maths of therapeutic house moving, $1 > 8$.

WAKE UP!

This was a dream within a dream, chapter within a chapter.

What I was seeking to illustrate was that the rules and defaults which energise our move go far deeper and reach far more broadly than most of us would ever imagine, even stand any chance of tracing. This is what makes them so powerful and why we will not notice that they have turned against us.

A house move, at least in cases when your house is more than a room, is a hundred-headed dragon. No principle, rule or default, or a set of them—such as extreme redistribution—can come out victorious unless you've refined its practice to extremes, including through 'static life'.

In all other cases, you'll see your rules and defaults crash.

In one of two typical scenarios, your principles will guide you marvellously for a fairly long time. It will even be inspiring how smoothly they work, how creatively you can apply them, and how much you discover along the way. After a while, it will become tiring and boring and repetitive and soulless, but it will still be ok, you continue, continue, drag your feet, but continue.

Until—

BANG!

In the last few days or hours

it

ALL

disintegrates

into

chaos! &9&-=c= qhpt7

The one who thinks of every penny will be paying small fortunes.

The eco-conscious will be stuffing everything that remains into bags for landfill.

The sentimental will have no heart space for yet another kid's drawing.

The single suitcase will weigh 28 kilos and there will be a bag and a rucksack that go with it too.

The other (die-hard) scenario is as you've read earlier—you blast your body exhausted and go to such extremes of responsible living that you carry two carrots and three spring onions, or was it three carrots and two spring onions, from one end of Europe to the other.

What's the solution?

Let me give you a clue: the foundations are only two.

HOW TO MAKE IT EASIER?
TWO THINGS TO DO THAT DON'T NEED
YOU TO LIFT A FINGER

Most of us arm to the teeth for the challenges of a house move. Channel time and money, sturdy boxes, loyal help. Ignite the motivational self-pep. Cut out moaning, slowing, 'how?!' – 'must do, will do, end of story', NOW. Still, one of the most frequent comments you hear from people who've just moved is that they are never moving again.

As we've discussed in the previous chapters, this happens, first, because we almost always have (wildly) more things than we believe. Even the least consumerist-minded of us do. The familiarity of environments and routines makes their components fade away. We become semi-blind to what's normal to have around. My show-flat demonstrated that even a two-bedroom uncluttered home can have close to 17,000 objects.

Second, everything we own requires a decision or a chain of decisions, at the very least whether we are taking it forward or not. While many will be split-second, automatic decisions, a fair number will make our brain choke. It is because they are drawing on (often implicit) principles of acquiring, keeping and letting go of things which come into conflict with one another. It is also because of undefined, uncertain parameters (Do I love this?!) which block the flow of a decision-making process.

Third, we tend to underestimate the number of microprojects that arise in a house move, from discontinuing contracts and memberships, through repairing smaller and bigger damage we've done to places, to handling awkward objects, and a lot more in between.

Fourth, we are sabotaged by emotions we avoid facing up to or which we miss, as if they were transparent clingfilm wrapped around both thing and thought. Most of those emotions have entered the game when we acquired an object. But here-and-now we are still likely to cover up/ reverse engineer them so as to avoid unpleasant truths. For instance, we begin to 'like' or 'intend to use' things. Look closer and rather than a rational intention, we have the Inner Miser in cold sweat at the thought of donating or underselling something that expensive. It's impossible to make good decisions if we ignore emotional truths relevant to them. Yet many truths cost us dearly before bringing in dividends.

And, fifth, we advance a house move through a range of personal rules, principles and defaults without sufficient appreciation of their downsides. Such guidance comes from our deeply held and partly subconscious ideas of what's good, effective, normal, right, easier, enhancing our quality of life....Yet in a mammoth project like a house move, any principle will be pushed to the limit. And anything that's pushed to the limit will show its dark side or fall apart, unless tempered to extraordinary levels of endurance and flexibility.

So what can we do other than stay put, ossify the roots?

Channel even more time, money, sturdy boxes, loyal help?

Bite our nails and pick the peeling skin around them, eat yet more triple chocolate trifle and smile through gritted teeth?

We can, in fact, do a lot while hardly doing anything. If you look closely at the above five reasons, we will see them merging. The first three are forms of underestimation. The latter two are forms of emotional or ethical (semi-)blindness. We thus have two generic ways to prepare. Start using them early on and it can make all the difference. And you don't need to lift a finger.

1. PUT ON THE INFRARED GOGGLES

The first generic way of preparing is to reactivate your ability to see, *really* see, what's in your house. It is to instruct, maybe trick yourself into coming home with fresh eyes. It is to find ways to let familiar objects and arrangements jump up and out of their background blur; regain their bright colours, forgotten beauty, weird shapes, wounds of usage.

You can do this through intense focus or mindful presence. You can borrow the eyes of a guest, somebody who wants to soak up all they can soak up about you – a new date, a crime scene investigator, the neighbour behind the pinch-lifted curtain. It can be somebody who has a strong opinion on how you should live, even if they believe they are only objectively observing, not judging – your mum, dad, mother-in-law, grown-up kids, said new date....Listing things is also an eye-opener, as I discovered on counting the possessions in my mum's flat (it took one to four hours per room).

It helps to watch for individualities and subtypes, not broad types; to go in and out of rooms, not keeping it "a room at a time".

Then register:
- the dining table chairs
- wooden stool for stepping on for high cupboards
- home office ergonomic eyesore
- rickety stools to extend your legs on
- the 'thing' beneath the ironing pile,
    a white cap of bedsheets that never melts enough
    to reveal the chair holding it....

- books you've loved so much that you fear re-reading
- books you've started but know you won't finish
- those you will start again *to finish*
- books under your care but not (felt as) yours
    borrowed
    received as (misjudged) presents
    meant as presents
- double copies
- the ones bloated from having been too close to
    the open window in the thunderstorm
- cookery books in the kitchen drawer
- the pile on the bedside table
- the one on the floor by the sofa
- travel guides in your rucksack
- mini-library in the toilet
    (which sits on a chair you missed counting above)....

Watch out for equipment and decorations which have fused with their space but are movable and belong to you: the reading lamps, chandeliers, microwave, curtains, cord extensions...

Undress the spots to their bare walls, before the paintings, photos, wall clock, calendar, heart pendants on the window handles....

Extract the objects out of routines and life's chores—the pegs that hold the clothes on the line, the basket for the pegs, the ironing board flat behind the door....The big rattan basket where you throw the recycling, but which is an object (beautiful) in its own right....

The tea towels hanging from the oven door, the unwashed pan on the hob, the scissors you've been searching for astride on the worktop....Your favourite mug. The non-descript water glasses which are, normally, as transparent to you as the water in them. The hand-painted glass that (temporarily, coming up to two years) is holding the toothbrushes.

I want to tell you to put this book down and walk around if you are home or close your eyes and imagine yourself opening the front door if you are not. I want to insist. To tell you that it's important, that it's really curious, that objects acquire a new light, shine a forgotten beauty; that I'll wait.

But it's annoying when a book tells you to stop reading. Just like a lecturer opening a talk with an 'interactive exercise', right when you've sunk into your chair and listener mode.

So put this book down or don't put this book down but take the time to rediscover your home. When you've done it, you'll be way ahead. Your brain will have started readjusting. Tick-tock, change tracks, regroup, prepare. Ready, steady, MOVE.

2. BEFRIEND THE SHADOW

If you want a house move that feels therapeutic, easier, more adventurous, more liberating than what has ever been or what you could have ever imagined, you need to open the door to the skeletons in the cupboard; to the chaos in your mind, heart and soul; to what is dark and 'wrong' about you and the opposite of what you want to be; to your Shadow.

No doubt, it will be scary and unsettling. There are house-moving times when, if you don't keep the lid tight on, you risk descending into inner chaos that will render the outer chaos laughably tame. But most of the time, a house move is a perfect opportunity to venture deeper into the darkness and return with gifts from there.

You've already braced yourself for trouble. You know some of it will be emotional trouble. You are ready to take a lot on.

You also have the externalisation advantage. There is some-thing sublimely protective, mundane and symbolic about seeing the dramas of your life, the madness of your mind, and the fears of your five-, fifteen-, X-year-old self reflected in the day-to-day objects you keep. You can hold them at arm's length. You have the power to throw out, pass on, leave behind, smash, burn, flush down the toilet both inert objects and negative experiences they have become associated with.

Crucially, you'll have a positive model for the transition from chaos into order. You'll see it come to life notwithstanding many moments of panicking that it's IMPOSSIBLE. The physical drama of a house move has a reliably happy end, even if accompanied by exhaustion and a bitter aftertaste. You will have moved. The chaos that looked unmanageable will be contained. The piles of rubbish will be cleared, the boxes of treasures kept. You will inevitably leave some of the past behind. You will inevitably open some space for the new. You may get help, but you'll do it mostly yourself/ yourselves.

When you trust you'll resurface, and when you trust there are treasures in the darkness—and affirming it for your house helps affirm it for your soul—you even want to befriend more of the dark, wrong and chaotic about you. You can do it in hundreds of ways relevant to a house move. But let me suggest one generic: inspect your house moving rules, principles and defaults for flaws.

Think of what you believe would make a grand move. Enjoy specifying it, seeing it applied in the best ways imaginable. See yourself in the flow of doing things/ having things happen that way.

You may be sipping white wine with a friend, cherry blossom and April sunshine in your hair, while the packing and removals guys are buzzing away in the kitchen.

You may be on fire optimising a methodical, systematic process; admiring the genius of Lakeland's storage solutions; or rejoicing in sticking 'fragile' cello tape under perfect right angles.

Here comes the good fairy, spring in her step, beaming a smile here and there, giving away everything she won't be taking with her.

Enters the cost-cutting ninja, legendary for slashing expenses and monetising on past loves.

There goes the one-suitcase girl, light and colourful as cotton candy as she turns the front door key to yet another latest flat.

You need those principles and ideal move visions. They are your North Star. Even if you don't think you have them, you have them.

Now see their dark side.

The cost optimisers amongst us better notice that costs are not only financial. They are of time and opportunities to use it differently; of mental and emotional exertion; of physical effort and the exacerbation of physical traumas (think bad back for half a year while saving £60 for a porter); of loss of sleep, rest and peace; of favours called upon that need to be returned.

The single-suitcase/ carload, new-page-turners may need to remember that often the best way to turn a new page is to re-read the old ones and take copious notes from them. Otherwise we re-write too much of what we've turned the page on and re-buy too many replicas of what we left outside the single suitcase.

The outsourcers may begin to wonder why it's beyond them to deal with their possessions, why what's supposed to enhance their lives has become a burden to pay their way out of, no longer a river of joyful plenty to splash in.

Don't overthink it. Just let in thoughts that go against your usual thoughts (you already have them, by the way, but have a habit of pushing them away or standard arguments to defeat them). Remember it's not about dissuading you from doing what you thought was a good thing to do. It is a good thing for you. It's about breaking the inertias which stop you from adapting better and from experiencing more of what's good.

If, in this house move, you can learn a bit more about being yourself and your opposite, which makes for a more expansive you; of sticking with your principles when they become inconvenient, but also breaking them so that you uphold principles that are even higher and truer; of facing your inner chaos while trusting there is an indestructible home in your soul, even if you are yet to discover it, you'll find your house move times easier, more liberating, more satisfying and adventurous than you could have ever imagined.

And whatever happens to your house, YOU will have moved.

CHAPTER 6

THRESHOLDS OF PAIN

There comes a day in each house move when the Pain kicks in.

It can be the sweet kind of pain, where everything and everyone you are leaving behind is so dear, so lit up, so open, where you are floating on air carried by love, joy, and a sense of magic for all that's been and all that's to come. You hurt with a love of life.

But it's also (mostly? only?) the pain of all losses—of breaking up; of DYING; of losing people, friendships, support circles, stability, identity, LOVE; of being left, abandoned; of leaving, of abandoning.

It's the steely, cold, free-falling pain. Of being a fleeting, forgettable, dispensable thing in a fleeting, all too temporary existence. A shadow on the stairs you used to climb home to. A name on addresses only Amazon remembers in full. It is the pain where the house you are leaving, the decor of your existence there dismantled, becomes unfamiliar, impersonal, lifeless. It is the pain of being a nobody to yet another new place—to be unseen or overwatched; tested, tasted and spat out.

It is the pain with tentacles to fear. Panic. Numbness.

Contraction. Preoccupation. When they become one, a monster is born.

It pounces from time running out—to sort, to pack, to choose, to book, to give away, to wait, to clean, to leave. It feeds on the vapour of money, the only state of house moving money. It snarls and calls the home you are seeking 'a chimera'. It swells if broader life ticks and demands and deadlines you.

It locks your face, strains the smiles, strangles the laughter. It deepens your wrinkles, dries your hands, blisters your feet, freezes your neck. It turns your mind metallic, stuck on compute, calculate, compare, weigh up, run in spirals, constantly failing to square the circle of the home and future you want with those you can have. It commands you to walk alone, wade a river of loneliness, miss the bridge to solitude. It turns your energy into a dark hole, empty chair, even if you are sitting there, amongst all the normal, lighter, smiling, rooted people with a home.

I was never prepared for those times. They always came. And when they came, I didn't know if I would be whole again, ghost-turned-real again. The evidence of my own life—that every move was ultimately for the better—didn't matter.

How do you cross thresholds of pain? Not sure. It seems it's one of those things that 'happen' rather than you making them happen. And I wonder if the royal road is of Pain meeting TRUST. You stay in the Pain. It doesn't matter if it's by determination or inability to run away. And you are visited by TRUST.

How does TRUST arrive? Not sure. It seems to be both by surprise and persistent invitations, by an excess of love and an excess of struggle. It blossoms from the softest of hugs. It lays itself over the rockiest of roads. It strides across the two. It often follows when we accept loss, failure, chaos while noticing that something still stands solid, still shines bright, still holds us.

I am again in a new café of a new city for a new degree. I am counting housemates—people who've never seen me fully and to whom I've never shown myself truly. (*Which comes first? Makes no difference. Same performance.*) I am estimating deposit raising years and can't bring them below a decade. I can't square the circle of owning a home. I can't, but they say that it's one of the ultimate circles of life.

Yet the café is warm, the machines are hissing, the coffee is velvety. The cup I hold starts holding me:

I am at home in my heart,

with some very special people,

and in every nice café.

I cross a threshold of pain. Then I rent my first flat by myself.

How long does it take to reach a new threshold of unbearable homelessness pain?

I don't know, eight years and about as many homes for me.

I've moved to a new country for an old love.

I ended up in a mountain village of about 200 inhabitants. Most of them were born around the World Wars. I can't speak the language.

I hate the house in my guts. It wasn't the one I agreed on. 'Mine' has not been decorated yet.

I've lost my debit card on flying in. I have no cash. And even if the village shop could take a credit card (it can't), I can't live on madeleines and green olives. I haven't read Proust. Madeleines won't save me. And I take my olives BLACK this season.

The trip to the supermarket is 16 kilometres. I said 'mountain village'. I have a bike with two working gears out of eighteen. The fastest speed ones.

I have a bleeding heart. I've just broken up with the man I came here for. Ten days after I'd come. After four years of waiting. The man I felt so at home with. And, yes, the man with the car.

I am a young (?) foreign woman who's not even English- or French-foreign to make her normal foreign. I am that strange creature who always greets you, throws out bags of rubbish in another pretty dress, freezes and looks down when a dog barks at her, and rides her bike with bright red heels and matching toenails.

And yes, I can hardly drink the coffee. It's too bitter. It has no foam.

I am in the opposite of home.

When you are so unravelled, so absurdly not fitting in, so cut out from your basic forms of security, you either break down or break open. You either hate yourself for being such an idiot, so unwanted, so rejected, disoriented, helpless and dependent, then run desperately away to arrive at more of the same, or find sublime peace and a cosmic joke in being all of that, exactly where you are.

If you are graced with the latter, the armour falls. Your eyes soften. The trusting child returns. You cross paths with people as a human calling forth another human, across languages, countries, ages, judgements and appearances.

Months later, I belonged. I was learning the language. I spoke back when spoken to and spoke forth when not. We understood each other's human kindness. Sometimes we understood each other's words. My neighbours tied back their dog. The old man with the beret, sitting on a chair by the road, always waved when I cycled up the hill. I wondered if he timed his sit-outs, if I timed my trips, or if our lives were made to tick together so that we could wave at each other.

No, it wasn't months later that I belonged, dear reader. I belonged from that split second when I looked around the hills, from the top of the house I first hated, and felt that even if I were the strangest stranger, the outsidiest outsider, I am, just like anyone I am a stranger to, a sister of the orange trees, a child of the hills around, the hills as old as time.

Now whenever the pain of moving, of being homeless, of hanging between lives kicks in, I find my way home to the World and its People.

My roots are growing by the day,

to ground me, to ground you at our next threshold of pain.

[illegible] Between [illegible] a chair by the [illegible]
[illegible] up the hill. I wondered if he timed [illegible]
[illegible] and ourselves were made to [illegible]
[illegible]

[illegible] that I belong [illegible]
belong [illegible] and some [illegible] and when [illegible]
[illegible] first before, and tell [illegible] were
[illegible] the outside [illegible]
[illegible] as a stage [illegible] insisted the [illegible]
the [illegible] as old as time.

Now when [illegible]
hanging between [illegible] I find my way [illegible] to the World
and its People.

My roots are growing by the day
to ground me [illegible]

CHAPTER 7

PARALLEL CLEANING

A sharp turn. From pain to cleaning. From belonging to scrubbing. From eyes looking into a stranger's eyes to eyes fixated on a carpet stain.

A house move is not for smooth transitions. Nor is Life. That said, cleaning can be surprisingly therapeutic when the pain kicks in.

Please imagine the following forms of filth:

- mould/mildew on the bathroom curtain;
- spills of tomato soup within the microwave;
- dust on the bookshelves.

When would you first notice them (or at least two of them)?

A. The moment they appear. No, they can't appear!

B. When I do my regular cleaning.

C. At some random moment—when they've reached a tipping point of visibility or I've got time to notice the world around me.

D. When they become pretty impressive, not to say gross.

E. When somebody comments/ raises eyebrows.

When would you clean them?

A. Right when I notice them, or as soon as possible.

B. When I do my regular cleaning.

C. When I have more time and/or mental space.

D. When they are too disgusting to ignore.

E. Only if I need to do some radical cleaning, as in moving house or if my mum is visiting.

Which letter are you? Maybe you are more than one? Yes, it is possible to be a mess as a cleaning type.

If you are a D or an E and renting through an agency, please hire a professional cleaner. Your own efforts won't cut it. Most of the time, it will work out cheaper to pay for the cleaning than lose a part of your deposit. Agencies aren't sentimental. Or well versed in the history of each of their houses' stains, for that matter. I've been charged for carpet smearing I remember from the viewing. Now I take photos.

Money aside, you'll be cleaning and hating this filthy house you are now extra pleased to be leaving. Your home-to-leave deserves better. So do you.

If you are an A or a B, you may intend to do the final clean yourself. Maybe it's a good idea. But being able to do it and/or having always done it doesn't mean you should do it this time. Remember that sparing ourselves martyrdom often gives others their daily bread.

If you are up for the task but worry because your contract has a professional cleaning clause, my experience says you can ignore the letters. I wouldn't have known if a professional cleaner I'd called in for a quote hadn't told me that relative to the many, many houses he'd seen, I didn't need him. I moved out of the area before he could benefit from his long-term business outlook. But thank you again, in a book.

All my recent contracts have had a professional cleaning clause. I've always broken it. Since that story, I've also done it in peace and with confidence. Nobody has ever disputed the standard. On the contrary.

That's even though I am a mediocre B, with spill-overs of C and A. As an A, I believe physical chaos translates into mental chaos. I find cleaning therapeutic. I feel energy moving differently in clean spaces.

But as a B and C, I don't need cleaning therapy all the time. My anxiety-responsive wrinkle deepens in houses where fingers fear to touch and bathrooms are always dry. If I'm sharing with folk who are at peace with piles of dirty dishes, sticky floors and hairs in the bathroom (I'm not), I still won't initiate cleaning rotas and rules. Feeling at home is the rota and the rule. I'll learn to accept your mess. Or I'll clean. If I notice enough to meet the professional standards, any A, B and C can do it.

Finally, if you are a C, you are the one with a choice. The pure letters amongst us are too driven by habit, firm beliefs and personality traits, even if we think that we are choosing. Our past chooses. You'll respond to your needs and the circumstances of the moment. And you'll feel good, whether you outsource the work and go to a spa or end up waving at spider webs, pondering how the lives we weave for ourselves can go 'poof' from one moment to the next.

(ANTI)CLIMACTIC CLEANING

If you choose to prepare for your house move over an extended period of time (the premise of this book) and, whenever you sort through a set of possessions, clean the space a few notches up from 'normal', your final house cleaning will be a non-event. It shouldn't take you longer than two to four times the duration of your normal routine.

Spreading the cleaning out also helps plan the use of cleaning products. If you have too many remaining, my experience suggests you'll have them claimed quickly if given away for free. (I've used Freecycle. Most recently, my cleaning products were taken by a family who'd just started an Airbnb business.) I've also tried offering them to cleaners at work, but they usually have company standardised products.

I no longer need to clean by myself. But I want to. My toilet seat has supported my most stinky self thousands of times. My mirror may have been throwing back a new breakout or a clenched jaw, but always looked me in the eye. I want to say thank you and goodbye to the fixtures that have served me.

I leave the spider webs till the end.
One more down.
My tenant, the spider, scurries between the bed and the wall.
I've just destroyed, in a single sweep, her house.
Her source of nourishment too.
It's all right. She'll work it out.
She's like me and you.
Already, there in the dark, she's weaving home and life anew.

PART II
ON-YOUR-BACK THINGS

Materially, the chapters in this part are about the possessions that make up most of our luggage in minimalist (single-rucksack, clothes-on-your-back) moves:

- **Clothes (*Chapter 8*).**
- **Shoes (*Chapter 9*).**
- **Sports equipment (*Chapter 10*)** for some of us. If that's not you, replace with what you need for an activity that is optional (unlike eating or washing) but without which you can't imagine your normal week. The equivalent of my sports equipment may be your arts materials, for instance.

Psychologically, these chapters are about:

- **The fear of truly shining** and eleven other types of psychological chaos (***Chapter 8***).
- **Lessons we were confident we have really learnt yet continue to repeat for years,** even decades, as well as nine other types of psychological chaos (***Chapter 9***).
- **Harmful inner conversations** and ten other types of psychological chaos (***Chapter 10***).

Throughout this book, **you will be coming across categories, groups and juxtapositions which feel unnatural, even 'wrong', to you.** This may concern the order of chapters and how they come together in parts. It may be about the possessions discussed in a chapter relative to its main object. For instance, the main object of ***Chapter 8*** are clothes, yet I mention umbrellas, drying racks and ironing boards there. Or I talk of hiking boots in the sports equipment chapter, not the shoe chapter.

We group possessions in ways that may be wildly different

from one person to the next. This is because:

Our lives, use of objects and minds differ.

Our living spaces make it natural or, on the contrary, impossible for certain objects to be kept together. The companionship which some possessions develop, in the sense of sharing space in one's home, may make every sense to us. It may look like the pinnacle of disorder to another.

Importantly, no category captures all that matters about an object. There are numerous good ways to categorise 'things'. Philosophically, this is the position of 'promiscuous realism' (in case you've wondered). For instance, an exercise top can rightfully belong to the category of 'clothes', to that of 'sports equipment', and to that of 'things to donate'.

The groups and categories I suggest are not something I propose as 'correct', 'better' or even take too seriously. Their main goal is to bring to the surface objects you might otherwise forget about, and, at times, signal something about the decisions awaiting you. Occasionally, I just like rolling my eyes at the righteousness of much advice on keeping spaces, objects and ideas 'logically organised'. Generally, the more you debate with how I group things, the better. It means you are thinking about and remembering more of what you own.

So whether your on-your-back things are similar or nothing like mine, let's get started with the clothes on and off your back!

CHAPTER 8

"When in doubt, wear red"[1]

The collision had propelled him off his bike, bare skin grating against coarse-grained asphalt, head hitting a concrete wall, helmet cracking open. Three hours later, his face is yellow-greener by the minute. Blood and dust, stuck to the skin of his arms, to the hairs on his skin, resist to come off to the wipes I'm cleaning his cuts and grazes with. I rub harder. He tries to hold his body stiff, his pain voiceless. Staccato shudders flow from him through me, rising, hitting, dissipating. The cycle re-starts. When the village doctor tests the mobility of his lower body, he wails as if broken bones are ripping muscle and skin apart. Still, while waiting for the ambulance, he climbs two flights of stairs to fetch his favourite red-and-blue top. I want to kick him. I only shout.

I can't tell you if he didn't ask *me* instead because he felt I was already helping beyond reasonable expectations (that was my ex-boyfriend turned friend, who'd recently messed up the

---

1 Quote attributed to Bill Blass (1922–2002), an American fashion designer.

honesty and trust assumption of the friendship too) or because he thought it was a ridiculous request to repeat. He had already asked for his red-and-blue top. I'd packed, apparently, the wrong one.

Yet I would have packed ten more (and ten times uglier ones) if needed, until I get it right. The desire wasn't stupid. When everything is going wrong, we want a piece of home with us. Some clothes *are* home.

My own legendary items of clothing are a pair of yellow trousers and a floral summer dress. The trousers I had from an age when they were loose and below the ankles. I wore them until my mid-twenties, ultimately as knee-high leggings, tight and threadbare on the bum. I might still be wearing them if my mum hadn't thrown them out. (Don't we all have stories of secret evil disposal of our treasures!)

Which are *your* legendary clothes? These are your reference point for what it means to love a piece of clothing. The further your sentiment is from such a reference, the less sense it makes to carry, or pay for the carrying of, a wardrobe item at moving out.

Now open your wardrobe or imagine its contents. Which of the following categories of clothes fill up most of it?

- Clothes you love—some just bought, some hopelessly worn out by the love, some only for special occasions, but all of them amongst your 'favourite things'.
- Clothes that you don't have much of an attitude towards, which are typical, normal, ordinary, maybe crossing over into the invisible or faceless. But they do the job.
- Clothes that you feel super comfortable in, hugged, held and consoled by, but which better be worn in solitary confinement.
- Clothes you look fabulous in, but the fabric scratches

your skin, or they make you sweat too much, or they 'do' or 'don't do' any other thing because of which you move onto the next hanger.

- Clothes you can't bear to put on again, on another Groundhog Day, are bored to death with, yourself in them, your life in them.
- Clothes that are mostly lovely if it weren't for a silly ribbon that's impossible to remove without damaging the fabric, a collar that's 'too round', sleeves a tad too puffed on the shoulders, [insert an irritating visual feature].
- Clothes that need special care which you aren't willing to give them—such as difficult to iron or needing to be handwashed or dry cleaned only (or even just ironed!).
- Clothes that need repair.
- Clothes that no longer fit you or never did—too tight, too loose, not flattering on your bum, breasts, waist...
- Your default garments for weddings, funerals, interviews, receptions and other momentous occasions. Some you can't wait to put on again. Others are as if infiltrated by an intense event: *the outfit I wore at my cousin's wedding/ when we broke up/ at Laura's funeral.* The energy of only a few hours refuses to wash off.
- Clothes you've worn only once or even never.
- Anything else?

WHY DO I HOLD ONTO YOU
IF I DON'T LOVE YOU?

Why, in this world of plenty, do we have anything other than clothes we love? Why don't we commit to having a wardrobe, and more generally a house, dare I say a life, where everything we have can make us smile? (If we pay attention, sure. Things inevitably recede into the background.)

If you've answered with a version of "because clothes don't matter", you might skip this chapter, or at least the psychological aspect of it (the pragmatic ideas are in boxes towards the end). Clothes still externalise some of your inner chaos but more subtly than for many people. It will be easier to catch the same issues through other possessions.

If you gave a version of a 'not enough' response (not having enough money or time; not being in good enough shape, etc.), think again. I didn't ask why you don't have all the clothes you've fallen in love with or lusted after across centuries and shop windows. I asked about the clothes you have. Don't commit a category mistake.

Test your money hypotheses
Clothes money test 1:
Open your wardrobe and drawers. Throw on the bed, or the floor, the items which you don't quite like or don't have much of an attitude towards. Sort them by standard types this time (trousers, shirts, dresses), roughly for the same type of context (e.g. work, exercise, home).

Does any of the piles have more than a single member? Three items per pile? Five or more? What's their rough combined cost? What one or two things could you have bought with this money?

Buying OK things tends to be followed by buying other OK things. Your mediocre collection has the price of luxury.

Clothes money test 2:
Make a (mental) list of your most favourite clothes throughout the

years. Indicate their rough price (it's ridiculous how many clothes prices we remember, or at least the range). Add the number of years you've worn them.

Have your most favourite clothes been the most expensive ones? Some of them — certainly. Though relative to the number of years you've worn them, even they have ended up average priced.

But you must also have a story or two of a dress, jacket, jeans, something which you bought from the sales, H&M, second hand... and you've worn threadbare or are still wearing, almost a decade later. For some, the washing powder you've needed throughout the years has cost more. The yearly cost of my favourite nineteen-year-old dress (bought from the sales too) is about £1.20.

Clothes money test 3:
Can you remember the last time when you've been ready to pay at the top of your range, even stretch that up, for a core item of clothing (such as a winter coat or an evening dress) as long as you truly loved it? Then you simply couldn't find anything to thrill you enough? Has this happened more than once?

Clothes money test 4:
Can you remember the last time when you hesitated whether to buy a piece of clothing, then 'go on', buying it, because it made such a little difference to your budget? *It's not a car! A third of the money I've just paid for a concert ticket. Five coffees.* Has this been a single event in your life? I didn't think so.

Money's not the issue.

The straps are invisible
And yet it is. It may well be THE issue.

My brother, an auto-motor sports TV commentator, including of Formula 1, refuses to buy clothes from anywhere other than second-hand shops. Even the outfit for his wedding reception was from there. He loves breathing life into discarded things, but I also suspect his past of driving him. As a kid, he often inherited clothes worn by his older cousin, then his sister, then his younger cousin.

If money has ever felt finite in your life, you are likely to have hundreds of inner ceilings about what's acceptable to pay for what. I do. I've cracked hundreds. Hundreds more remain. I've grown up during the collapse of the communist bloc in the 80s and 90s. Shelves were empty, food was rationed, inflation was in the thousands, and my country was receiving aid for, give and take, fifteen years. I've also been a student through six degrees (when 'student' stood for 'out-of-pocket', not 'privilege').

You don't need such extremes—and some of you have seen far worse—to develop inner money ceilings. An extended period of constraint is enough. Then we "CAN'T give that much money for a dress, it's obscene." We "don't shop from those shops". We've also developed the skills to make (clothes) money stretch, like waiting for the sales, repairing old attire or remembering the days for new stock in second-hand shops.

By itself, most of the above is not dysfunctional. We all have priorities and pet hates in spending money. We all have shops that feel like home and others that don't. Having restraint is eco-friendly. It becomes dysfunctional when our past steers us into buying clothes, or anything else for that matter, that stop at 'this will do'.

Because 'this will do' is investing in kind-of-love. And whether it's human love or clothes love, kind-of-love is always, in the long run, more expensive than investing in true love.

The 100-arm Goddess (or the Renaissance Man)
and excess of 'universals'

One way in which old money issues can shape our wardrobe is through a preference for 'universals'. This is what I call clothes that fit several, even contrasting, contexts. A hectic lifestyle – trying to be a 100-arm Goddess or a Renaissance Man – imprint the habit deeper. The philosophy of 'a capsule wardrobe' gives it the stamp of glitterati approval.

I noticed the excess of universals in my wardrobe once I was looking for a summer dress that was 1) smart and 2) casual, with a touch of 3) sexiness and 4) femininity, but 5) only a touch as it had to be 6) entirely appropriate for work too, even if 7) fitting for a party or 8) a Sunday walk on the towpath, as well as 9) comfortable to cycle in, 9a) without showing my knickers to the upcoming traffic yet 9b) not getting caught in the spokes of the wheel either. Retracing the history of my high expectations to my twenties, I came up with a list of twelve contexts I needed to glide across with the same clothes in a normal week, ranging from the office, through mountain rescue team training sessions, to classical concerts.

Some magic clothes can do that for you. My favourite universals used to be a navy-blue dress with a golden buckle and a black plaited jumpsuit with a low décolletage (adjustable towards propriety with a safety pin). But all-rounders are usually a compromise in each distinct situation. Fitting anywhere means not attracting the wrong type of attention by excelling somewhere else.

I cut down on universals the moment I realised I was leaning towards them and why. My love for my wardrobe has grown exponentially.

Will it work for you? I don't know. You may have just realised you need a navy-blue dress with a golden buckle.

It is not a book of rules, it's one of mirrors.

Ghosts of once-denied love

We may be asserting that "money can't buy you love" and while most of us rarely try to do it directly, most of us also try thousands of ways to do it indirectly, including through clothes. The rules of money and love are tied in a knot. In clothes, it's one of the most visible.

Some of us ration the number and/or quality of our clothes relative to how limited we experience the (self-)love. If we don't feel that we deserve to sparkle and shine, to have and be given, to be sublimely loved and cherished, we are likely to default to quite-nice-isn't-it, sensible, affordable clothes. Practical. Responsible. Focusing on what matters. All that's deeper than appearances.

Others grow the number and/or quality of our clothes in an attempt to assert and express the fragile (self-)love. We value and love and respect ourselves and it shows in how damn good we look. What we dress in is a statement of style, class, elegance, beauty, quality. And on some days, it absolutely is that. We own every aspect of our brilliance. On other days, well, most days, we are obsessively registering if we've been noticed, admired, complimented enough, recognised as one of a tribe, on a par with others, above others, thumbed-up, head-turned, envied.... We acquire clothes we cannot form a lasting connection with, don't wear enough to experience eternal moments in, but without which we feel insecure, invisible and not belonging.

It doesn't need to be anything extreme. We may only be doing it in one area of life, such as date nights, special occasions or our favourite sport. The defining feature is not how many and how much. It's that we buy believing we've expressed self-care and self-love, while (subliminally) hoping we would be accepted and appreciated more.

We dress the ghosts of once-denied love.

Bodies to hide

We may also feel nothing, or anything but love, for our clothes because we are ashamed of our bodies. We may still be proclaiming love and acceptance for them. Yet the true acceptance and love for our bodies—which make us care for them, nourish them, inhabit, move, explore them, have them loved in ways that electrify the wholeness of us, treat them as a temple, precious gift, ultimate home—pass us by.

There are forms of shame to revolt against; to refuse to experience; to face naked and vulnerable and owning all of yourself.[1] But there are also aspects of body shame that call for sweat, discomfort and commitment. For catching ourselves in lame excuses, high values and harsh judgements all at once. Inner beauty. The wise acceptance of the passage of time. The only twenty-four hours in a day which we, sadly, need to distribute so thinly, with our family, work, social media, world peace.... The food industry. The built environment. The neural circuits wired by past habits. Exercise kit that's too expensive. Sports clubs that are cliquey. Yogis that are woo-woo. The body obsessed that are shallow and artificial and photoshopped and stupid.

Some of the best places to buy clothes you'll love are exercise

---

1 Brené Brown has written of these with clear-sightedness and depth I won't try to condense. Read her if you haven't. Her books can be life-changing.

studios, cycle lanes, mountain paths, dance floors....The more frequently you visit, the more clothes you rock in. In fact, the more likely you are not to care if you have clothes on.

Ultimately, clothes are a temporary presence. The naked truth will always show.

Invisible cloaks for fearful souls

Still, there are softer parts of our Being than our squishy bellies.

Most of the people I see regularly, including myself for many years, wear clothes that are ok, perhaps even lovely, but non-descript and non-identifiable. You can exchange them with the person next desk and no-one would notice. There is no stamp of you.

It makes sense. It's safer to be invisible, or at least a diluted watercolour version of yourself. The more you are noticed, the more likely you are to be ridiculed. Accused. Shamed. Singled out to complete a task. Shouted at. Asked for more money by more beggars. Shot dead.

Typically, we don't pick what to wear in the morning by weighing the risks of being taken hostage at the bank or angering a bull at Trafalgar Square. Yet most of us dress to blend rather than to kill. Even when it's time to shine, we do it a few notches down from our inner image. Attention feels sweet. THAT much attention is scary. All our soul cracks, life lies and hanging skin around the knees will be there for the world to see. Clothes that draw too much attention expect of us to trust, own, shine, discover and re-discover the beauty of our soul and body well before and after we've been dressed in them.

That is not to say that the healthy, adapted, strong thing is to be visible by default. There *are* times to hide.

Sometimes we need the space and anonymity to go deep within, to rest, to heal. Sometimes we move the swiftest when we attract the least attention. Sometimes we create the greatest magic, the best of arts when we disappear to the world. But if we find too many invisible cloaks in our wardrobe and drawers on moving out, it's unlikely we are simply creating the space for going deep within ourselves and the worlds beyond this world. Far more likely, we've learnt that it's safer to hide.

Time pushes and field pulls

Of course, the psychology behind our not-so-loved clothes is often far shallower than our fragile self-concept. It is in the realms of narrowed awareness and field effects.

Sometimes we buy clothes we hardly connect with when we are racing against the clock.

You have a job interview tomorrow.

You donated your winter clothes last season, yet the icy winds are here earlier this year.

You have a date!

It's time for the office Christmas party, a wedding, hiking trip, a holiday....

We go for quick fixes and wear them once. Occasionally, that's life. But it's a sad life when our wardrobe is a permanent exhibition of constant running.

Other times, our unloved clothes happen at the click of our emptiness with the shops' fullness, our heaviness with their lightness. Clothes commerce, just as any commerce, always steps in readily in our struggles with inner chaos.

If we frequently let it 'resolve' them for us, our wardrobes become the sum total of our field stimuli rather than an expression of us. Our clothes show off the strongest vectors in our environments as opposed to our essence, best assets, living spaces and moods.

It happens easily. And while it's honey-dripping righteous to focus on how manipulative and exploitative of our insecurities clothes commerce is, it happens easily because it is both that and a masterpiece of talent, beauty, passion, creativity, efficiency, human psychology, brilliance upon brilliance, including in the skill of making it so evasively manipulative and exploitative. There is nothing better at controlling our behaviours than such double-faced leviathans, whether it's the fashion industry, social media, money, technology or opioids, for instance. When heaven and hell converge in a creation, it's easy for it to claim our soul. It doesn't matter if we embrace or reject it either. If you spend too much energy on being against or shutting away something, you are still controlled by it.

The only way we can ride, even fly, on such dragons rather than be burnt by them is to be deeply connected to our true needs, tastes and desires; to be constantly renewing our efforts to switch into these; to hold fast onto them when flooded with external stimuli. As unlikely a path to psychological balance, not to say enlightenment, as it may seem, buying clothes is a practice of connecting to Self.

Ask your wardrobe.

Memory circles
Let's add the spirals of memory.

I am shifting hangers on a sales rack. The woman next to me pulls out a blouse—blue and white stripes, relaxed fit, broad neckline. She inspects it at arm's length. I find it so pretty that I swell to say it. Then right when I open my mouth, I realise it's a variation of what she wears. "Get something different," I say laughing. "This is too similar to what you have on!"

"Perhaps that's why I am looking at it," she responds curtly.

Maybe she was right. "If it works for me, I'll have more of it" is a familiar logic in buying clothes. Maybe my intuition — that she was unconsciously falling into a pattern, forgetting she already had what she was looking at — was right. Maybe she was irritated with me for being right rather than for violating her "me and my clothes time-space reality". Whatever. Just another attempt to connect falling flat on its face.

Yet whatever the truth of this case, the point is valid. You too must have found yourself drawn to a piece of clothing, trying it on, having the feeling of it being "exactly what you wanted", buying it, and soon after being struck by how similar it is to something you once had or even still have. Same nuance of green, same wrap-up style, same polka dot pattern even if in a different colour.

It wasn't perfect fit. It was perfect familiarity.

DECIDING ON BOUNDARY
(KEEP OR NOT KEEP) CASES
Separating (or not) from true loves

Please don't agonise over the fate of your ridiculously faded, ripped-at-the-front, hole-between-the-legs, transparent-on-the-bum, moth-eaten, etc. favourites. Both keeping and throwing them is a sensible choice. You are projecting onto such clothes a positive emotion you can summon back any time if you wish to, but unless you have to minimise your luggage, there is no overwhelming reason to do so. Rational reasons don't count for more than emotional reasons. Emotional reasons can be fully rational. Don't conflate love with some of the unhealthy forms of sentimentality and attachment though *(see **Chapter 20**)*.

If you need to let go of clothes (or anything else) you've loved but can't take with you, consider creating a ritual. I take photos of favourite clothes I am leaving behind. I spend one last special day wearing them. I fold them caringly before putting them in a donation bag. I say thank you and goodbye. There is no limit to how sentimental and silly you can be in separating from objects during a move. There is no requirement to be so either.

Feeling into the depths of boredom

If you are bored with a piece of clothing, gauge the reversibility.

There have been periods in my life when I would wear some clothes so frequently and for so long that, after a time, my body was as if emitting a repellent on feeling them creep on. They might still be perfectly wearable. I might be receiving compliments for them. My money fortunes might be 10,000 metres (pounds) down a debt hole. I wouldn't take them forward. Groundhog Day props must perish in a move.

Sometimes, however, clothes we've loved but have become bored with (though not to the above level) regain vitality when combined differently or when they sit out a period of disconnection. Matching clothes in new ways, even if only in your imagination, is a good measure for the reversibility of boredom.

That said, 'bored with' is one of the best reasons to let things go. Find the contexts where the need is acute. Somebody out there will be screaming with joy at your here-we-go-again clothes.

DEALING WITH THE VARIETIES
OF HARDLY WORN/UNWORN

If a piece of clothing **needs alteration or repair,** don't wait for
the madness of a house move to look for a tailor or sit yourself
down to do it. Or do (as I do, it's practically the only time I have
clothes repaired). It's still good. A liberating house move clears
away intentions, not only space. More pragmatically, you don't
want to be carrying forward items in a coma. You want to be
certain that everything you are taking with you has a future
in your future.

If a piece of clothing is a **pain to maintain**—for instance,
awkward to iron or only requiring dry cleaning, take a risk against
the instructions. If I don't wear something because of the hassle
and expense of dry cleaning, I wash it. Not a single item has been
damaged so far (wash may mean hand-wash). Such clothes will
get worn out quicker. But they'll be worn. I've also stopped buying
any 'dry clean only' clothes, with the exception of winter coats
and jackets.

If you have clothes which are beautiful and **hardly worn
but feel stamped with an experience**, consider respecting
the uniqueness of the moment. Recently, I sold the dress which
won me the 'best-dressed dinner guest' prize out of seventy plus
magnificently dressed people. (I must have been the cheapest
dressed dinner guest too, but that's another story.) If you've
always been praised for being smart rather than beautiful,
you'll understand why I keep the certificate in the same folder
as my diplomas. Still, I never wore that dress again.

I begin to avoid occasion wear if I've gone through an intense
experience in it. It's never intentional. It's only that such clothes
feel locked in the past. I started to respect that. I let them belong

to the unforgettable moments they've co-created in my life and to somebody else's wardrobe.

If you find **no particular reason not to have worn** a piece of clothing, start wearing it right this day if it's in season.

Similarly, if you've been missing the clothes or accessories to combine an item with, start window-shopping for them. Ideally, add nothing new to your luggage. Only use the attention to revive the piece (or not).

When right before a move you begin to use something you've never or hardly used, you simplify decision making. You find welcome variety. The ease to leave behind. Old intentions releasing their hold.

Decisions are simpler when you've bridged the gap of strangeness.

On peeking through the restaurant window two years later

We sometimes can't let go of clothes we've hardly worn because they haven't paid off their price. You can always try to sell them rather than donate (more on that later). But if you get nowhere with the trade, make a thought experiment before you pack them in.

Imagine you've been out for a dinner for two in a fancy new restaurant. You were buzzing with excitement to go, yet you found it overpriced, over-praised and underwhelming. Imagine it's two years later. You still remember the experience, even keep the receipts. It was so disappointing that, every now and again, you go back to the premises, circle around them, peer through the windows, read the menu posted on the entrance, and weigh up the pros and cons of booking again in the hope of diminishing the disappointment from two years ago.

That's what you are doing with most items you can't let go of because you've once paid good money for them. Overthinking a few disappointing dinners. Think again.

REDISTRIBUTING THE CLOTHES
YOU ARE NOT KEEPING

As you have, mostly likely, been redistributing clothes, whether you've been moving house or not, I assume you have enough of your own ways, hacks and principles. I've moved mine into boxes to make them easier to skip.

Boxes 4 and 5 have ideas on selling and donating clothes, respectively.

Box 6 has examples of my personal ethics of donating and giving away clothes.

Box 7 discusses what to do with items from the broader family around clothes: accessories, clothes care items (such as ironing boards and drying racks) and underwear.

BOX 4

SELLING CLOTHES POINTERS

- **Selling clothes is rarely worth the effort (if money is your main motivation)**

  Relative to what you've paid, the return on clothes sales will be typically disappointing. Your potential buyers have too many other options in clothes trading. The money might be meaningful if you are selling designer clothes (I don't know), but then your idea of meaningful money will be different too (and good for you!).

  Unfamiliar labels, even if the clothes are beautiful and almost new, are particularly hard to sell.

  If you insist on selling, I suggest you go for direct contact, as in a garden sale.

  Alternatively:

- **Look out for local shops selling high-quality second-hand clothes—some will buy yours out**

  I've sold clothes most successfully to local boutiques for high-quality second-hand items. The latest one I used offered a 50:50 split of the selling price and six–eight weeks of display time. It might not be visible that they buy things out. Ask.

- **Some of the clothes-focused apps/online services you can try (in addition to generic ones like eBay, Gumtree or Facebook Marketplace) are below. Interestingly, Vinted and HEWI have been started during house moves:**

  - *vinted.co.uk*–a community of over 50 million users, operating in 13 countries in Europe as well as in the U.S. and Canada.

- *depop.com* — lists over 2,200 brands, though this includes non-clothes brands (from beauty to photography equipment).
- *hardlyeverwornit.com* — or HEWI, for luxury items. Lists almost 1,800 brands (again, includes brands specialising in other products, such as shoes, bags and accessories).
- *corporate.remixshop.com/en/* — available in 9 Central and Eastern Europe countries. Over 10,000 items added every day.

I've found the last one, Remix, exceptionally easy and simple to use. You create an account, check if they accept your brands and put the clothes in a bag they deliver to you. They do the rest — taking photos, advertising, posting to buyer, etc. I sold all I offered within days. Expectedly, the profit was underwhelming, at the level of several coffees for a once worn Laura Ashley dress.

Depop and Vinted I've had recommended, with the disclaimer that it's a slow process and, ultimately, 'all' down to you (though I wouldn't say that a platform that links you to potential buyers and enables the transactions leaves it 'all' down to you).

Figures as of Jan 2022.

BOX 5

Donating clothes basics

**If clothes donation facilities have been
off your radar so far, look out for:**

- **Donation banks/ containers:** the typical locations for
  these differ across countries, but I've seen them most of-
  ten at recycling sites, supermarket car parks, and in and
  around permanent open-air markets. Tourist areas, espe-
  cially by the seaside, tend to have more of them.

- **Donation/ recycling facilities in clothes stores:** there
  might be donation/ recycling boxes around the store
  entrance or counter, but it might simply be 'a process',
  whereby you give a bag of clothes to any staff member.
  Typically, any brand is accepted, not just the clothes of
  a particular store. You often receive a 10-20% discount
  voucher in return.

- **Home recycling collection:** some local authorities
  have made arrangements for textiles to be collected and
  recycled, even if it's far from obvious (for instance, the
  black box of Cornwall is generally for glass, but it can be
  used for textiles).

- **Charity shops:** I'd never seen a charity shop before com-
  ing to England. Shops for second-hand clothes are busi-
  nesses in the part of the world where I was born. Donat-
  ing clothes at a charity shop can be a blindingly obvious
  solution or a complete oddity for you!

- **Donation bags coming through the post box:** to be
  filled up and collected a few days later. Such schemes
  are managed by commercial companies. As charities re-
  ceive a small proportion of the profit, I use them rarely.
  That said, nothing wrong with a good business and ex-
  ceptional convenience.

- **Projects using donated clothes to teach skills**, such as clothes repair, sales skills and customer service – see, for instance, the concept of Africawad (*africawad.org*).

If the chain for reused clothes is not so well organised where you live:

- Consider making the redistribution task **special** (for instance, commit to giving your clothes where the need is greatest or in a place you have a connection to) rather than as easy as possible (such as leaving a bag of clothes next to the neighbourhood rubbish containers). You'll love it far more and often find yourself in an adventure.

- In places with no clothes recycling facilities, **try places of worship.**

  You would think most religious institutions will be facilitating, if not doing, such charity work, but at least in my hometown's churches, this was not the case. Prepare to be asking around.

- **Refugee centres** or refugee support groups are another obvious place of acute current need.

  I have both picked up leaflets asking for clothes donations for refugees without moving an inch outside of my routines and spent hours searching for information on refugee centres. Donation intentions lead just as often to perfect encounters as they do to failed quests.

- **Orphanages** are also a typical place to contact if you have clothes to donate.

  Precisely for this reason, some receive quite regular and high-quality donations. I remember being a volunteer in an orphanage in my twenties and having some of the kids wear far newer and nicer clothes than me. If you want your donation to reach those most in need, seek institutions with **no website and far away from big cities.**

**Loading up and turning up
is not necessarily efficient:**

- Even if a place generally accepts clothes donations or did so 'last time', **it may not be the case now**.

  For instance, quite a few UK charity shops were not accepting donations long after the pandemic lockdowns were discontinued. Too many people have had extra time for decluttering. Trade had been limited. Store-rooms were small.

  Many magnificent donation/ sustainability initiatives run out of capacity, becoming a victim of their own success.

- Check **working hours.** Bags of neatly tied clothes at the doorstep in the evening are a sad sight of scattered rubbish in the morning.

BOX 6

SOME OF MY PERSONAL ETHICS AROUND DONATING AND GIVING AWAY CLOTHES

- **Corrode your attachments
  by looking into the abyss**

  If I see/ read something viscerally disturbing about people being cold, wet and tattered, I lose any attachment to clothes I hardly wear or am bored with. It no longer makes sense to keep clothes half-heartedly. Such stories usually 'find you', but you can seek them out too if you want to corrode irrational attachments.

- **Presentation matters**

  I never throw or stuff clothes in donation bags. I wash and carefully fold them. A gift needs to look like a gift too.

  Overly worn-out and irreversibly stained clothes, hosiery and underwear I put in a separate bag. I stick an 'industrial use'/ 'rag trade' label on it. I have no idea if it's helpful. I even doubt it (why would the people who review the donations assume that my criteria are the same as their criteria?). But it's my way to signal, "I don't take your beneficiaries as subhuman".

- **When giving away to family and friends,
  start with the love, not with the 'don't need'**

  I don't offer any of the clothes I am redistributing to family or friends. I don't suggest it as a universal principle. In my case:

  I don't want to see clothes I am bored with ever again, whether in the mirror or across the table.

I don't like some of the underlying messages: "It's too big for me, but since you've always been fatter, sweetheart, it might work for you?"

I've also found that, whenever I've accepted clothes in this way (and have been thrilled to), 95% of them have remained 'foreign bodies' in my wardrobe. I've ultimately always donated them, typically at my next move.

That said, I gladly take clothes of my mum's, friends' and housemates' which they don't currently wear. Goes vice versa too. But it doesn't start from "I no longer wear that". It's from "Oh, I love that!".

- **You shall be judged**

Since I had a bag of clothes reviewed by a stern-looking, God-fearing woman in a local church, I am borrowing more conservative eyes in preparing church donations. If you are in the habit of feeling judged, including when trying your best to do something good, you will feel judged when donating during your move. The more you donate, the more judged (though virtuous too) you will feel.

It's a perfect opportunity to work on restructuring your habitual patterns. More controversially, you can have fun providing stern-looking, God-fearing people with opportunities to practise non-judgement.

- **Showing care can make you decide differently**

If an item of clothing or an accessory has a sorry appearance but is fully usable, consider giving it extra care before making a final decision—wash, iron, dry clean, repair it...

A few moves ago, I hand-washed and ironed a shawl I had put aside to donate. (I needed a last-minute matching accessory.) I was amazed how beautiful its delicate flowers were. Three people complimented me on it the same day. It had a second life with me. Both seeing things while taking care of them and the results of that care can make you change your mind.

BOX 7

THE BROADER FAMILY AROUND CLOTHES

ACCESSORIES

- Accessories such as **bags**, **gloves**, **scarves** and **belts** are normally easy to donate alongside clothes and shoes.

- Fancy **hats** often need a box which takes up a third of a suitcase. You can make up for lost space and protect their shape further by stuffing them with scarfs and clothes and putting light clothes around. Recently, I started to let hats go. I happily imagine myself as a regatta-style hat-wearing lady for an event once a month. I'm beginning to acknowledge it's more like once every ten. Years.

- I've searched on and off for almost two decades, but still haven't found a good way to recycle **umbrellas**.

  Years ago, I detached the cloths from the spokes of several broken umbrellas and sent them to the U.S. A Philadelphian lady was using them to make dogs' clothes. Carbon emissions were hardly a topic of conversation then. Please don't go searching for "umbrella recycling dog clothes Philadelphia" though! If you have plastic, metal and textiles recycling around you, you can dismantle the umbrella and recycle the components separately.

  Then buy an umbrella designed to last. I am a convert to Blunt, "wind tunnel tested to a Category 1 Hurricane (71mph)".

CLOTHES CARE ITEMS

- Irons, ironing boards and drying racks I've sold, donated or left in houses which needed them (or took with me during bigger moves). Those are some of the 'most wanted' items in the world of affordable personal commerce and community sharing.

UNDERWEAR

* **It's easier to sell yourself than your underwear!**

    If you decide to sell your (obviously unworn) underwear, be warned that you'll run a social experiment rather than a trade.

    When I tried, I got, within hours, half a dozen requests to model the lacy bra and bodice I had advertised. You'll get invited to a few homes too, including ones where "the girlfriend's away for the weekend".

    You decide if this is a warning or a top tip.

* **Give a second life to bras**
  (whether your own or forgotten at yours)

    Bras are, it turns out, a significant design and sewing challenge. They are a high value recycling item. Bra banks are often managed by breast cancer charities, but have a local coordinator, which means you can find them in unexpected places (e.g. actual banks, offices, cafés, even pub toilets). Lingerie shops can have them too, but surprisingly sporadically in my experience.

    The bra banks of lingerie shops for women with bigger cups do accept small bras (in case you've been wondering). They don't look down on you either! They seem to know about breast size insecurities, whatever their nature.

* **Buy underwear bags—for your move and for ever**

    If you don't have them already, consider buying proper lingerie/underwear bags, even if moving out is not the time for new purchases. In case it sounds unfamiliar, those are not lingerie washing bags, although they are a useful possession too. Rather, they are usually drawstring bags for storing and carrying underwear.

They simplify every move and every trip. Mine are amongst my six oldest possessions.

- **If on your clothes-sorting nights you are more likely to be going to bed with a movie, rather than with somebody who would notice your lingerie, try *The Dressmaker* (2015)[1].**

On the surface, with so much more underneath it, this film is about the transformative power of clothes; the 'rubbish' who remain rubbish no matter how beautifully they are dressed; homes you were never at home in but need to return to so that you can find your true home; a boy's murder in the past and a love in the present that...

I won't spoil where it gets,

but it starts with a striking red dress.

---

1 Directed by Jocelyn Moorhouse, starring Kate Winslet, Liam Hemsworth, Hugo Weaving and Judy Davis. 7.1 on IMDb.

The floral summer dress I mentioned and didn't continue the story of is a short strappy dress of red-pink-grey-black flowers on a white base I've had for nineteen and worn for eighteen years.

I recently collected it from repairs after I'd butchered it. I'd cut out a piece of it to give to a man to remind him he's far better than what he believes about himself and that the evidence is all around, even if he can't see it. Moreover, it is not only that he can't see it, but he often argues against it or even twists it into its opposite. He does so not because he's twisted, but because that's the first thing we do when evidence contradicts the most deep-seated beliefs we hold.

That dress knew of rationed confidence, irrational self-doubt and twisting the evidence. I was confident it made me almost beautiful to those who loved me. Yet when strangers were staring, even turning heads (it's a body-hugging dress, and it looks red, and I first had it in my twenties), I thought that they thought, and one of them would finally say, and the rest will hummmm and confirm at the next crossroads or construction site that "That girl is spoiling the dress! Over 60 cm waist! Under 90 cm boobs! Boooo! Take it off her! Give it to the hourglass figure woman!"

I changed into the dress to tell him the story and thus impress its message. I gave him the piece I'd cut off the dress as an 'anchor' for the message. He said it was a good story. I can't remember what he said about the dress. But the clip that held one of its straps in place snapped, flew off, hit the concrete floor. One of my shoulders went naked. I thought it was the energy behind his eyes, regardless of the evidence of their stillness and his distance.

If he remembers anything, it's more likely to be the dress

than the lesson. Learning to believe that others see goodness and beauty in us that go far beyond those we can see doesn't happen with one sermon, or a hundred. How do you begin to see yourself fundamentally differently when you've been seeing yourself a million times as you see yourself? It's one of the most difficult things in life. You can't force a new perspective, even if you can prepare the possibility for it. It reveals itself to you.

Even more likely, he remembers nothing. He had a concussion shortly after. He fell off his bike.

Clothes can change everything and nothing.

They can be a home and a foreign skin.

They can matter immensely and not a fig.

They can hide us and reveal us and expose us, and reveal us and expose us when we think that they hide us.

They can show our essence in ways we feel reflected back at us and, in turn, begin to embody more of. They can show our essence in ways we completely fail to comprehend, both for the better and for the worse.

They can carry stories and memories and the touch of those fingers and the roving of those eyes only after a few hours. They can carry a price tag five years later.

How come clothes create such contrasting realities?

Simple.

You fill them in.

CHAPTER 9

"SHOES SHOULDN'T HURT"

"You think you deserve that pain, but you don't," he says, touching a scratch on her ankle. Love has just made an entrance. Over a shoe, as it has a classic habit of doing. Have you noticed that both putting feet to extreme tests and showing care to them at their dirtiest and ugliest are symbolic of a great love?

This pick-up line of shoes' wisdom and compassionate psychotherapeutic assessment is from *Me and You and Everyone We Know* (2005).[1] When I first saw the movie, love was hurting to total emotional freezing and a partial physical one. (If I insist on being precise, I will tell you that love never hurts if it deserves its name. It is the stirring of old wounds from what was not love when it should have been love that hurts. But since hardly anyone of us will experience love as never hurting, the precise language around love and pain becomes almost impossible to understand.) One way or another, it was a time when I felt life could only be a Burden for

---

1 Directed by Miranda July, starring Miranda July and John Hawkes, 7.3 on IMDb.

the rest of it. The best I could hope for was for the Burden to feel occasionally lighter. Maybe it would work through being useful to others, feeling into their happiness, and becoming so fed up with dissecting my pain that I stopped noticing it, that old boring all too familiar heavy omnipresent but also irrelevant shadow.

My sizeable, elegant shoe collection became one of the centrepieces of decision making during this move. In a reversal of the Cinderella story, my shoes had to pass a test. It was 'shoes shouldn't hurt', somehow intermingled with 'love shouldn't hurt'. The way my foot would slide down and into them had to resemble that yielding, vulnerable, quiet, totalising state when fully accepted by another.

I left with the shoes on my feet only.

UNLEARNING TO HURT IS DIFFICULT

The rule of 'shoes shouldn't hurt' was sublime in facilitating decisions at moving out. But moving out was late. I needed to learn to apply it at the point of buying shoes. It took me no less than four years and five moves, after committing to only having shoes that don't hurt, to make my shoe purchases pain-proof.

Unlearning to hurt is difficult.

Our feet are a prime example of how disconnected from our bodies and how accustomed to avoidable pain we can be. If you've ever had blisters, corns, bunions (how ugly even the words sound!), the bone of your big toe sticking out, slight changes to the arch of your foot, continue the list, you've spent some of your walking life ignoring the pain and discomfort from your feet. If you have had such mini-traumas anything other than infrequently, then you are a specialist in switching off pain sensations from your feet. And if you are a specialist in disconnecting from the pain in your feet, it will be unusual not to do it in your broader body and life, too.

Your feet tell a story. Look at them bare. Feel into them when you are next walking. Translate their silent story into words you can hear. If you are not sure what to feel into, *see **Box 8** at the end of the chapter.*

If your feet tell no story of repetitive pain, good for you! You've learnt the value of ultra-comfortable shoes. But I won't let you off just yet. I'll let you off only if it's exceptionally rare for you to repeat painful lessons you thought you'd learnt. Otherwise keep reading. My shoes can teach you a thing or two.

WHY ARE WE SO TUNED OUT?

We've learnt to disconnect from our feet (you can generalise to bodies; you can generalise to painful sensations and emotions, too) long before it was up to us to decide what to walk in, or long before we could decide well. My earliest memory of a radically bad shoe decision is of descending from a train, seeing my mum at the beginning of the platform and not being able to walk to her. I'd just returned from a school trip in the highest mountain of the Balkans. I'd hiked for two weeks in shoes a size smaller than mine. I was like the Little Mermaid: "You will keep your gracefulness... but at each step you take you will feel as if you were treading on a sharp knife, and as if your blood must flow."[2]

For most of us, similar experiences, often from weddings or feats of tourism, are an extension of a normalised day-to-day discomfort and a standard form of being disconnected from our body. Extreme extensions from the normal creep in dangerously

---

2 *Fairy Tales* by Hans Christian Andersen—Illustrated by Arthur Rackham. Pook Press, 2013. Kindle edition location: 3183.

easily. When shoes hurt or something else hurts repeatedly, we've often followed a predictable trajectory:

A. We make a rushed initial decision we can't backtrack on easily.
These were my aunt's hiking shoes. They were perfectly comfortable in the thirty seconds I'd tried them on in the kitchen, on the floor. By the time I knew they were killing me, I was more than 500 km away from home.

B. We notice the pain, but we notice it intermittently. The road we've embarked on carries us; its joys and challenges distract us. What we love is more than what hurts us. We also discount what hurts, as there are far more excruciating ways to hurt.
It was rare to notice my feet other than when putting my shoes on, taking them off and walking the first 500 metres. There was a path to walk. There were rugged mountain tops, tiny high-altitude flowers and boys from bad reputation schools to fixate on (with changing priority). There were cherries to steal, secrets to hear and much more painful stories to brood over (like that of the guy who stopped himself from raping a girl after he looked into her eyes. Nobody could tell me what he saw in her eyes.)

C. We have limited opportunities to choose against the pain unless we accept to leave altogether or show ourselves in ways we don't want to appear (weak, ugly). Either way, there will be drama.
What could I do? Hike barefooted on rocks, thorns and snakes? Moan and be carried? Return home? Give a chance to the uncool trainers I had in my rucksack? No way. I've been both stoic and stylish from an early age.

D. Other people may notice our pain, but mostly won't. They too are in pain. If they notice ours, they'll typically offer you balm for the symptoms rather than a solution for the causes. It will often be balm for their symptoms. It won't even work for them.

One of my teachers, whose bed was opposite mine in one of the dormitories, noticed how bad my feet looked and offered me some of her balm for cracked heels. I politely refused. I didn't like her. My feet were bleeding. I didn't have cracked heels. Looking at hers, the ointment wasn't working for that either.

Sliding into pain is easy when the latter is at familiar levels. Leaving what we've slid into is so costly at the time of the rupture that most of us prefer to put up with it. That's why unbearable pain is often better than tolerable pain. We cannot not act against it.

THREE LESSONS ON NOT REPEATING OLD AND PAINFUL LESSONS

"Life will be teaching you the same lesson until you learn it."
I was slow to learn how to choose the best shoes ever. But I tried to figure out why I was slow. The answers apply to many (most?) things that hurt, often far worse than uncomfortable shoes.

The elements of Lesson 1

There was no way I could start buying sublimely comfortable shoes from the moment I decided to. My ability to feel signals from my feet had been numbed for decades, in ways both minor and extreme. Comfort was too abstract a concept. "Shoes shouldn't hurt" was too unspecified a principle.

There is no way we can choose into supreme comfort, ease and beauty—far beyond what's relevant to shoes—from the moment we decide to choose against pain and suffering. We've chosen the abstractions. It will take time to master the specifics.

When we decide we want something BETTER, our original visions are abstract and patchy (provided we are taking a meaningful step up). It doesn't matter whether these are about sublimely comfortable shoes, a nurturing and uplifting relationship, a true home or a fully relaxed body, for instance.

You've made up your mind that shoes will no longer hurt, won't give you blisters, won't deform your fine foot bones, won't tire you to walk in. You've made up your mind that you won't ever again be with a partner who push-pulls you, takes you for granted and projects his or her ancient wounds onto you. You've committed to a house you are never uncomfortable, constrained or depressed in. You've started asking your body not to contract, not to hold its breath when you stretch it beyond what it's learnt it can do or when the (big) man you love tries to nestle himself within you. When we commit to cutting the cord to something painful, we start by knowing what we don't want far more clearly than knowing what we want.

We've had flickers of experiences with that thing new, better and glorious. But flickers don't lift the darkness. We don't quite know what composes and signals 'the thing'. We don't quite know how it feels to truly have it—as yours, as staying there for you, not as a brief taster to be taken away when the time's up.

Those shoes don't fit.

Lesson 1

We keep being confronted with painful lessons we thought we'd learnt because it's the 'minor' details that give substance to the big principles. Don't conclude that there is something inexplicable or doomed if you keep repeating the same mistakes, while you thought you'd learnt your lesson. The low-level mistakes are different, even if the big lesson remains the same. Have patience with the details of the GOOD you are after. The dots will connect.

The elements of Lesson 2
We also repeat bad decisions when we have, supposedly, learnt our lesson because of what I call 'subliminal dealbreakers' and 'treacherous convenience'. They often come as a pair.

A couple of summers ago, I refrained from buying a pair of exceptionally comfortable, while also feminine and elegant, Ecco sandals. They cost about a third more than what I would typically pay for shoes. I was already paying more than most of my friends.

Instead, 'without noticing', within a couple of months I had bought four pairs of cheaper sandals. Please have patience with their stories. There is a point beyond the trivia.

One pair were hip green-golden-brown flats. Grounded in evidence or not, I go by an orthopaedic surgeon's advice that flats should be worn for up to two hours a day. Otherwise they deform your tendons and delicate foot bones. Whenever I put flats on, I have a clock ticking at the back of my mind.

The next pair were exorbitantly-expensive-before-the-sales ergonomic sandals with fancy strapping. In theory, they were super comfortable, primarily because of how the straps wrapped the ankle. My feet were not persuaded. I accused them of being desensitised and plebeian. Thousands of research hours and decades of design experience had gone into those sandals. What did my dumb feet know?!

Besides (an as-if-peripheral thought which hijacked the decision), I didn't want the hassle of returning them. That summer, the post office was 8-9 kilometres uphill, in 30-45° C. A shoe box wasn't fitting easily into my rucksack. I would also be back to square one with the search.

The third pair were white wedges, a good fit for most summer clothes. Wedges don't work on a bike. Yet that same summer, no matter where I sat, white wedges dangling from crossed legs, I had to cycle there first.

The final of the four were bright red velour heels. I bought them for a birthday lunch and all the special events that would follow. Yet I was a stranger. I was invited nowhere special. In cycling to the birthday lunch though, I found that the block heel clipped the pedal dead steady in place. The red heels became my crazy bike shoes substitute. They were finished within two months.

I threw the heels and donated the other three pairs when I moved at the end of the summer. On dropping the bags, I realised the contents cost close to two pairs of my unbought Eccos.

Why did it happen?

In making three of those purchases and in the failure to return one, I had compromised on what should have been my dealbreakers, whether ever or this season (no flats, since they start an irritating inner clock; undebatable comfort; most shoes fit for cycling). I had also succumbed to treacherous convenience (avoiding the 'return' task). I had fleeting, feeble thoughts that I was making compromises, but I didn't drag them out of the shade.

Whenever we find ourselves unhappy with decisions we have promised ourselves to make differently, in need to re-learn a lesson we thought we'd already learnt, we usually have 'subliminal deal-breakers' and 'treacherous convenience' involved. There was something which mattered to us, but we ignored. There was something which was unimportant and lame in the grand scheme of things, but we let it take over.

The summer after that, I bought the Ecco sandals.

Lesson 2
If you find yourself repeating the same lessons again and again, try to lift to the surface 1) the subliminal criteria which end up being dealbreakers in the long run and 2) the lame reasons that trick you into bad decisions.

The elements of Lesson 3
Back to the red heels for a little longer. Add a flowy occasion dress some of the time and sure as hell I was the most absurd cyclist in the area.

Yet I wasn't trying to prove a point with my shoes and dresses, or to be noticed. On the contrary. I had to make peace with standing out. I was aware that for most, maybe all, minds that register me, I would be the cliché of a woman who wears heels on mountains paths, a dress in fenced-off fields and nail polish when peeling potatoes. I had to accept that people will stare, take photos, whistle, clap – and they did, all of that. As I found out later, even one of my closest people was dragged into laughing at me in the company of others, while either hating himself or defending me, all the time thinking it was none of his or their business.

I didn't want to be laughed at. I didn't want to exist like a silly woman in anyone's mind. At first and as ever, I was driven to shape the image and change how I looked, approximating the proper cyclists' look. Former and current people pleasers amongst you know how vital it is to try to manage the images of us which exist in the heads of others. If we don't and if they reflect a distorted image back at us, we believe them, not ourselves. If we can't change their truth of us, we'll accept it as the truth, then grieve how inadequate we are.

Luckily, my pocket was empty. I had no money I could direct towards cycling gear without serious compromises. I had to refocus on my priorities. They are not cycling shoes.

I also wanted to feel life was normal and I was me when I entered a café or a shop at the end of the road. It was all the more so as life was anything but normal and I felt like anything but myself.

Most importantly, it was high time I trained myself in trusting what I knew about myself. No matter how I appear, I am not that cliché of a woman — clueless outside of her usual environment, flinching at pain and intense physical effort, damsel in distress the moment civilisation drops away, and a black hole that sucks attention. Not now, not then. My legs were strong. I soon knew the hills. I could overtake a fair number of the Lycra-clad, professionally shod cyclists. Several have been trying to detect the motor of my non-motor bike. A few complimented me on how strong and fast I was. Don't imagine the rise of the underdog, Wonder Woman type of movie. It wasn't. But I was a decent average amateur cyclist who was transcending her decent (above) average generic and cycling-specific self-doubt.

In an afterthought, I also accepted that I was that girly girl who may end up in heels on mountain paths, a dress in fenced-off fields and nail polish when peeling potatoes. I love being a princess from time to time. My peers from teenage times despised it. Many of my current peers do. Not me. I like princesses. I have many identities. One of them is a Princess, the girliest kind.

And in honouring the truths I knew better than any, I came to realise that the clapping wasn't ridicule. It was encouragement. Some of it was admiration.

Lesson 3
We wear shoes and make decisions that don't fit us because we are still mustering the courage to stop fitting in. Sometimes we need to make a leap. Sometimes it's enough to keep building the courage muscles. The time to stand out will come.

DEALING WITH THE PHYSICAL CHAOS
Whether or not your shoes speak of a habit to accept unnecessary pain and/or repeat painful lessons you thought you'd learnt, you are unlikely to carry all of them into your next life stage. Here are some practical and occasionally psychological suggestions for dealing with the excess.

Plan to complete your unfinished, or start your unstarted, shoe business
Carrying items that have not paid their price on my back and never using them after has taught me to let sunk costs go easily. But the issue with never-, once- or hardly-worn items is not just the money. It's unfinished business. Some of us complete things. What if all that was needed was a couple more days or nights of mutual accommodation?

It may sound easy to let go of such possessions now you are reading. Yet the need to complete the unfinished or start the unstarted can be absurdly firm when you are packing.

It's more rational to override it, but if you cannot (I often couldn't), don't fight it. Let it wear itself out. After you've packed something two or three or four times, without having used it at all in between, you'll ultimately leave it behind.

You will leave it behind because, when you don't integrate an object from a previous home, from a previous life phase into a new one, your connection breaks. The thing fades. You stop seeing it. You need to re-enter those old, other spheres to feel it come back to life. Then you can snap it back in and use it again. Otherwise you become strangers. You may keep moving it for some time, for old times' sake, but then you stop. You'll stop. I promise.

Much better, begin to wear those shoes (what an idea?!) in the time you've got left in a place. Take out the boxes. Plan your outfit, even if imperfectly matching. Two days will often be enough to know if a pair will ever be comfortable. An hour will do to catch sight of the pretty finish to your legs and decide that you want more. A moment of true presence will shine your appreciation before you set another pair free.

Walk in the shoes of your potential buyers
In my experience, shoes don't sell well online. This includes marvellous, worn-only once, expensive shoes (by which I mean ones you buy on an above average salary but not in Harrods). I always get a high from crafting the text of the ad, perfecting the photos, then seeing the sleek listing published and the number of visitors ratcheting up. Then I sell nothing.

With my feet planted in the customer's shoes, I understand. I never offered the option to return. It made sense for me as a moving-out seller. My address was an imminent past or an unhappened future. It didn't make sense as a buyer. I would never buy shoes without trying them on or having the option to return after having done so. When I next have shoes to sell, I'll welcome a return. Alternatively, I'll offer them in a context of direct contact, most likely to the same local 'preloved' boutiques which have worked magic for my clothes.

Remember the peripherals

Remember to plan for footwear in the shed (mountain boots), under the bed (home slippers), in the bathroom (flip-flops)....

Remember the shoe polish, brushes, leather moisturises, nubuck sprays...(unless they are mostly a marker of good intentions). They fit easily into the empty spaces of shoe boxes.

Donate with a twist

You can typically donate shoes in or around the same places where clothes are accepted. *See **Chapter 8** for more.* It's easy. It's boring.

Years ago, I lived close to a cobbler's shop which was managing a shoe donations box. The guys would repair the offerings and donate to people in need. Perhaps ask if your local team does something similar. Even if not, drilling a hole in your comfort zone is never a bad idea.

You can also donate by buying shoes for your next life stage. *Tom's Shoes* donates one pair of shoes for each pair you buy off them. *Start Something That Matters* by Blake Mycoskie, the founder of Tom's Shoes, is a perfect thematic read for your shoe sorting days. You cannot read it and remain ungrateful for having shoes, any shoes. You'll donate far more easily too.

If you've only seen Disney's *The Little Mermaid*, you may not know that Anderson's original tale has a sad ending or, at best, a 300-years-delayed almost-happy one.

In Andersen's tale, the prince does, ultimately, marry the princess chosen by his parents, the neighbouring king's daughter with her "long dark eye-lashes and laughing blue eyes" shining with "truth and purity". He mistakes her for the woman he is seeking—the young maiden who had found him on the shore and saved his life. He says that that maiden is the only one in the world whom he could love yet is unable to recognise her in the Little Mermaid.

On the morning after his wedding, the Little Mermaid is destined to die. Her heart will break, and she will become foam on the crest of the waves. This is what she had agreed to in her deal with the witch. She either wins the prince's love and, through this, an immortal soul or dies when he marries another.

The sisters of the Little Mermaid try to save her. They exchange their beautiful long hairs for a knife. Before the sun rises, the Little Mermaid must plunge the knife into the heart of the prince. When the blood falls upon her feet, they will re-join into a fish tail. She will be able to return to the sea and live out her three hundred mermaid years there.

The Little Mermaid takes the knife. She enters the tent of the bride and the groom. She kisses the prince's brow. She glances at the knife, then fixes her eyes on the prince again. He whispers the name of his bride in his dreams. The knife trembles in the hands of the Little Mermaid. It trembles, then she flings it far away into the waves. She throws herself from the ship into the sea.

But she does not dissolve into foam. She finds herself amongst the Daughters of the Air. The Little Mermaid has raised herself to the spirit world, as she's tried, with the whole of her heart and despite all the suffering she's endured, to do what the Daughters of the Air do: good deeds. Unlike mermaids, who can only obtain an immortal soul if they win the love of a human being, the Daughters of the Air can earn it with three hundred years of good deeds.

After three hundred years of good deeds, the Little Mermaid can float into the kingdom of heaven. We all know that she will. (It can be even quicker depending on whether she meets mostly good or mostly naughty children but that's a pedagogical add-on we don't care about.)

There are many ways to read *The Little Mermaid*. A typical one, which was long mine, is as a story of unconditional love. I was determined to nurture love in its most generous and purest forms, like the Little Mermaid, and also train the strength of character to let me throw the knife away every time I felt it trembling in my hand. I have been like her, or at least tried my best, on more than one occasion.

The role is beautiful and tragic. I now think that much of it is unnecessary (or, rather, necessary for us to learn from but not model). Unconditional love doesn't require pain, even though at times the love will be so powerful and overflowing that you won't notice the pain. When the pain becomes persistent, shouting at you that you are being harmed or you are harming yourself, it's time to make a change. Paradoxically, it is precisely the call of love that's asking you to step away. It is love protecting you from harm.

The Little Mermaid should have chosen against pain far earlier, far before the dilemma of whether to plant a dagger in the prince's chest or turn into a pink cloud for 300 years. The prince never truly saw her. His vision was hijacked by a hazy memory and an earthly princess, no matter how we all know that the Little Mermaid was the woman from the memory and a truer princess. She never showed herself fully and 'spoke' her truth either. Presumably, it was because her voice was taken away by the witch. Yet there are always ways to speak your truth and show yourself, even if no sound, no words would come out of you.

Back to the story as we have it. In it, feeling pain with one's every step is a price paid for love. It is a price paid to be with and around somebody who, by a tragic inability to recognise you and own the love he feels for you, cannot love you back with the whole of his soul and in a way that grants an immortal soul to you too.

Perhaps it is also a price paid for trying to be somebody you are not. A human rather than a mermaid. A nobody, a mute castaway, rather than a King's daughter, the Princess of the Deep Blue. It is a price paid to be walking in somebody else's limbs (or shoes), far smaller than your measure.

Shoes that fit you don't hurt. Nor do selves. Nor does love.

As for earning an immortal soul, you don't need to earn it, whether through love or good deeds.

You are not a mermaid, nor a daughter or son of the air.

You are a human.

You were born having one.

BOX 8

WHAT DO YOU FEEL IN YOUR SHOES?

- Have you entrusted your weight down onto your shoes? Or do you walk somehow higher up, slightly afloat, as if you don't want to step fully into them? It's usually to avoid feeling the subliminal discomforts more acutely. Though there is something to be said about not standing your ground in the metaphorical sense, too.

- Does the sole of the shoe touch the arch of your foot throughout? Or do they have a gap in between? Maybe it's the opposite, the sole is pushing against the arch rather than offering it a place to rest on?

- How do your toes touch the sides of your shoes? Do they have enough space to move? Have they imprinted their shape onto the contours of the shoe?

- What about the back of your foot? Is there a rub?

- If your ankles are covered, is the contact a light touch or subliminal pressure?

- What else can you feel?

- If all feels fine, is it perfect comfort? Could it be difficulty receiving sensations from your feet?

- If you find that you are used to pain and discomfort from your shoes, can you remember when you first started to switch such sensations off? Where else are you switching off daily pain and discomfort?

WHAT DO YOU FEEL IN YOUR SHOES?

[illegible]

- Does the sole of the shoe touch the arch of your foot throughout, or do they have a gap in between? Maybe [illegible] pushing against the arch rather than offering it a place to rest on?
- How do your toes touch the sides of your shoes? Do they have enough space to move? [illegible]
- What about the back of your heel? Is there a [illegible]?
- [illegible]
- What [illegible] you feel?
- [illegible] perfect [illegible]
- If you [illegible] remember [illegible] started to [illegible]

CHAPTER 10

"I SING THE BODY ELECTRIC": SPORTS GEAR AND INNER COXES

Early each morning, while I cycle to work between the sleepy fields and quiet river, I align with a tiny woman screaming hysterically at seven big men. Some of the men's faces are stony, others are distorted, but all men are bending over backwards and sweating to obey her.

The rowing teams are training on the river Cam. I had a theory that the coxes of so many men's teams are women because it taps into an atavistic response to the shouting of their mums. When I shared it with a friend trained at elite fitness levels, he crushed it with a blow of common sense v. depth psychology. Women are lighter. Your cox may be guiding you, but you also carry him or her.

The failure (or not) of my theory aside, all of us who exercise carry a cox in our heads. Even if you don't train competitively, you won't improve meaningfully, won't rejoice in seeing a page of a human anatomy atlas upon yourself, and won't get HIGH on endorphins if you don't push consistently beyond your comfort zone. And this happens either when somebody else is pushing you onwards

    staaay down, keep going, keep pushing!

or when you do it for yourself. Typically, it's both.

You don't even need to exercise to have an inner cox. You only need
an area of life where you must or want to perform, win, succeed,
get better, reach the top. It's also almost by default a team of coxes
rather than a single homunculus.

(S)HE SINGS THE BODY ELECTRIC

    Tell me:

Do you run, pedal, row, push, lift, jump, sit up,

    hold stronger, faster, longer because first and foremost

    (moments of suffering, pain, injury, fear,

    panic notwithstanding)

you LOVE

the power

the energy

control

millimetre precision

muscles coming alive, hugging each other closer,

    kicking in harder when the going gets tough

vibrancy of your body in strain, post the strain?

You 'Sing the Body Electric'

the miracle of movement

flickers of awareness:

    (it's easier) push (stronger)

    push (swifter) push (more-precise)

    push (than-last-time-yesterday-when-I-first-started)

your body in its beauty

definition

grace

uprightness

standing tall, taller

your body, the ultimate miracle

ultimate home, even

in its limits, in its walls

stiffness, inflexibility

narrow range

still home

HOME.

Mind clear, empty

troubles of the world away, your world away

disconnected by the rhythm

flattened by the weights

muted by the effort

faded by the focus

resolved?

The exhilaration of success

of victory

or gracious loss.

You won inside

a threshold crossed

of time

of weight

of height

of PAIN.

Crazy happy endorphins

the sweet fatigue

the pride

a smile held back, trembling to burst
'twas nothing, really, not quite there
laughter when you've cracked it
or you couldn't, but were all in
childish, stubborn, pointless, that's the point.
Noisy gulps of water
the tastiest of hungers.
Drop dead in bed
no, not yet, before that:
hear the hummmm
of all the energy
in motion...

You can go now, fall,
to rise again
feeling more You.

My A-team Cox salutes you. She's also quite similar to my favourite instructors and teachers. But I have others too.

THE SPORTS INCARNATION OF THE INNER CRITIC

May I now introduce Cox B, the sports clone of the Inner Critic:

I am out of shape
had let it slip again
so out of breath
flushed, heart beating, snot trickling
after this, really, how could you
so stiff, inflexible.
Looks ugly
preposterous

UGLY.

Wrong body, wrong joints
you will never be able to do that
push as hard as you want.
See her?
Teacher loves her, helps her
of course, strong, pretty, hard-working
beautiful outfit, beautiful body.
He, there, started after you
clumsy, awkward, taxi driver, roll your eyes
now even teaches, certified.
That one too, white hair, ass thrice the size of yours
can stand on her head
you can't
you could, once.
Look around, the worst of them all.
Hurts, uh? Shaking?
You can't wave the flag of victory
without the flag of pain
don't even think of slowing
releasing
resting
would rather you faint
than give up.
Where were you those months?
Where?
Moving
houses
slacking.
Back hurts, right

crappy abs, that's why.
You have more than that to give
dig deeper
you're pretending
pretending you are trying hardest
pretending you are focused hardest.
There is more
always more
more that you can bring out of you
more that you can hurt
you have to pay
pay to get there
for not being here.
Body in pain
Old woman, wreck.

THE RESIGNED

Still other times my cox has checked out. She's looking at her watch, the distance left to cover. She's resigned at my mediocrity, just wants me to finish. But I don't want to finish. I want to quit.

So much more to go
I hate it
I can't
It hurts
I don't want, don't want to
I want it over
Can't wait for the end
How much more
Too much
I want it to finish

End, over, stop
Why am I here
Why the hell did I come here
Such a drag
And I'm not even halfway

There are far more coxes spurring me on or coxless versions of me dragging my feet through a hard stretch. But those three are the core team.

How about yours? Again, it doesn't need to be sports. You may not be exercising. You may have long purified the inner conversation there, by now mostly singing the body electric. But if you are like most of us, there is an area of life where you want or need to achieve and do well and excel, and perhaps you often do, but can't do it consistently, joyfully and without anxiously looking around for what others are doing or thinking of what you are doing. Or maybe there was such an area, but you gave up on doing well in it. Would you stop and write down some of what your inner coxes are/were telling you there?

Who are they? How do they reflect the voices, words, messages you've heard, time and again, when you were younger and had to try harder, persevere, cross a threshold, deal with pain, achieve? Who in your life talks to you like that now? Where?

Would you stop?

I'll wait.

Okay?

Okay.

Did you open a file, or fetch a pen and paper?

Or said 'later' in your mind?

You know there will be no later if it's 'later', don't you?

It pays off immediately if you do it. The day I wrote to you of my inner coxes, I rode up a brutal slope with speed from a different world. I was testing the words of the "Sing the Body Electric" cox while cycling up. And I could catch and throw away the words of the Inner Critic as just that—words.

Once you distil your inner conversation, you'll also acquire almost supernatural skills in mind-reading the sporty types around you. You'll register the harsh inner dialogue, constern-ation, suffering, restriction, self-criticism of far too many of the runners, cyclists, regulars of exercise classes, yogis (or managers, academics, entrepreneurs) that you've always thought were better than you. Yes, you've sensed a dryness about them—the juices of joy have somehow gone, often from their body too. You felt a 'don't touch me' vibe—*I am focused, determined and don't have time for silly distraction*. You were repelled. But you were intimidated too, felt less than them too. Yet you'd better be compassionate. Too much of their power is rooted in pain.

You'll also see (the obvious) that the truly great ones don't emanate pain and self-torture. It is sublime power, control, focus, ease, confidence, presence, oneness with what they are doing. And no, they didn't get there *because of* the pain although they've gone through pain and will continue to go through more. They got there because they've learnt to leave pain behind. Yet most of us, normal achievers, will fight tooth and nail for the need to be in pain and suffer to achieve.

Are you still reading? It's just as good. You've remembered how sometimes the most difficult thing is to stop, pull back, refrain from pushing on.

DEALING WITH THE PHYSICAL CHAOS

Below are some suggestions of what to do with your sports gear. The first also continues the theme of choosing the voices driving our achievement or underachievement programmes.

Shed old skin you've suffered in

Dare yourself to let go of any sports outfit or equipment which makes you feel the suffering or underachievement of exercising rather than the thrill, joy and success of it. Of course, redistributing the gear which reeks of dysfunctional inner or outer conversation, self-torture or taking it waaaay too easy will not in itself change anything. But there is something classically symbolic about the radical shedding and replacement of an outer skin. It can be the signal, expression and anchor of an inner transformation.

Giving up my default top for HIIT (high-intensity interval training) was such a signal. My body hated the class, or at least how I went about it relative to the shape I was in. The message failed to reach consciousness for months. Yet when I was moving shortly after, my once favourite pale green bamboo top felt like being shouted at, old and split inside, hurting in a fight of myself against myself. The top stayed behind. I moved on, including how I exercise.

Value is two-thirds context

Recently, I advertised a forty-year-old bike which had both breaks malfunctioning and only three 'theoretical' gears (practically none, as all three were stuck). About a dozen Gumtree enthusiasts got in touch in an afternoon (the ad was fully transparent). The first person who viewed it was the person who took it.

Context matters though. Bikes are a currency of their own in cycling cities.

I've also donated bikes for refurbishment. Most memorably, it was a bike ignored by the person who stole its lock (super robust unless you leave the key in). When I was moving, I donated that bright red bike with a floral saddle to a local charity employing and training persons with disabilities. If it were a better bike, I would have donated it to one of the projects shipping bikes to Africa (you can run a search for 'donate bikes Africa', or any other location, of course, but the bike charities working with Africa seem best established). The last two places where I had my current bike serviced were also either selling refurbished bikes themselves or advertising a bike recycling scheme, both in the context of social enterprises.

Most of 'my' places[1] will be irrelevant to you. Bikes may be irrelevant to you. The point I am making is that even hopelessly battered sports equipment and accessories can find a new home. Value is two-thirds context. You can think of your old sports gear relative to contexts where it'll be laughed at (or snubbed; I was angrier at that thief for offending my bike than for stealing my lock). Or you can imagine the same gear in contexts where it can improve, even change, lives.

Stock up your community gym
One of my favourite ways of donating sports equipment is by leaving it in community gyms. Their shared stock is almost unfailingly tatty, filthy and limited. I've done it for mats, belts, blocks and weights. I don't even ask (sorry). I know where they sit. This has been my gym or studio. I leave them there.

---

1 But in case you live somewhere I've lived, these were, respectively, Owl Bikes, Cambridge (*papworthtrust.org.uk/owl-bikes/*); Re-Cycle (*recycle.org*); Julian House Bike Workshop, Bath shop (*jhbikeworkshop.org*); Clive Mitchell Cycles, Truro shop (*clivemitchellcycles.co.uk*), and who were advertising Cornwall Life Recycle (*liferecycle.co.uk*).

Keep the germs in the family
Small accessories which go with hygiene warnings, such as swimming goggles and caps, I've passed onto willing friends. We've already shared enough bacteria in our times together. Nobody has ever been worried about an extra colony or complained subsequently. That said, most of us have changed, post-pandemically, in our sensitivity to microscopic threats.

If exercise has ever helped heal your soul, help other souls be healed by it
I've sold, on eBay, hardly worn hiking boots after intensity of bidding and for prices exceeding my highest expectations. Yet the joy of those trades was far inferior to having a pair welcomed by a 'walks' charity[2]. The latter enabled 'walking, talking and taking action' as a route to improving mental health. Annoyingly, my boots got lost in the post and never reached the charity. Yet I'd stumbled upon my favourite way of redistributing sports gear: let it help troubled souls. If a form of exercise has done wonders for your mental health, consider this option. There is a growing number of charities that use sports and exercise to achieve social and mental health goals in addition to physical health ones (as if they were ever separate, but that's another matter).

Bite the bullet
If you are moving sports equipment which requires disassembling, and if you've always outsourced the task, maybe it's time to bite the bullet. If you are not reading in order, **Chapter 2**, *the Bullets to bite section*, talks about that.

---

2 Walk Talk Action. *walktalkaction.co.uk*. Last accessed Aug 2022.

Recently, at a dinner in an Italian restaurant with the sea behind us, white wine, pizzas and candles in front, I was listening—my chin trembling, eyes welling, voice shaking in my brief responses—to suggestions about, hmmm, bike cleaning. It was to the eye-widening confusion of the man I love, who was telling me something entirely matter-of-fact and helpful about how he cleans his bike.

We take it for granted that the greatest physical challenges are to be taken up when we are best prepared, while we often sift through emotional mud, looking for gold there, when we are at our most vulnerable. Yet some of the best windows of opportunity to clear old shit open when we catch ourselves in incomprehensible reactions during good times. Incomprehensible reactions always carry a trace of psychological gold. The good times, in turn, give us the inner strength, lucid mind and emotional distance to follow it to its source.

As it was a remarkably good time, later that night I chose to continue crying (by myself) and explore the slippery road from tears to clarity. I found myself in a Shakespearean soliloquy against, occasionally dramatic dialogue with, Inner Cox B, the sports servant of the Inner Critic. The argument my Inner Critic lost, bruised and bleeding, was how useless I am in sports and exercise; how I don't deserve nice sports gear; and how I am not allowed to talk, write (and, as of tonight, listen) about it, even if only in the context of moving houses.

My Inner Critic had strong evidence in support of his claims. I've never trained professionally. I've never competed other than at school sports events. I was mediocre-to-useless at ball games, the marker of sports skill at school. True, I ran fast, was graceful at gymnastics, and could do more sit-ups than most, but that was only for Physical Education tests. Moreover, as our teachers reassured us regularly, it was natural to be good academically and fail at sports and vice versa. I was one of the best academically. Don't even think of overreaching into the land of the Truly Talented.

In later years, I never stopped exercising, but was committed to keeping it a space of non-achieving. Academic life was enough with its own forms of getting 'there' first. Anything physical I did had to be about enjoying movement, looking after my health, keeping in shape and busting stress. More recently, it's also become about exploring my body. No achievement, no competition, no comparison was allowed. Other than when it was. You don't just disable the achievement programme. I've crossed more thresholds of pain than I ever thought crossable, even if I hung in there mostly through my (trained) mind, far less on muscle and technique.

I've also always preferred the Sherpas to the Gore-Tex-clad Westerner, the native of the hills to the cocky visitor on a carbon steed, the yogini who moves with grace and loses balance and holds on or falls off but does so in whatever T-shirt she'd picked this morning rather than the one in *de rigeur* yoga top with crossing stripes. That is, I've always sided with dark horses who under-signal their brilliance.

Cynically considered, I had chosen roles I could fill in. They were the ones financially available to me. They fitted with being (super) shy when younger. More sympathetically, I was responding to representations of the Good in books and films I loved. I wanted to train an instinct for the substance against the surface, true gold as opposed to shiny objects. I wanted to be able to pick the modest, unobtrusive grail from *Indiana Jones and the Last Crusade* rather than the hundreds of gem-studded goblets around it that were not it.

Snap. Lightbulb. My Inner Critic has co-opted my values and was using them for its own advantage. That's why I hardly have any sports gear and never compete formally. I tell myself it's not what matters, and I trust that, but I also believe I don't deserve it or live out of a past where I can't have it. Otherwise I would have noticed there's no need for either/or. I can choose both the form and the substance; the play and the achievement; the ease and wisdom of the local and the bike and determination of the visitor.

Our weakest parts often take cover under our values and ideal selves. Those values and ideal selves are real and solid and true but, unwittingly, also end up camouflaging our most destructive and fearful fragments. Importantly, it can be exceptionally difficult to disentangle one type of mental content from the other.

We try to touch the skies from the peaks of our values and best selves while, simultaneously, standing on the crumbling rocks of fears and subpersonalities. That's why so many of us never make the leap that they have in them.

Now look at your luggage:

Is some part of it too small relative to how much this aspect of your life means to you?

Do you have both a dark story to tell why you don't deserve more and a beautiful one why it's all you need?

It needn't be sports gear. It can be musical instruments, arts supplies, house decoration....It can, of course, also be something less tied to specific objects, like love, success, intimacy, happiness....

If you do, STOP. Stop, even if stopping is often the hardest thing
to do.

Sometimes we carry too little of what is ours because a lead-
heavy cox has taken up half of the boat we are rowing in.

PUT THE OARS DOWN
TAKE HIM BY THE COLLAR
PLOP HER IN THE RIVER!

Driftwood of your past...

Alone in the boat
you are winning the race,
Singing the
Body
Electric.

PART III
HOUSE-BOUND AND
ROOM-BOUND THINGS

On the one hand, the chapters in this part are about **possessions you might not have at all**. If you are moving from one furnished accommodation to another, you might have no or hardly any:

- Furniture (*Chapter 11*).
- House decoration (*Chapter 12*).
- Bedding (*Chapter 13*).
- Cooking and eating utensils (*Chapter 14*).

On the other hand, the chapters here are about **psychological issues that are fundamental to our experience of being at home:**

- **Our perceptions of the essence of home,** in the sense of possessions and physical features which speak of a home more than anything else—the key psychological topic of the furniture chapter (***Chapter 11***).
- **Pains and traumas from our childhood** we have learnt to cover up—the key psychological topic of the house decoration chapter (***Chapter 12***).
- The **accidental, but often rock solid, associations** we have developed **between a physical home and an emotional home**—the psychological red thread of the bedding chapter (***Chapter 13***).
- **Roles we have adopted in nourishing** (or nothing like it) **our body**, our ultimate home in this world (***Chapter 14***).

Whether you are seeking pragmatic ideas or psychological insights, or both, prepare for some heavy lifting.

CHAPTER 11

TIE YOURSELF TO A TABLE.
IF TABLES ARE FEW, WALL COLOUR WILL DO

The first item of furniture I bought in my life taught me that unless I learn to sit with anxiety—let its sticky, vibrating fog clear away before I do something—I will destroy, single-handedly or in a chain of events undeniably started by me, some of the most beautiful things in my life.

I had bought an antique chest of drawers, failing to account for a curve in the last flight of stairs leading to my bedroom. It was from a shop with Treasure Island-like suitcases strewn around (the big black ones with silver pins), creepy dolls and talking parrots behind the counter. Expectedly, it didn't have a returns policy, even if I didn't want any money back. I couldn't wait for two weeks for a charity collection. I called in a local removals and recycling business. 'Fast, friendly, affordable'.

The removals guy moaned I was giving him a cheque rather than cash. He was measuring me up head to toe and mostly in between, without making any effort to do it furtively, as polite men do. He had several front teeth missing. And while I was anxiously apologising for not being more thoughtful and not having withdrawn cash, and chasing away the inner question of what had happened to his teeth, he bent over, snapped two of the legs off the chest of drawers, then snapped each leg in half in front of his chest.

I didn't mean 'done away with' like *that*.

The chest of drawers story is full of perturbation and insight. It is the only experience in my life when somebody—two young Polish porters—returned half of the tip I'd given them. It carries the almost similarly rare memory of my dad being of help straight away when I rang him, without the usual counterforces of sarcasm, guilt-inducement or redirection for help to my mum, granddad, uncle, neighbours, random passers-by, the authorities or anyone else but him. It brought me the insight that my ability to get into a mess has always been equal to or smaller than my ability to find a way out of it.

It also had me formulate the initial core principles of the *psycho-mathe-physics of big household items*, a discipline and a forcefield you'll inevitably be sucked in when moving house. Here is their current version.

1. Factor in the heavy magnetism

The decision to keep or sell your furniture usually 'happens'. The inner processor spits an outcome depending on whether the furniture is yours (mostly obvious, but not so obvious in a break-up for instance); how attached you are to it; how big and heavy it is; how expensive; what distance you are moving at and how much it costs you to; the features of your new home; whether you have found it at all; how easy you believe selling or donating furniture is...

If you still don't know, may I humbly share a conviction that furniture has magnetic powers. It pulls us into status quos. If I sniff that a status quo has outlived its usefulness, I sell my furniture.

The first time when I sold almost all my furniture, I was downsizing to a cheaper, furnished place (with sea views though; a fundamental rule of downsizing is to upgrade wildly on at least one house feature so that it never feels like a compromise).

The second time, even if it looked like (pessimistic) pragmatism (I was going on an extended research visit abroad, and although I wanted to return to my university, I had no new project secured), I was burning my bridges. There was something wrong with my life. There had been for some time. I thought that the glitch was in me. I still believed it. But I was beginning to wonder if it was not, instead/ partly, living a life which was small for me.

No new path was calling me. Nor had I suddenly decided I needed to start searching for my inner truth or some bigger one, not least because I don't know another way to be. But I didn't want for a set of beautiful furniture in storage and the memory of how peaceful and grown-up I felt in the flat for which I'd bought it to magnetise me back. I had to block my return to a new version of what's been.

I don't know whether it worked partly because I had no big possessions to come back to. But it worked.

Some life transformations start from selling the chair you are sitting on.

2. Measure, or backs shall be broken and nerve cells shall die

When I say measure, I mean measure. I mean buy a measuring tape if you don't have one. Sometimes furniture has entered our homes before we have. New fixtures have been added and narrowed the space; doors changed; partitions created. The way we go out of a place is not the way we go into it. Ditto for furniture.

A few flats ago, I had a three-seater heavy leather sofa, which had me cheating on my bed and had guests outstay their welcome. It was a crown jewel (I lived at the top of a former Tower) I'd bought off the previous tenants. I never worked out how they'd brought it in. It was a single unit. The doors were narrower than it was. A kitchen bar was protruding into the only route it could take.

I failed to sell it (with an honest explanation of the difficulty of removal and making it the buyer's responsibility; somebody should know the tricks). I couldn't donate it either (no slots for two weeks by the time I called the furniture charity).

I was also beginning to doubt if taking it out was sensible, despite the contract requirement to remove all your possessions. It couldn't work out without unhinging three doors. There were five flights of steep narrow sharp-turning stairs to be navigated. It would scratch every white wall on the way and chip every corner.

With only a modicum of bad luck,
porter trips down the stairs.
Railings shake
Chaos
Clamour
"Compassion for the objects we sit on:
It could be the other way round"
Was the phrase 'performance art' or 'art performance'?
Thought-provoking
if it weren't for the

Blood
Disconnected
Spinal cord.
IT WAS MY FAULT.

To avoid such possible futures, a friend's engineer husband offered to lower the sofa with ropes and levers through the window (high third floor). Glasses on, four excited eyes glinted. I thanked him. I thanked the narrow window more. 'Sofa ex machina' was going to be over the top in more than one way. Next option.

I ruled out paying another furniture killer. Next.

I gave up. I prepared to pay in the hundreds for the breach of contract. It was ok. I only wished I had measured the sofa and passages early enough and accepted the loss right from the start. It would have prevented an inner nuclear war of stress, nerve cells dying in their millions.

When the estate agent got in touch, she only passed on a message from the new tenants. They were asking if I wanted any money for the sofa.

3. Bend the time between
rough sleeping and abandonment

Responses to furniture sales ads queue in minutes after you post them (recently, I've only advertised on Gumtree, but classifieds in local online publications as well as physical notice boards have also served me brilliantly). But with most of us playing a losing game against time and to-dos, the practical arrangements with buyers may drag on dangerously close to the Big Day. If you play it too safe and sell too early though, you may be sleeping on the floor or eating from your lap for weeks.

I play it safe-ish. Items which are expensive, present a logistical challenge (beds, tables or big carpets) and are dear to me, I advertise about three weeks before my move-out date. Current pattern is that I sell them on day one or two. I have them removed by the buyer towards the end of week two. I am left with a week to eat like a horse, walk on cold floors, and sleep 'rough'.

This pea-feeling princess suffers when her legs or neck are over-curved on some small futon or when she's in a sleeping bag on the floor. Luckily, she's chanced upon a solution—have a guest mattress and sacrifice it.

I had bought a simple single mattress, delivered within twenty-four hours, when I first moved in my last unfurnished flat. I was planning on buying the bed of a lifetime, so I knew I would need an interim solution. After my bed was delivered, the mattress served guest overflow needs. When I sold my bed at moving out, I slept on the mattress until my very last day, having advertised it on Freecycle the night before (a free newish mattress will always be snapped in minutes). Circle closed. Princess unbruised.

I don't regret the trade-off of good sales v. inconvenience. I've loved the quiet company of any furniture I've kept. I sought it out. I waited for it. It held me or my extensions.

I won't sell it for peanuts. I'll be picky about its new owners. I won't abandon it under the rain.

Because I've done it and it hurts.

A six-month-old bookcase I sold last minute had to go for one-sixth of its original price. It didn't have a scratch on. To add insult to injury, the buyer, who was supposed to come on the evening before I left, cancelled the deal. She had misjudged the distance. She had a little baby. I transferred the money back.

Told her I understood. And then shouldered my bookcase and took it out. I left it under the rain, TO A GOOD HOME letters leaking their red down. Or was it blue.

I'll sleep on the floor. I'll eat from my lap.

4. Square your stress

One of the reasons I was so uncomfortable with abandoning my bookcase was that, if nobody collected it, people would hate me for littering. Frowning at the eye sore on the green grass. Calling the council to remove it. The council people shaking their heads at all those irresponsibles. Where is the world going?

Until I thought that this is the job of some people. Just as the job of others is to remove heavy furniture. Just as the job (or pastime) of still others is to contact them. Let alone that sometimes the new tenants want to pay for what you've left (and then they don't, that's the almost complete story; the complete one is that I let them choose whether to pay me or not depending on how they felt about their money situation). Or that an early bird locks his front door in the misty morning, turns around, and rubs his eyes against a white bookcase on the green grass. Then unlocks his front door again.

Until recently, I never added my stress to the equation of what to do. My calculations were skewed towards being environment-ally and socially responsible, a most considerate tenant and, ultimately, a good girl. They were also skewed towards not paying more than I could pay.

I've added the 'minimal stress' parameter. To the house moving maths. To life maths.

Then I started squaring it.

I can't believe the difference.

5. When you respect the difference between absolute and relative loss, you stop losing

Potential buyers rarely haggle about the price of furniture. But on the couple of occasions when this has happened, I've been served by a lesson I taught myself incidentally on hiring a taxi in Nepal.

My Mount Everest of negotiation skills is to accept a potential loss—of a taxi ride, of a furniture sale, of anything other than my core values—as nothing more than a different way ahead. Then the lightness with which you walk away gets you everything you asked for (the fair taxi fare, seven times lower than the starting one; the asking price for your black dresser, just as you advertised it).

Even if it doesn't, you can't care less. The alternative is just as good and possibly better. I love an easy ride. But I also love walking. I love a good trade. But I also love donating. It's only a relative loss if I can't take a taxi or sell my dresser. Yet I'll suffer if I betray love, even if only for furniture. I'll suffer if I betray the expectation to be treated as a human rather than a (golden) goose, even if only by a taxi driver. Those are absolute losses.

I've never needed to reduce my asking price for a piece of furniture. Anyone who's haggled, has felt the same energy that the Nepalese taxi driver did. I'll walk away. Lightly. I'll lose the relative, not the absolute.

Then I lose nothing.

6. Divide the labour, even if you 'can'

You don't have to make it easy for the buyers of your furniture. Just honest.

I have been at my most unhelpful and unaccommodating when selling furniture. Quite the contrary to what I normally am. It's so beyond my carpentry skills and means of transport that I don't even try. I only give the facts around the practical arrangements in the ad.

You are not disadvantaged in selling items if you can't disassemble them, can't remove them, can't offer transport. You are picking different segments of the market—the people who can. Many potential buyers bring up the ease they offer (to come and pick something immediately, dismantle it quickly, remove it today in their van) as an argument that you sell to them rather than somebody else.

Even if you can take your bed apart, carry it down with your best friend from floor three, transport it to your buyer—even if it feels satisfying and virtuous to do it—remember that you don't have to.

Calculate the best labour distribution for you, under current circumstances, of having to make 16,000+ move-related decisions.

Let the buyers calculate theirs.

Meet your match.

After all, you'll have slept in one and the same bed.

7. Interest in furniture is a constant

With two exceptions that taught me their lessons forever, I've always bought high-quality, beautiful, immediately favourite furniture, even if it generally meant four to six weeks of waiting and even if it was relatively expensive (though nothing exorbitant). As it happens, the furniture I've sold, across homes and moves, has always been less than a year old. I've looked after it well. I've touched and cleaned it with love. It might have vibrated differently from the love.

All the above (or exclude the vibrations) has allowed me to charge a good price. Typically, I would ask for 60% of what I'd paid.

The first person to view an item has always bought it. I have even received 80% for sales items I'd advertised relative to 'the original price'. I've wondered if I can get away with 100%. But it feels unfair. Even 80% I find ethically questionable now my fortunes are better.

My experience with furniture is quite particular, but stories I hear make me think it's one of the easiest possessions to sell, no matter how old or used. Again, it simply picks a different segment of the market. My mum recently sold a sofa-cum-bed that was over fifty years old. This is the bed in which she had slept as a teenager. Then I did, from around the time I found out, in sadness and in rapture, that you can't bring anything from Dreamland into waking life to the time I left home to do exactly that. Then it was my brother's. Then it was for all the guests (or us again freeing up better beds for them) throughout the years.

Now, we hear, it's gone on to have a new career as a sofa in a sustainable living kitchen.

Interest in furniture is a constant.

8. Deal with the remainders

Remember to plan for 'occasional use' furniture that may be hidden or folded away: inflatable beds, garden chairs, folding tables....Ditto for big lamps and other movable lighting.

When I go home home in May, I will find none of the old furniture in the 'kids' room'. Not only my bed has gone, but there has been a complete clear-out. My mum may have furnished it anew, but since she takes her time with home infrastructure decisions, I may still find it as it is now, shortly after Christmas: freshly polished wooden floor, freshly painted walls, a computer desk with a chair, the rocking chair of a cousin, in brief storage at ours (four years so far), and a forest of exuberant plants.

For twenty-three years since I left home, I've always gone back and found the kids' room as I knew it, a lamp changed, a carpet too, but mostly nothing new. Nonetheless, I'm not troubled by the loss of the furniture of my childhood. It was time for it to go. Childhood has gone too. And it's a good thing I am not stuck in it.

Yet my heart sank when I saw the photos of the walls. Our room was half a rainbow. A summer and a song. Each wall was of a different colour: yellow, pink, green and blue; pale, harmonious hues. Now it's Blue. I fear it would not feel like 'my room'.

Colours matter to me, in general and on the walls of a home. In my last year as an undergraduate, my roommate and her boyfriend had painted our room loud turquoise. It was over the wallpaper me and my brother had put up two years earlier. My soul left there and then, as much as I lived there for another nine months. A few years ago, my live-in landlady repainted the kitchen walls into a purple and orange combination which surprised her too. Same experience. Soul walks out to seek its true colours. Body follows a few months later.

One woman's wall colour is another man's furniture. Many years ago, a friend 'lost' the home he grew up in, as his dad had decided to move. When I expressed my heartfelt compassion (he was the first of my friends to lose his childhood home), he brushed it off. "Ah, when you see everything taken out, it's four bare walls. And also, most of our furniture is in the new flat. Home's just moved."

Furniture seems to carry the essence of a home for many. Such people take their furniture with them, arrange it in the new place, and feel it's 'home now'. Not for me. Yes for my friend. Not for my previous landlady who voted for her cat and the photos on the walls. Perhaps yes for my aunt who had furnished her living room as a Versailles bedroom. Not for my friend with a stable of four bikes and a fifth for indoor training. Your turn.

We differ in the possessions we have imbued most strongly with the essence of home—the ones which, once removed, make us disconnect from a place, and vice versa, once reinstalled in another, allow us to feel at home, or at least begin to.

It differs between houses, too. Without my granddad's books (more on that in **Chapter 19**), it will no longer be grandma and granddad's flat. Without the views of 'my' marina apartment, it will no longer be the rental home I've loved the most and would have bought if I could.

It also differs between time periods. For decades, it was books for me. Once I survived an unthinkable separation, the fetish died away. Then it was photos of family, friends and mental states embodied by nature or expressed in art. I let go of that need in a flat where nothing was allowed on the walls. Now it's perhaps the sheep Maria, which I often take out first and pack last—the last soft toy I've kept, a present from Maria (Margo) and Maria (the Dressmaker) from over nineteen years ago. But if a friend's kid (or a friend, even if I doubt it) asks for Maria, walk out they will with Maria.

Even our most treasured possessions are simply a shortcut to the essence of home, not it. Let alone that, if you ask my philosophy of science PhD supervisor (the legendary John Dupré, for the record), there is no such thing as an essence. Everything, a home included, is many things, has many true natures.

Why do I care about wall colour and my friend cared about their furniture? I can keep guessing. But whatever the reasons for our respective attachments, a dramatic change in their objects pushes a partial and difficult to admit awareness over a threshold. Then you suddenly KNOW.

I knew from Day 1 that both those places, the one which became turquoise and the one that turned orange-purple, were a physical and emotional compromise, even though the colours were originally right. I also know that I've left home home long ago. But in all three cases, the knowledge was half-suppressed. I had to see it written on the wall, in colour, so that I KNEW.

My friend knew for months that the home he grew up in would no longer be his. The inner emotional disinvestment had begun underneath the surface. It hit home when he was faced with the bare walls in their flat. But he also needed or wanted to feel at home in his dad's new flat. He carried the feeling through the furniture. If there was no furniture, I am sure his dad would have been more than a perfect vessel for it. Or a cat, a photo, a bike, a toy sheep.

It's useful to have things that store the essence of home for us. We can always create a home without them if need be. It's a projection we can call back in minutes if we are clear that that's all there is to it, but it helps. It keeps the gravity of belonging holding you fast and the black hole of disconnection away. The laws of psychophysics are not at their most reliable in transition times. It's not a bad idea to tie ourselves to some old table.

It will be light and easy if those things are photos for you. It will be dusty and time consuming if it's books. Heavy and expensive if it's furniture, but achievable nonetheless.

But what do we do, those of us for whom it's the colour of the walls?

We laugh through tears and
it brings up a rainbow.

CHAPTER 12

HOUSE DECORATION AND PAINTED-OVER SOUL CRACKS

I wonder if, by the time they can finally come home, the (naked) women entrusted in his care will choose to do so. Maybe after all those years they will have made a home in the little house by the lake,

where pink clouds and blue waters widen your morning eyes;

where you are never irritated to need a pee at night, as the bathroom ceiling opens up to the starry skies above, reminding you that the galactical distance between your shit and the Sublime is often crossed by lifting your gaze;

where you will learn to light a fire, no matter how CERTAIN you are that you CAN'T, because somebody will give you, in a way your analytic mind still fails to 'deconstruct', instructions mixed with calm faith in your abilities (and because otherwise you will be as cold as you've never been in your life).

Then, firewood cracking, a book of poetry on your lap (courtesy of the host's fine library), hands and lips rhythmically seeking-receding-from a thin-stemmed glass of wine, eyes sinking in mud

and love of centuries past and the bay across, you will hope that
the laws of physics don't lie, that the cold of space did not, indeed,
get lost but turned into the cold of time and is freezing this
moment for eternity.

The lake house is where two paintings of nudes by my uncle,
one of the best-known artists of my hometown, have found a
temporary refuge, five years so far. It's the island abode of a man
who, from what I can feel, hides more of his power, wildness and
poetry than is good for him (and, by being untrue to himself,
becomes untrue to others) and to whom I have more reasons to
be grateful for than he's aware. I didn't want my paintings locked
up in a loft for the few months I was going to be abroad. I later
requested that they be cared for until I have a house of my own,
until I can hammer in as many nails on the walls as I wish. In the
flat I was leaving, no new nails were allowed. My naked women
were in a canvas bag by the bed.

Awkward, entangled, excessive and invisible

Good art stirs the soul and troubles a move. Although most
house decorations are not collectors' items and most of us are not
crossing country borders when moving, house decoration is a
moving-house headache.

It's often awkward to take down, pack and transport:

- **fragile and delicate**, while also reliably **irregular** in
  shape and size—vases, bowls, chandeliers, lamp shades,
  mirrors, statues, seashells, Christmas tree balls...
- **voluminous**, even if light—decorative cushions, bed
  throws, rugs, rattan baskets...
- **ridiculously heavy**, even if relatively compact—iron-
  cast candle holders, door stoppers...

- **a faff** to take down and wash (that's why you've not done it for years), even if it's **never as bad** as you expected – think opulent velvet curtains;
- **a faff** to take down and untangle, and **always worse** than you thought – like long garlands of decorative lights;
- **non-recyclable** – most Christmas tinsel;
- **alive!** – like flowers or fish bowls.

It's also a typical source of dilemmas pitching the sentimental and pragmatic against one another:

- **Too dear to part with and actively serving as decoration,** but crazy to carry around – it took me years to stop stuffing suitcases with stones and rocks I'd brought back from beaches and mountains.
- **Too dear to part with, yet consistently residing in cupboards** or drawers after a few weeks of being displayed – like the drawings of your nieces and nephews or the calligraphy brushes from your friend's trip to China.
- **Not particularly dear but** being a 1) gift and 2) familiar – such as a serving plate you never genuinely liked but became used to using.

It is also almost by default:

- **Too much,** even if you thought you lived like a Spartan.
- **More invisible** than the idea of decoration suggests. It's astonishing how quickly we stop seeing that which went up to be seen.

An underestimated invisibility is not unique to decoration though. First and foremost, it's a feature of every good home and everything at home.

THE PRICE OF HOME-LIKE CERTAINTY
IS A BLUR OF THE SENSES

Home is where you can walk with your eyes closed. You take
out the black pepper mill without looking up from the pan. You
go peeing in the middle of the night and don't turn the lights
on (even if your ceilings don't open onto starry skies). You glide
between the bed and the wardrobe without a bruise (because
you've had one so many times).

But what gives us the certainty of inhabiting space with our
eyes closed also blurs our senses.

It may be that the familiar becomes the good, right, beautiful.
Ceilings are the optimal height. Decorations—true art. The love
expressed, the pain admitted hit the golden mean, no more that
should be shown and seen. The salt of food, the spice of life are
spot on, perfect, right.

Or it's all wrong. Home is where the beautiful becomes lack-
lustre; the grass the wrong shade of green; the rooms too small,
no, pointlessly large; the food of today as that of yesterday; the
conversations scripted, suffocating; the people looking too
provincial, thinking doubly so.

Or maybe it's all quite all right, at the level of a shoulder
shrug. I had to visit some of the best museums and galleries of
modern art to realise that my uncle belonged to the global world
of the arts, not the artistic obscurity of my hometown. Suitably,
he was dead by that point and most of his paintings damaged
in his damp atelier. Important as it was, that was also a minor
discovery about what was exceptional in the home where I grew
up and never thought much of.

There are many metaphorical homes—within our minds,
bodies, social circles, jobs, knowledge, habits...—we need to leave

behind, burn, take apart stone by stone to force our eyes to see, ears to hear, fingers to tremble at the touch of the World, again or like we've never known before.

There are also many metaphorical homes – of safety, acceptance, love, belonging, peace, truth... – we need to rediscover, recreate, extend in our adult lives, even build from mud and straws, so that we can see, hear, feel, touch the World in all its incomprehensible variety and fullness.

Most of us will not. Most of us will only be living in clones of homes past. Memory narrows our dreams, paths and imagination more than we can ever conceive of. We need our Inner Child's disconnection from reality and the energy of other lives, wildly different to ours, to loosen its grip. Few will open the doors to either.

We also sniff, with the nose of fear, that if we peer into homes we've never had or feel into the one(s) we have long lost, there will be blood and tears.

We shall be torn to pieces before we find our True Home, the one we can never lose.

Paint over the complexity once again. It's time to pack.

DEALING WITH THE PHYSICAL CHAOS

My pragmatic suggestions are impressionistic, as house decoration has not been a major concern in my moves. I don't buy decoration easily. I have inherited a mental allergy against kitsch and objects that mostly collect dust. Ceramic dolls (unless in museums), potpourri (unless at a spa), artificial flowers and fridge magnets top my list, if you are interested. I also rarely receive house decoration as a gift. People who know me are disarmingly mindful in choosing presents of minimal weight, size or longevity.

All this means that, in standard moves, I take most of my house decoration with me and, in one suitcase moves, I take extra care in matching it with its new owner.

Let them cherrypick
In minimalist moves, I invite friends to a 'cherry picking visit'. Those are for anything I won't be taking with me, but since bed throws, blankets, decorative cushions, vases and the like are particularly hard to stuff in a single suitcase or sell (or post if sold), they are often a dominant category. I make sure to remind my friends only to pick things they absolutely love and need. Lightening my load is a bonus. The goal is of fireworks of love between people and possessions. (That said, because my possessions are pretty and well looked after, such visits are usually like raids.)

I send things home home if I can't separate from them, can't store them AND know they'll be a perfect match to something specific. The super soft cream bedspread from my flat a few moves ago is now the normal cover for my mum's lounge sofa. It landed there so naturally that it even inspired the purchase of more super soft pastel blankets.

Increase the audience
As my paintings have shown you, I seek an audience for the art I own. More accurately, it seeks me. It all started from a friend's husband's friend saying that the one thing he needed for his island house was better art. He rents his house to tourists too. My naked women are, I hope, regularly appreciated.

The cushions from one of my flats went to a couple who'd just started offering a room on Airbnb. If their business has been even moderately successful, they will have propped several hundred guests by now.

Find the courage to go through a proper adoption process

With my flowers, I find master gardeners and ask if they would 'adopt' them. Well, I've only done that once, but here's the script.

On a beautiful sunny afternoon, I roam the streets of my neighbourhood looking for its most magnificent garden. I smell the flowers. I brush my fingers over the green foliage. The next opulent garden is always more impressive than the latest one. Until it isn't. This is my flowers' new garden. I take a deep breath. Knock on the door. Complete strangers, but so sweet—an elderly lady and her husband. I tell them I loved their garden more than any other in the area. I wonder if they might welcome my five pots. They beam. They'd be 'delighted'. I bring in the pots a few hours later.

I wonder how my flower kids are now.

If you can't possibly imagine knocking on strangers' doors and asking for your flowers to be adopted, I can reassure you that I couldn't either. The first psychology book I bought, and took extra care to hide, was on overcoming shyness. It didn't help. It took me about twenty years, many self-dares like this, a young man who thought blushing was cute, and, mostly, radical self-acceptance to leave that behind.

Make your office more home-like (unless it's already at home)

Much more boringly, I've taken flowers to the office.

I also add my Christmas decoration to the office collection.

There is always an unserved need in ugly functional buildings.

...or keep it simple

At least in Britain, charity shops welcome house decoration.

I asked myself what I didn't tell you this time out of fear or embarrassment. What was it that I embellished, decorated, covered up when I should have laid it naked? I asked and immediately remembered two stories of (almost) art on the walls at home.

Many years ago, on returning home after one of the dramatic ruptures between my parents, we found the walls used as sheets of paper. With colour crayons and in big letters, my dad had written messages of pain and anger, of love turned sour and revenge. The words were sometimes his, sometimes quoted. You open the front door and right opposite, above another door, you read: "This is the end, beautiful friend" (yes, it is The Doors). You go into the kitchen, sit on the heater, and the wall you have your back against whispers of a clock ticking loudly on the floor and a "sensation of pointless counter fight" (*Isn't every fight a counter fight?*, I asked myself every time on re-reading the wall message I knew by heart).

With the distance of time and transferred onto the pages of a book, this may sound like (an attempt at) art. Scary, raw, ugly, stirring—but riveting too. The quotes were art recognised by the world. In the right context, my dad's original writing was also poetry incarnate.

For those of us who couldn't decline the audience participation it was, however, life.

The walls spoke of a drama more real than real and one that, it felt, might have ended up with counting the bodies. As some of you know all too well though, extreme drama goes with a surprising number of mundane difficulties. How do you weasel out of your friends' suggestion that they come over, especially since, until yesterday, it was so normal for them to? Or if they ring the doorbell uninvited, giggling at the genius of their surprise, how do you explain why your parents leave each other messages on the walls? How do you tell the neighbours' little kid, "I'm afraid we don't have cello tape," as calmly and naturally as you can so that she hopefully un-hears the "Put the knife down!" coming from behind the closed door?

My dad's writing is covered up by several coats of paint by now. It took ages before the first went up. I would say at least three years. It may have been three years of subjective time. Whatever the objective timeline, we had practically stopped noticing it until another visitor came by and wondered at the eccentricity of my literary parents.

We had stopped noticing not only the words on the walls but also the pain in our hearts. After all, you live with and within painful experiences, you don't encounter them as exhibits in an art gallery or as stories in a book. When the time came, the coats of paint—pigments, resin, solvent, additives—did the job beautifully. I don't remember for sure, but I think the letters were first scrubbed away. The coats of psychological and social paint—smiles, disconnection, masks, determination—did the job less beautifully if you had eyes to see the cracks.

Even more, many more years ago, when home life was normal, at kids' birthdays we were allowed to draw on the doors (if we promised to scrub clean the drawings a few days later). My brother and I, our cousins and closest friends each had a door to turn wildly creative on. Total abandonment and freedom of expression. The coolest of parents to allow that. As much as I am no longer (that) fussed about my birthday, I still believe the bells and whistles celebrations are one of the best things I've been taught at home. In victory and defeat, in mourning and in joy, in peace and in war, you need rituals and decoration to keep you afloat, grounded or moving, whatever's called for.

Same pastels, same rooms, some of that same wild, unrestrained self-expression. Not exactly the same spots, as we were too little to stretch that high or weren't allowed to draw where it would be close to permanent, but almost.

Art is of the beautiful and the ugly, the comic and the tragic, of contrasts and ambiguity.

So are most real homes, even if in different proportions.

When you leave some of them behind, or even well before you are able to, you will find the psychological and social paint that made them inhabitable starting to crack.

You may paint over the cracks quickly. Seeing and feeling the truths of your home is not for the faint-hearted. For those who dare try, it may take years of scrubbing away at old words and old pains before you reach the glory of your soul.

But sometimes, and every time on a clear starry night,
the galactical distance between
your shit and the Sublime
is crossed by just lifting your gaze.

CHAPTER 13

LIAISONS DANGEREUSES

I am one of those people who've left their home country with one suitcase for one year, CERTAIN that they'll return. Then, many years later (nineteen in my case), we still haven't, having come to believe that the best way to return home is to keep going forward. It's not that I arrived at the conclusion quickly. On the mornings of at least six years, I was refinding, in the pit of my stomach and as acute as the morning before, the dilemma of whether to 'go back home'. It sat side by side a sense of irreality, guilt and emotional shrinkage, a self-contained tree trunk pruned of wild, loud and over-reaching emotional branches. The noodle-fication of roots was an older process but intensifying too.

In the one suitcase I travelled with, I had clothes, shoes, toiletries, cutlery, dictionaries (six thick hardbacks, photos and goodbye cards in between the pages) and a set of bedsheets. Something in the discord between the bubbly voice and trembling chin with which one of my aunts gave the bedsheets to me 'just in case'

meant I am taking them, even if I thought them superfluous.
I soon found out that they were, instead, closer to lifesaving.

Much furnished accommodation comes without bedsheets. Even if it has them, they are strange bedfellows for long or forever. Time and again I'd lay down my sheets and create a home space I could enter, not just watch (photos), hold (little spoon, big spoon and fork from the home set), eat (the meals you can almost recreate with the ingredients of a different country) or conjure up as an inner image. I gave up this set of bedsheets fourteen years later, one of my last six possessions from home home. Both the flat sheet and duvet cover had become so thin from use and washing that they kept tearing up, until each got a tear of about a metre within weeks of one another.

There are pathologically many bedsheets and towels, redolent of home, billowing in my memory space.

The dowry my grandma was sewing and embroidering for me, with me chipping in with the embroidery, even though a woman with a needle is now a most peculiar alter ego. The dowry's long been used and gone out of use. If I cared about marriage (other than of hearts and bodies), I would have thought not waiting has brought me a curse.

The source of my love for worn-out sheets—the story of another one of my aunts who, as a newly married (also a big city girl, journalist covering the sectors of culture and education, tailor-made clothes, shoes bought with the dollars of my grandma's 'American' sister), visited with her husband relatives of his. The sheets in the bed made for them were yellow, threadbare, *that's so inhospitable.* Yet, on slipping in between them in the evening, my aunt found herself amidst the softest sheets she'd ever slept in.

It's a story of bedsheets getting better with use. It is also a story about the invisibility of much hospitality. When somebody opens their home to you, they've spared more thought and care than you'll ever notice.

The habit I borrowed from Arthur Dent, the inter-galactical hitch-hiker, who, some of you will remember, always had a towel in his bag when travelling across worlds. As does my dad. At sixty-nine, he hardly uses another form of transport, claims to be the longest serving hitch-hiker in the country, and I'd bet a year's salary he believes he's the best of all although he's never said it. That's always been his downfall—expecting, needing, demanding others to acknowledge how exceptional he is in things far more and far more important than hitch-hiking, while the only thing he needed was/is to own it himself.

I have a lifetime mental catalogue of bedsheets and towels. If I need to return home, in the sense of feeling loved and taken care of, somebody quietly thinking of and watching over me, or if I need to feel a profound loss yet simultaneously the consolation that all is well, bedsheets and towels I lay down for me.

MEMORIES AND DREAMS AIN'T ONLY SWEET

Yet bedlinen and towels tell dark stories too.

My bedsheets have seen more blood from my body, and the shame of it, than anything and anyone in my life. No, no big trauma there, I am lucky unlike so many women and men, though it has, indeed, several times, been blood from manipulative but still consensual sex at the edge of a period. We learn integrity and boundaries as much as pleasure between the bedsheets.

The blood and shame I mean is entirely menstrual. *It's ok that you bleed, sweetheart, it is nature; it's only bad, REALLY BAD, if anyone*

sees it on your clothes or you spot the bedsheets – is an implicit
cultural message enough of us have grown up with. If you cringed
at reading this or found it tasteless, or if you objected vehemently
against its message, you've only proven its strength. There was
something powerful to cringe at or object against. I had to have a
partner criticise me for failing to contain the blood which came
out of my body, when it came out while having sex with him, to
revolt internally.

Now I bleed, and sometimes it trickles away, and it may spoil
the bedsheets, and it may wash away fully or not, be Vanished out
or not, and it is as it is. And, come to think of it, I hope it continues
for as long as it can.

My bedsheets have also whispered of more loneliness than I
would easily confess to. You must know this whisper. Everyone
knows this whisper, even if from brief periods though usually
not – of the arms of a great man (or a great woman), of the home
like no other which they are, and that they are not here to hold
you. Or that you've known arms of not-so-great or almost-great
men, or women, but not of the truly great ones. The truly great
ones you only know from worlds other than this, but you know,
you know, YOU KNOW they are there, yet not here. Then your
pillow gets soaked in tear-rain or, worse, stays as dry as a desert,
no matter how ardently you pray to be able to cry.

IT'S NOT ABOUT THE BEDSHEETS, IT'S ABOUT THE ASSOCIATIONS

My bedsheet stories shouldn't matter to you in their contents
unless they've reminded you of similar experiences. But what
should matter to you if you want to be free to create the best
home you can have and to feel at home as frequently as possible

are two features of their *form*.

The first is that these memories foreground a particular type of object (in this case, bedsheets, towels and 'other huggables', as I call them), yet the heart of the memory is not in the objects. The essence of the memory is somewhere in the love, peace, family, familiarity, repetition, sweet everydayness...they came with and out of. But, for whatever reason, the objects define the memory.

The second formal feature of the stories is that, whether within themselves or in another unrelated story, they contain a negation of the main positive emotion. And no, the negation is not there because I want to show you a truth—a hard, heart-breaking but true truth that every beautiful thing can fall apart (yes, and grow up again), but because I am trying to unsettle your standard associations of *home objects–sweet home feeling*. More broadly, I am trying to unsettle your associations between a physical home, on the one hand, and home as a psychological, emotional, and, if you wish, soulful and spiritual space, on the other (or, briefly, emotional home).

If we manage to break enough of those chance associations— which are as hard as rock in your psyche but as precarious as ash at the end of a cigarette without your personal history and a world of social pressures—we'll put your next home on solid ground.

You can't create a true home without repairing the rotten foundations you've inherited from your parents' home, if you carry such mental baggage. The ghosts of that space will undermine any home you attempt to build until you exorcise them.

And, please, don't feel disadvantaged if the home of your childhood was extra rotten. People who have started life with the most beautiful, love-filled homes are just as prone to struggling to find their True Home. They often believe they have IT, only to see it crash at a time of crisis. They are controlled by black boxed associations just as much as you are.

LABORATORY DOGS OF SORTS

Much, maybe most, of what we experience around homes and home possessions involves the mechanisms that develop Pavlovian reflexes.

We have felt at home or seen others feel at home:

safe, protected, nourished, warm
LOVED
accepted—with our tantrums and our sweetness,
noise, tears, ignorance and illness, and contained in all
helped, encouraged, prided on
true, unguarded, peaceful, 'You'
scared, hurt to be consoled
free to express, free to experiment, fail, fall

when our parents tucked a soft blanket around us, making a
cocoon of us, leaning to kiss us goodnight;
when your mum made pancakes on Sunday and you and
your brother were splashing jam on and all around them,
arguing whether 'the tortoise' or 'the whistle' is the 'right'
pancake shape;
when you sat on top of the heater, warming up your bum
alongside the clean clothes spread to dry (OK, with the
clothes partly underneath your bum, as it was too hot
otherwise, even if you'd sat with the same trousers on the
school stairs);
when you rocked back and forth on the dining table chair

because it just calls you to rock and because no one of
those who forbid you to rock is around;
when...
when...
when...

With enough repetitions of the right kind, we, like good
laboratory dogs, start salivating of a home-coming when we see
soft blankets, jam jars, pancake pans, fireplaces, rocking chairs...

Unlike laboratory dogs, we can begin mistaking the bells
(sofas, cushions, bedsheets, curtains, right up to the brick and
mortar of a house) for the food (the emotional safety, nourishment
and love of being in a true home). Many of us are not simply
alerted wrongly. We begin chewing the bells and insist on
continuing. It sounds ridiculous. It is. And it isn't. It is tragically
easy, natural and logical for it to happen.

WHY WOULD YOU CHEW THE BELLS?
1. Because some of them are milk and honey
First, there is an undeniable truth in the association, a necessity
of the connection. The physical is emotional. Home spaces
and objects do, obviously, at a physical level, enable comfort,
protection, warmth, peace, care, relaxation, love. No spiritual
home will serve our basic bodily needs for long, even if, in
the midst of physical bliss, we are easily overflowing with
indescribable lightness, profound ownership of the truth that God,
the Universe, the Earth or Humanity are, indeed, our Home.

Let the risk of a disaster hang over you for a week (before it
passes, I won't wish you worse to prove a point). Find yourself
without a roof at 2 a.m. under the rain after a delayed flight, B&B
locked, phone dead, owners deaf. Wriggle for space in a tent

with three snoring men, terrified you'll start screaming with claustrophobia yet scared to sleep out in a brown bear area. Sleep with a bucket over you, water dripping from the ceiling. If you exude peace, relaxation and good humour within minutes and while stuck there without the end in sight, I shall listen to what you have to teach me (determined coping, hysterical laughter or sombre resignation won't do).

More positively, the difference in bodily sensations between basic and luxury versions of home 'things' can be life-changing. (Think of sleeping deeper on a top-quality mattress.) The more attuned you are to your body, the more acutely you feel and crave subtle differences in home comforts. Bodily care is mental and emotional care. Never underestimate the ways in which the body can nourish the soul.

2. Because they are in the ancient soup

Second, we bear the consequences of the pre-conscious amalgam of having a home and having parents (or others who've taken up that role, or even seeing who 'normal', happy kids turn to) and finding our parents at home.

Our physical home was, for most of us, our most reliable emotional home too, because our parents were there. It may have been movie-like good. It may have been just average. Yet even if the cracks in the relationships and expressions of love were as broken windows to an Arctic storm, being with our parents was still, for most of us, on most occasions, better than any other alternative we had. Even if it wasn't us who experienced an exuberance of safety, love, support from being with our parents, we saw it in others who had a home with such parents to return to.

Protection, nourishment, love, encouragement, consolation came from going home, for us and/or for others. They didn't come first and foremost because of the physical space. They came mostly because of parents or parental figures in it. Yet way back, it was all a soup whose ingredients we couldn't pick apart. Then we simply continued to half-think the same way.

3. Because they are all around

Third come the totalising, all-permeating social and commercial messages around 'home'. The solidity of the association physical home – emotional home is not something that the world of grown-ups would blow up for you, unlike so many childhood illusions. Why would it?

It's a commercial perpetuum mobile.

It must run till the end.

It reflects the social status quo.

It must stay. Forever, if it may.

4. Because the opposite does not attract

The fourth reason why the physical-emotional home association is so strong is in how it's opposed.

The voices against the commercial machine and status quo frequently target the objects and spaces that come through them. *You've sold your soul. You've drowned it in your home swimming pool. You vacuum cleaned it from your Persian carpets. Hung it on your Parisian chandeliers. Locked it in one of your twenty-one rooms and now can't remember in which one. While your True Home is God, your true home is your soul.*

It absolutely is. A million times. Always pick that one if you must. Yet most of the time you don't need to pick one or the other.

Many of our over-the-top spaces and objects are not only quite all right and harmless, but in fact an embodiment of the human spirit and creativity, of somebody's love, longing, time, soul, God's inspiration and the muses' singing. There's nothing wrong with them. There's nothing they are guilty of if you don't expect them to do what is not their job to do. We sense that, even if materialism troubles us, even if we renounce it at times. Something warns us against trusting the voices against our home in the material.

5. Because they are easier to handle

Fifth, most of us have far superior skills in handling the material objects from our everyday lives than the energetic qualities and complexity of emotions. The former have buttons or gentle fabric and mostly don't talk back. The latter can tear you apart, knock you down wailing on the floor, and even kill you.

When we are prioritising colour schemes, bedsheets, sofas, cushions, kitchen surfaces and bathroom tiles, we may be turning to tangibles and constancy to help us handle intangible, uncertain, undulating emotions and experiences. For many of us the emotional experiences that make up the 'I'm home' feeling—safety, protection, support, warmth, love in their pure, true, unfailing versions—have been hard to find, hold on to, or make sense of throughout our lives. They have been coming and going. They have been hurtling us up to the stars, down to the ditches and everywhere in between. For some of us, they have been by default unreliable, intense, costly, dangerous even if occasionally—for brief spells—the sweetest things of all.

5½. Because substitution creeps upon you

Now please take a seat at a table. Pick your fork. It's a fork in the road. Down one of the roads, life robs you of your loves. It may be ham at the time of austerity. It may be true love buried by cancer. It may be your mum's arms languid with depression. Down the other road, you were given in excess. You ate and became fat. LOVED another and lost yourself.

Which road you've picked, or was picked for you, doesn't matter. They'll cross and run as one and fork out again and meet and split many times. Yet they'll both pass through the parched land of substitution.

Somewhere down one road or the other, you'll try replacements: chicory coffee when there were tanks in the streets and nothing on the shop shelves; soya ham when you wanted no more blood shed for you; tender sheets when you couldn't find the tender touch; solid furniture when you lacked the solid ground. You may have been reluctant and suspicious; you may have been resigned; hopeful and curious; righteous perhaps. It's irrelevant. You tried.

You tried. They helped. They helped partially or (almost) fully. It was partial or complete depending on the degree of deprivation; the power of the persuasion; the difficulty of obtaining the 'real thing' or the perceived danger that came with it. You kept replacing, for whatever reasons mattered to you or circumstances that 'forced' you. You trained the longing out of your system. You lost the taste even.

Then one day you woke up and found it's quite ok, quite nice, easy, natural, better—really!—to drink chicory coffee, eat soya ham or not water your artificial flowers. Just as it can become quite ok, quite nice, natural, better—really!—much better to fuss about bedsheets, memory foam mattress, wooden floors and colour scheme at home rather than seek true love and deep connection.

Let's summarise, as I fear that what I write comes in and out of understanding, so familiar yet so elusive. There are at least five-and-a-half reasons why it is so easy to believe that if you create an amazing physical home with amazing physical things, or even just a decent physical home with decent physical things, you are paving the way to your true emotional home:

1. the fact that the physical is also emotional-psychological-soulful-spiritual;
2. the conflation, coming from the time we were born, of home as a physical space and the space where the source of all life, nourishment and protection (our parents) was/were;
3. the intensity of the commercial and social message;
4. the fundamentalism, righteousness and hypocrisy of many voices talking of our home in God, the Universe or our soul;
5. the ease of handling objects as opposed to feelings;
5½. the slippery slope of substitution.

It's so easy to believe that an amazing, or even decent, physical home will lead to an amazing, or even decent, emotional home.

IT DOESN'T WORK.

HOW DO WE KNOW IT DOESN'T WORK?

Let's cut out a likely misunderstanding. I am not saying that the right order is to start from your emotional home and not care where you live or what objects surround you, or at least not care until all good things align and you can have spirit and house in one. Rather, one's physical and one's emotional home should nourish, strengthen and enable one another. Ideally, we need to attend to each of them simultaneously or in close succession. Realistically (and still ideal enough), you often have one lead, take priority and bolster up the other. You also keep a watchful eye so that the relative priority of one doesn't undercut, sabotage or leave the other falling behind or apart.

The problem is not of having a magnificent home or spending time choosing and doing it up before you've reached your feeling of homeness in the world. We don't need to put life on hold to find the light. (If anything, I'd say the opposite is truer.) We've lost the balance not if our physical home is hugely important to us or currently taking precedence, but if it is sucking disproportionate amounts of money, time, expectations, dreams, mental and emotional energy to the expense of almost all else. We've lost the balance when we've sacrificed or put on hold—for the sake of a brick-and-mortar home—too much of what matters to us, lights us up, and makes us who we are.

1. We'll see it collapse

In one version of the drama, we may lose sight of our sacrifices because we see our dream home take shape in front of our eyes, under our own hands, with the help and appreciation of those with whom we are co-creating it.

My brother split from his wife not least because he became intensely focused on creating their perfect home-space. My sister-in-law missed the love, the presence, the attention. My brother, in turn, missed his boyish adventures and routines. When the relationship collapsed, he left behind a shithole-of-a-flat-turned-palace by the work of his hands, and, symbolically, the ashes of a second house he'd transformed the same way. (Who started the fire is another story; it wasn't either of them if you've wondered!) He left with a bag, a bleeding heart, and the sense of having been betrayed and having lost himself.

My brother is healing, not least through transforming another ramshackle house. The attention to a physical house, or the work that will buy it, is not the problem. It can even be the solution. The problem is in what falls away because of it.

2. We KNOW, even if only in the middle of the night

In a different classic version of the drama, not to say tragedy, nothing external happens. No skies fall. The protagonists are quite all right in their magnificent house, always with another home-improvement project lined up. Life's routine, sometimes hard, sometimes sparkly, most often normal, lacklustre or a form of prison, depends on how alive you, the observer, are. There isn't much to notice, much to think about the price you've paid until
those moments
of a. b. s. o. l. u. t. e c. l. a. r. i. t. y
in the middle of the night
or vis-à-vis the Truly Alive
when we know everything.
EVERYTHING
about ourselves
about the lives we've chosen
of whether we are us,
the person we came here to become.
Whether we are with
the one we love,
as love was first promised.
Whether we are home
or playing make-believe
in a house of cards.

3. *The hook tears our entrails*

In a third classic subplot, we hurt palpably, starkly, with no need to wait for the middle of the night to know. We know that the high ceilings, bay windows and winding staircases, or even just the (half-)ownership of an average house, have worked as fish baits. We followed appearances. Or desperate hunger. Now we have our entrails torn.

THERE ARE MANY WAYS TO TRAIN A DOG

We need to make the argument even more complex before it becomes simpler.

Partly because it is the most commercially effective, the classic association for beautiful home spaces and possessions is of safety, protection, love, warmth, security, support....Nothing wrong with that. For most of us it's the perfect combination. The challenge we discussed is that one does not follow from the other and/or depend on the other. As a result, we may sometimes, even often, need to disconnect the two so as to create them in their grandest versions and combinations.

There are, however, at least three other classic scenarios that link features of a physical home to those of an emotional home. Again, we may be deploying their scripts unconsciously and limiting-to-harming ourselves in so doing.

Loving home–poor home

We may have grown up in safety, love, warmth, acceptance, encouragement, laughter but also in ultimate simplicity, even poverty (if we knew that counted as poverty in the Big Wide World). If we begin to see the two as inextricably intertwined, causally related rather than randomly associated, we may grow up to glorify the most basic environments, as if they were the source of love. We may vilify our richer lives, as if love and connection left because of the plenty. We may have nothing but a shoulder shrug for the beauty and ingenuity of material objects.

You know the romantic stories of replacing a palace of riches for a hut of love, or tragedies of poor talents rising to the top and losing their souls and meaningful relationships. Such scripts latch precisely onto this type of physical-emotional home association.

Alternatively, having grown up in poverty, we may see no glory in scarcity, no trap in riches. We may succeed in creating homes that are both loving and materially abundant. But if old associations keep their grip on us, a worm of fear will be eating away at our hearts. We will fear that both the love and the plenty hang on a thread. It was never meant to be that good. Those were never meant to be together. We glued them through single-mindedness, wild ambition, God's Grace, fickle luck.

But the glue may unglue itself
unglue itself
UNGLUE itself.
It is up to us to check
check
CHECK
how safe it is
today.
Every day.

Beautiful home of cold hearts and closed minds

Others amongst us may have had picture perfect, enviable physical homes (normal nice and pretty will also do) where hearts were fearful, love rationed, freedom dangerous and emotions either too flat or too chaotic. Well-groomed and well-fed, sinking into funky bean bags or buzzing along electric trains, we've spent years freezing on the inside, breaking into little fragments or drifting away from what's here. Numb, contained, controlled. Volatile, extreme, unpredictable. Scared, angry either way.

We may grow up to devalue home comforts as they were never imbued with safety, human warmth, love, acceptance, encouragement for us. We may despise or reject them. At an extreme, we may find ourselves glaring, sneering at, turning away from innocent, inert objects as if the crimes of love were theirs.

We may also join the ranks of the volunteer-humanitarians to the Global South who witness how happy and connected poor people can be and begin to blame our plenty for the loss of community and connection. We may join a community in our own part of the world, committed to the simplest of material lives and making most of what we have from scratch. We want nothing to do with the soulless world of material abundance.

Or just as plausibly, we may hang onto home comforts and trimmings as if our life depended on them. We've learnt to trust their stability. We feel their reassurance. Once upon a time, we hid underneath patchwork blankets, behind the pillow wall of our underdesk house, in the company of our teddy bear, trying to shut away the hurricanes in our parents' lives. Now we've expanded our hiding places, multiplied the sources of fear, and replaced the teddy bears with remote controls. I am safe in my castle.

Dark emotions in dark spaces
The two negative poles can, of course, intersect. We may have grown up on the inside of crappy relationships, experiencing abuse, neglect, abandonment, addictions, trauma. We may

have also been surrounded by cold, mould, concrete floors and cardboard windows.

The most natural trajectory then (though 'natural' is not a sentence, not a necessity, 'just' a frequency, a brutally high frequency though, and hat off to you if you've deviated from the prediction of a broken life) is to lose trust in homes and homeness. We mistrust the existential possibility of both a physical home with a soul and of a psychological-emotional-soulful-spiritual home with a reality, solidity that won't fall apart when pressed to extremes.

And we *shall* press to extremes. We must test, we must show how fragile, skin-deep and ultimately non-existent in the promised way any home-like thing is—unconditional love, warmth, accept-ance, compassion, generosity, etc.—when you poke its goodly surface. We feel triumphant to have opened its cracks. Relieved we didn't fall into the trap. Superior in being 'bad', deviant, cynical, resigned, but real, true, clear-sighted too. It's better to be sad than sorry.

If only we could cut that thin red string of hope playing down our spine. Or have it pulled by an (human) angel.

Or it may be softer, more personal. It is not that we mistrust that having a good, true home is possible. Of course it is! IT IS. But not for us.

There are many in-between types of association we default to in linking home as a physical space with its material possessions and home as an emotional-soulful-spiritual experience. We are also prone to mixing the types of associations. This too is natural. For many of us, the quality of home relationships goes through different phases, sometimes polarly opposite. The same applies to the levels of family/ household abundance and, in turn, the quality of physical home environments. They too are more likely to fluctuate than not.

So many of us work from contradictory associations, yet never see this as a reason to question their validity.

CUT THE CORD

Break the associations that do you no good:

between the home you were born in and

the ones you are creating

between the homes you've had and

the ones you'll choose from now on

between your material and emotional home

if they undermine each other

between the people

who've left, who've never come, who are not enough and

the reality, possibility, proximity of a home of love.

Cut the cords.

Unravel the scripts.

They are random

personal history

social patterns

thin air.

Links created by the repetition

of training laboratory dogs.

You are not one.

A home is felt in 10,000 ways; created in 10,000 more.

You can start almost anywhere, almost anytime.

From a mug or from a hug.

DEALING WITH THE PHYSICAL CHAOS

I may need to remind you that we were talking of bedsheets, towels and other huggables before it became about associations and laboratory dogs! Here are some of my experiences of dealing with the excesses that may trigger your (better) solutions.

Magnify the pleasure

I use house moves to increase the proportion of bedding and towels that are nothing but pure joy to own. This means redistributing the rest, typically items with some synthetic fibres in their composition or boring (and I don't mean soothing) colours. After repeating the exercise a bit too many times, I've learnt to buy fine bed linen from Day 1 in a new place, if I need any. No until-I-have-time-and-money solutions allowed.

Some of it is easy

Clothing banks in the four (European) countries where I've been vacating houses have been accepting bedsheets and towels.

I've never tried to sell bedlinen, but with fine bedlinen expensive as new, I trust (and have been told) it has a willing market if unused.

If we keep breaking the rules and 'they' keep writing them with bigger letters, maybe it's time for the innovators

In contrast, no clothing bank around me has been accepting duvets or pillows.

On one occasion I stuffed a pillow despite the explicit rule. It is, of course, irresponsible and annoying, but apart from shaking with anxiety while running late to leave the flat, I thought that if enough of us continue to do it, maybe they'll change the rule or at least explain it, rather than write it with even bigger letters.

To deal with the same problem, I once sent my (almost new) duck feather duvet and pillows home home, at the other end of the continent. I may now think it silly, but my mum continues to send the occasional note, more than three years later, to thank me for the warm goodnight hugs on cold winter nights.

Sleeping less rough

I've left a sleeping bag to a homeless guy (he was sleeping when I did, so no memorable story to tell).

If I need to redistribute bedding now, I'll seek refugee collections. When I last read a leaflet of a local group, blankets and duvets were on their most needed list.

Remember your last night

Remember to plan for the bedding you'll use on your last night.

You may need at least half a suitcase if you are taking it with you. That's why I often sleep in a sleeping bag on my last night. I've shipped the rest of my bedding off. I like my last morning simple and transition light.

If you are donating your bedding and don't want to contribute to even BIGGER letters on charity containers, you need to have time to wash and dry it. When I don't, I assume it's better to deposit it with DNA material on than damp.

If the bedding is of the house, I like to wash and hang it to dry before I leave, even if I'm not expected to. It's yet another symbolic way of not leaving myself behind.

If I've carried yellowish sheets with little holes, house after house
after house, until I finally tear them with some dramatic jerk of
the leg; if I've asked my mum to send me, 3,000 km away, the
decade-old face towel I'd forgotten to pack; if I have at least a
dozen similar stories to tell, I've obviously needed to hang on to
home and family in a way that can be held and touched, that
can hold and touch me. I was, of course (or mostly), aware it was
a game. I would laugh at myself for playing it. But if I were a bit
more aware, I would have taken my family out of my bedding,
towels and other huggables before they had turned into rags.
I wouldn't have ferried them back and forth the roads and air
corridors of Europe.

Or maybe not.

Maybe there are times when you cannot be or shouldn't be
more aware, when it's far better to let tatty, obnoxious objects,
functionally dying yet still emitting home-home-home signals,
serve as life jackets rather than take the thin air out of them.

Maybe the clear-minded disassociation won't allow us, force
us to swim, buoyed up by the faith that home and homeness
transcend any particular object, but drag us further down towards
the bottom.

Maybe it's ok to buy a new set of bedsheets then.

Doesn't sound like a 'maybe' to me.

DEFINITELY.

Embroidered.

CHAPTER 14

HUNGER GAMES

I am waiting for the Tuesday drinks crew, a bright blue exclamation mark under a white umbrella. The warm wind is simultaneously kissing my neck and twirling leaves around, more and more kisses and more and more leaves each day. A boy kicks a ball high. It gets stuck on top of a shade sail. Five men push beer glasses forward, chairs back, get up. They start jumping up and down, fingers overextending, poking at the shade sail. A square of bar customers is watching.

Is there a social norm for how many times you jump, how long you let your food go cold, to help another? Is there a significant difference if an audience's watching? How about when you are jumping, leaping to help yourself? If there's such a social norm, it's creeping. It's at the line. For perfect dramatic effect. Loud cheers, laughter, patting on a back. The boy thanks sheepishly, sits on the pavement, curves over the ball. A minute of a still embrace, then he begins to kick the ball again.

A table has just been cleared. I choose a chair amongst six.
I take out a box of melting core muffins from my rucksack. It's the
excess of eggs and chocolate in the house I am leaving. I rest it on
my lap. I change chair four times. It's muffins on – muffins off lap
under the table. Somebody may shout at me for bringing in my
own food, even if I don't intend to eat it. I balance sun and shade.
I calculate probable deviations from the normal ball trajectory.
The boy is now playing it safe. But that's never for long with a boy
and a ball.

It's a beautiful Mediterranean afternoon by any description but
the internal one. Yet a perfectly looking environment, especially
when it's a perfect cliché, is like a home. It's the safest of places
to hide from others even when you can't, or don't need to, hide
from yourself. My hands are shaking. They'll still for the photos.
Stomach's in a knot. Knots stay quiet, tongue-tied. I am as blue as
it gets, but the azure of my dress will blind you to the rest. I fit by
mimicry. I'm safe.

The only risk is if somebody from the drinks crew asks for the
backstory. People ask for your story at moving house/ leaving the
area/ "have a good life" farewells. I tell the truth when I am asked.
In spring, I moved in for a love like that in the movies. It lasted
as long as a trailer. In the summer, my heart had moved on (I am
wrong to think it, but I don't know that yet). Now, in the autumn,
as a migratory bird, I need to move. Or, mostly, my landlord needs
his house.

There you go, I can share the bones of the story. But I can't spit
out the flesh. If I do, it will choke another from the drinks crew.
The flesh was shared.

Relax your face. Those are expats. All of them have crossed out
part of their backstory.

They know how to ask. They'll guard their eternal sunshine, your spotless mind.

Tuesday after Tuesday from spring to autumn, I had tried to like the drinks crew. I was building a semblance of a social home away from mine. You know the practice of open-heartedness and appreciation of the Other when it's not the right others and when you want to leave, you could choose to leave, but it's still better to have a social circle. By the end of every single night, I genuinely liked them. Of course I would want to bake muffins for them before I go; drink farewell drinks and pay for them before I go; let my soul grope, one last time, for soul traces under the suntan and life on display. Yes, trapped souls always leave a trail of crumbs for soul-seekers to follow.

Or maybe I needed respectable use for the eggs in excess. One shouldn't be throwing food out. Moving house is not an excuse. Or was it that I was self-protecting against stuffing myself with muffins.

It is good to cook and share the outcomes when you are moving out. Cupboards need emptying. Farewells need food. It's healing when you are moving out with your heart bleeding. It's hard to stuff yourself with twelve muffins (or was it a sixteen-hole tray?) you cared about while making. And when you are out sharing them, you're not home alone, crying. All the more important since 'home' is not even yours for much longer, just the alone.

Whatever. I'm here. I look normal. Plus, the psychological answer to either-or is often 'all'. I don't need to doubt having wanted to bake for the drinks crew.

I wave at the first two.

MENU OF THE DAY

Please give your attention to today's reading menu, as described in this section. You need to be aware of what you'll be served later. The ingredients are mostly familiar. The combinations may feel weird.

Materially, this chapter is about the food and kitchen equipment we have at home and how to handle them at house moving.

Psychologically, it is about our internal affair with food and eating, some of which spills out, laying out our inner mess to the world, and some of which is undetected, cropped and filtered out, including from the screen of our own awareness. This internal affair is presented through roles we've adopted in performing the life task of seeking nourishment, both physical and emotional. These roles often feel like home in their familiarity and rootedness. But it's just as often a dysfunctional home. It can be dysfunctional even if, on the surface, it's one of the healthiest and most attractive.

The first section of the chapter resembles a personality questionnaire. (You don't need to fill in or score anything, but it will guide you towards self-inquiry in a similar way.) It introduces three out of seven general personality dimensions and 'imbalances' on them. It also describes fifteen–out of twenty-eight–imbalanced eating personality types.

The three dimensions concern:

- how we listen to our body and inner signals relative to how we listen to signals from the world around us;
- how able we are to tune into inarticulate impulses in comparison to clear directions and principles, and how likely we are to follow one or the other;
- how responsive we are to the call of 'the good as right' v. that of 'the good as pleasurable'.

The remaining four dimensions and their thirteen eating personality types are not covered in this book (they'll either become part of another or I'll publish them on **milapetrova.com**). A three-course meal (section) is enough for the purposes of a house-moving book. I promise. If you want a glimpse of the remaining dimensions for other purposes though, they concern:

- how we prioritise or balance feeling good *now* relative to feeling good in the future;
- how we control the inner-outer boundary through which we admit things into our bodies and lives;
- how pronounced our punishment-and-reward relationship with ourselves is;
- how safe or scared we feel in the world, and how prepared we are for when the skies are falling.

Together, these seven dimensions define our eating, in my view, far more than the specific foods we eat and diets we follow. More interestingly, imbalances on these dimensions in our eating are often mirrored by imbalances in our broader lives.

For each of us, parallels between our eating and broader life exist or are stronger on some dimensions than on others. For most of us, however—which is a strong claim, but so my current hypothesis goes—imbalances on these seven dimensions share remarkably many similarities between our eating and our broader lives. And while our eating and its consequences may make us happy, unhappy or anything in between, typically, it's the broader life pattern that makes us happy or unhappy to a much greater degree. Imbalanced eating patterns are thus, often, a symptom of a much broader imbalance and that broader imbalance has the same form as the eating imbalance. (Nothing precious about the word 'balanced', by the way. You can substitute it with healthy, adaptive, functional, etc.)

Dynamic, individual, goal- and context-specific

Having a balance on the dimensions discussed here is not about finding a perfect stable point, not even the golden mean. It is about being able to move in and out of points. It's dynamic, individual, goal- and context-specific, and open to moment-by-moment refinement by tracking the consequences of our choices. The other side of this is that any point on these dimensions, including the extremes, has value. Wherever you are stuck, there is something beneficial about it.

While none of the sides of a dimension is, by default, better than the other, our positive associations tend to be lop-sided, to veer in one direction only. For instance, "listening to one's inner voice" (the tuning-in side of Dimension 1) is often taken to mean "discovering one's deepest truths". Yet we also have many stupid, lazy, broken, self-sabotaging, fearful, dangerous, perfidious, you name it, inner voices. Mine, for one, are a whole choir. We often need to kill our most darling stories so that we can tell ourselves better ones.

If you find parallels between where you are stuck in your eating and broader life on these dimensions, sometimes fervently proclaiming the superiority of your beliefs, you'll see paths to eating differently. You'll also remember that truth can be found in the strangest of places. Smiling frozen in your fridge. Crossing legs on tins of beans. Gone to mould on last week's bread. You may even become wildly impatient to start sorting through your food supplies so as to call forth their truth.

And if you don't find any of your dysfunctional patterns,

general or eating-related, described in this chapter, please, raise a
toast to yourself. Make it with a blood red cocktail or a dark green
juice. Stick a cocktail umbrella, a mint leaf on top. Yours is a flag
of victory so few can claim. I've not met a single person as perfect
(or as self-deceiving) as you are.

SOUL CHAOS IN FOOD AND EATING
Dimension 1: Tuning in–opening up
The first dimension we'll consider extends between, on the one
hand, an extreme ability to tune into the signals of one's body,
to hear 'the voice within' and, on the other hand, an extreme
openness to the invitations, messages and signals coming from
the Big Wide World. As mentioned earlier, every point on this and
any other continuum has value. Having found one's balance thus
means that you can move flexibly across points, depending on your
current goals and circumstances and while tracking the conse-
quences of your choices. Now let's check if you've found yours.

Test yourself for over-listening to external signals
Does any of the following apply to you?
- You are trying hard be a good, successful person; to
  have something to show for your life; to make it to the
  top, regardless of whether your top is visible success,
  inner growth or both; or even only to create a good,
  normal, ordinary life WHILE a part of you is weeping on
  the inside that there is something wrong with your life
  (or, indeed, Life), that something about you got lost or
  broken on the way.
- You always try to do the right, good, best thing and
  while working out what it looks like, you find yourself

swayed by the opinions of others. In fact, you rarely notice that those are 'opinions'. You take them as 'standards', 'better knowledge', 'truth'. It's especially the case if they come from your closest people or people you admire.

- You feel incredibly anxious in the context of uncertainty, contradictions and disagreement. You need certainty. You need spaces where opinions and experiences converge. You create and guard mini-worlds of like-minded people.

- You are constantly finding yourself resolving somebody else's problems or supporting somebody else's goals.

- You are bending over backwards to be an extra good girl/ good boy when your antennas signal that that's the way to avoid criticism or conflict, even if, realistically, you've already done more than your fair share.

- You wish you had more courage to stand up for what you believe in, but never quite manage. Or you do it admirably opposite strangers and adversaries, but never within your own valued groups.

- You have a tendency to become overwhelmed or burnt-out.

- You adapt, adapt, adapt; understand, understand, understand; accept, accept, accept; patiently, sensibly, creatively resolving negative situations for far longer than most people would even imagine possible. It may be in your relationships, work, housing arrangements, anything. Until one day, one hour, one minute you SEVER, STRIKE, GO. It is out of nowhere for those on the receiving end. It's entirely logical to you. The tension and intentions have been accumulating. It was only a matter of crossing a threshold.

- When a disagreement arises, you are keen to explain, justify, defend, assert, insist on, resist, argue for, etc. a position, opinion or choice, whether internally or externally.
- You find yourself over-reacting to any advice which doesn't match your leanings, whether you ultimately follow it or do the exact opposite.
- If you are persuaded by a vision, you will climb nine mountains to reach it, without ever stopping long enough to consider if it's your mountain.
- You know you can lead and do far greater things that you are currently doing, but never fully dare. The formal sign, appointment, permission, unfailing certainly hasn't come. So you don't.

If you've *not* found yourself described in any of the bullet points, you can safely skip the eating personality types that follow. It's unlikely that any of them will apply to you. Otherwise see if you recognise yourself in one or more of them.

The first two to three sentences should be enough to show you if a type applies to you.

Firebird Seekers
(even if they wouldn't eat the Firebird)

If you are a Firebird Seeker, you are willing to try every persuasive approach to eating right. 'Right' is whatever leads you to your primary goal. You want it all, of course, but at any one time a goal takes precedence. It may be being the version of slim you find most admirable. It may be improving your muscle-fat distribution.

Having more energy. Not dying in the six months the doctor told you you've got left. Getting rid of some soft overflowing padding, an undulating landscape under the shapewear. Goals may thus come into conflict, most perilously when health and appearance ones collide.

Whatever the goal and path though, the Firebird Seeker in you keeps walking. You walk with sterling discipline and sharp awareness. It shows results. Sometimes AMAZING results. Sometimes 'maybe results'. Not on a par with the effort, yet enough to keep the vision bright, the walking light. You will not slack, other than for brief moments that are few and far between. Yet an inner permission for a weakness, for a doubt, would have served you far better than unfailing military discipline:

I know that eating as I do increases your energy level. But does it increase mine?!

I do all that's healthy to do. I am healthy. I must be healthy. But how can somebody truly healthy feel so exhausted?

I am such a diligent little bee sourcing ingredients, sprouting, juicing, soaking, draining....But I used to BE more! To think of Living and Being and the youth of my Soul. Now it's of cooking a dinner, of Vitamin B, of Vitality and of Vegetables for you and for me.

You know those herbarium-rose shoppers in health food shops—yellow as the sheets of paper they were pressed between rather than the picture of health their habits deserve? Obviously, if that dry flattened rose is us, we won't think that our best efforts have done it. We'll believe it's age catching up at last; gaps of knowledge; drops in effort. If the body doesn't 'deliver' the promised outcomes, we'll refine and double up the effort. We'll spend even more on special products and advice. Sometimes we must even get sick for the penny to drop.

In another version of the Firebird Seeker, we are attuned to our body's signals. We listen and adapt. We emanate health and youthfulness. Compliments (and thin sharp arrows of envy) prove it. What we are failing to hear though are the signals from our broader self. It's telling us that if we were julienning fewer courgettes and weren't washing the juicer three times a day, we would have learnt to dance flamenco. If we were less disciplined about doing the right things right, we would have had the chance to feel into which things are right for us in the first place.

Again, remember, the balance is always dynamic, always personal and always goal and context-specific. As a former Firebird Seeker (mostly Version 2), I now wish I had spent less time grating cabbage and more time learning to dance, but that's not an 'everybody and always' relationship. You may be a chef, nutritionist or fitness instructor. You may have been diagnosed with a life-limiting illness—sure as hell you would want to try anything and everything! You may have DECIDED you are done with your excess weight once and for all. And nothing wrong with the occasional, even protracted, firebird seeking by anyone. The point is to be noticing cues and consequences apart from picking blue feathers.

The Called and Stimuli Controlled
(or the Eternally Tempted, or the Eating Meditator)

I[1] don't quite see it happening. It's as if a part of my brain is temporarily switched off. It's as if I've been CALLED. And when I'm CALLED

---

1 The perspective from which eating types are presented ('I', 'you', 'we', 'they') changes across and within types. I chose to risk a level of confusion but accommodate individual differences around forms of expression which help us hear what we don't want to hear. We may need company ('we'), a critical-yet-compassionate look straight in the eye ('you'), safe distance ('they'), a clear form for the words of inner voices or for silences pregnant with meaning ('I'). Perhaps by jumping around perspectives, I will accidentally hit upon the one that works for you.

(by food, though by demanding people's demands too), I respond. I can own what I've done or didn't do later. In the moment, I'm gone.

It's right there in front of me—in the supermarket, behind-the-corner takeaway, in the fridge, already on my plate. One reaches out. It 'happens'. It's offered too. I take all that's offered. It's an unfinished business otherwise. There is no call like that of the incomplete calling to be completed. No regrets like the ones for missed life opportunities.

You say I'm not taking enough information from my body, letting myself be controlled from the outside. You must be right. The proof is all over me.

I see it in the mirror. I see it on the scales. In the stretch of the buttonholes. In the extra XXXs of my clothes. In my blood test results. In the eyes opposite. In the dimmed light when I am undressing.

I feel it in the rub of my thighs. In the hugs that keep the other at a belly's distance even when I love them so much that I want to erase any distance, any separation.

I hear it farting, rumbling, gurgling. Shouted at me, whispered about me.

But I don't see it, feel it, hear it there and then. I don't see that my body is waving that I'm approaching the threshold of 'that's enough'. I don't hear the alarm that I have passed the threshold. I'm deaf to the screaming that I'm stuffed. It's quiet, believe me. Deafening silence even. I don't find a clear, lucid thought on the surface of my mind that that many bakewell tarts, Indian, peaches, whatever, will trigger my acid reflux right away or add to my weight later. When I eat, I live in the pure, pupil-like now. There is no tomorrow at the end of a fork.

You say that when I eat like this there is an anxiety, fear, guilt, confusion, fatigue, whatever I refuse to listen to; that I want to make it go away by eating (drinking, smoking, sex too, but you said that's for another time). You say it works because eating is such a powerful, *basic reward. It's true. And it isn't. There is something I want to make go away by eating. And it (almost) works. Everything other than the eating is a background when I'm eating. Though strangely, too, eating is also a background if you consider how little I notice of it.*

But you are wrong that I refuse to listen to fear, guilt, anxiety, whatever. I can't pick any clear voices, any defined sensations. It's a shapeless something. That's what I chase away by the ultimate draw of attention, the snap-of-a-fish-finger switch-off of thought. By the ultimate meditation, one could say. EATING.

Rise and Fall
(especially around New Year)

The Rise and Fall people mix the two patterns above. In some of them, the Called and Stimuli Controlled leads most of the time, but is banished in periods of intense dieting and, perhaps, exercising. At such times, the discipline and extremeness of the Rise and Fall can put even the most committed Firebird Seeker to shame. But, as we all know, in 99.5% of cases it will break down. In other Rise and Fall people, the Firebird Seeker leads, passionately following a right-eating vision and suffering for it, with brief periods of 'losing it'.

When you look at a Firebird Seeker and a Called and Stimuli Controlled in their pure form, both in appearance and when eating, it's almost impossible to believe that they are the same type of person. And yet, in terms of their inability to tune into themselves and their excessive orientation to external stimuli, they are two peas in a pod, two M&M's in a pack.

Test yourself for over-listening to internal signals
Does any of the following apply to you?

- You repeat the same mistakes, again and again, even if you've been warned repeatedly by others, suffered the negative consequences of numerous previous iterations, and possibly even tried something different as taught by experience (strictly your own or very similar).
- You hear others comment (shout, bark, grumble, tell you through tears) that you are stuck in your opinions, beliefs, habits, worldview, way of life; impervious to criticism; stubborn, headstrong, difficult; politely phrased—determined....For you, it's more about having an identity and an opinion. Plus, it's an objective fact that some things are True, Right, Real, Possible, Worthy...Or at least in your country. In your house. In your relationships.

If it sounds like you, see if you can recognise yourself in any of the following eating personality types, all of them imbalanced in the direction of over-listening to internal signals.

As Solid as Rock Salt
You eat today, tomorrow and yesterday what you've always or long been eating. You trust the tests of time. The beauty of the familiar. The ease of habit. If in Budapest for a single night, you'll probably go to Pizza Hut. Why risk failed experiments? Why change what works? Why spend so much energy on seeking joy in something that's just a need? Makes sense!

It doesn't make sense, however, if your body is SOS-ing for change with ailments, excess weight, bad breath, foul mood, boredom....It doesn't make sense if it goes with you being painfully disappointed. With people. With knowledge. With the Good. With miracles. With their combined taste (good knowledge, good people, knowledgeable people, miraculous goodness...). You are *certain* that no other person, no book, no article, no programme can tell you anything of value about food and eating (or anything else in life, for that matter). You know it all. You've heard it all. It's 98% rubbish. Or doesn't work. Or what's the point anyway. Both the certified once healthy and the certified gravely ill will be certified dead still. You'll stand. Ill, sad, perhaps fat, but rock solid. With a crust against Surprise. With salty tears that cannot flow. Or stop.

I'll Eat (It) My Way
(which is always the opposite to yours)

I'll Eat (It) My Way people, typically younger ones or grown-ups having a moment, are eating the way they are eating partly to assert themselves while staging a demonstration against you. If it's you who likes making a My Way eating statement, powerful choice, mate! I mean it. That's a weapon nobody can take away from you, always available, several times a day. It makes an impression, whether used against your mum or partner behaving/ cast as your mum. The annoying thing is that, if you look closer, it's self-defeating precisely in the goals of control, free will and differentiation. By doing the opposite to what somebody is doing or advising you to do, you are just as controlled by them as if you were submitting to them fully. Whatever you do, it responds to what comes from them, not to what's within you. Let alone that there are better ways to tell another how angry, hurt or resentful you are. Perhaps when you grow up.

Almost There
(now and for the past twelve years)

The Almost There people will explain with healthy self-confidence, a scoop of self-awareness, and a sprinkle of self-criticism (always of the rational, self-embracing, and thus largely impotent in spurring action kind) that they are eating in a very balanced, sensible way. It's almost perfect, really. You only need a few tiny adjustments to reach your best weight and resolve a health concern or two (nothing usual, everybody your age is on medication!). You're determined to try. You've set your mind on how you'll do it. You'll get there. You've done it before. You are Almost There now! As you've been for the past six-ten-twelve years.

Dimension 2: Clear rules–subtle signals

This continuum concerns our tendency to pay attention to what is clear, well-defined, loud, coherent, logical....v. what is vague, emerging, shape-shifting, mysterious....It is about our preference to follow subtle signals, nudges, impulses, emotions, temptation, magic relative to a preference to be led by guidance, rules, directions, plans, storylines, lucid and refined thoughts.

The balanced point is, again, dynamic, individual, and goal- and context-specific. If we go too far and too consistently in the direction of the clear, rational and principled, we lose the magic, adventure and revelations of the world. If we go too far and too consistently the other way round, we find ourselves in a chaotic, meaningless soup of stimuli where basic impulses and manipu-lation rule, and the light of reason only flickers, never shines.

In the context of food and eating, this is about whether we eat from the momentary, fluctuating needs of our body; prompted by nudges from the environment which affect our subconscious; or from well-articulated but rigid principles and programmes. Let's poke your balance.

Test yourself for over-leaning towards 'the clear'

Does any of the following apply to you?

- In sticking to discipline, principles, values, goals, rules... you are consistently pushing away improvisation, mystery, inner impulses, uncertainty, experimentation, things too good to be true, strange birds on your shoulders...

- You are feeling tense, rigid, as if dried out. Something's happened to your principles and values too. They used to give you wings, extraordinary power. No more. By now it's just a sense of feeling right for doing what's right.

- You tend to feel anxious, even scared, in situations lacking clarity, guidance and order.

- You feel a longing, a calling, a deep inner urge to do something different, be somewhere different, to explore, run, sing, laugh, love, live in ways you've sensed, never had, and yet consistently fail to follow. You remain 'sensible', 'rational', 'cool-headed', 'well put together'. Eaten on the inside too.

If that's you (one bullet point is enough), see if you are also, in your eating:

Food Soldier

(often working in tandem with

the Food Police or Food Academic)

Food Soldiers have firm beliefs about right or wrong, healthy and unhealthy, moral and immoral ways of eating. If you are one, you know that any enemy—whether red meat or the apricot tarts you see in the shop window of your local patisserie—requires self-protection, emotional control, safe distance and a level of denial of your humanness. As a Food Soldier, you are at a high risk of losing the joy of eating. You have a goal. A goal's achieved through discipline. You may achieve it, but you may also damage your health by failing to listen to your body, as it mostly speaks in subtle, bundled up ways requiring translation, rather than through clear orders.

Some Food Soldiers also behave like the Food Police, over-monitoring and chastising others for their transgressions in eating. If they themselves 'transgress', they'll do it in private. 'It's only human'. It's ok. Or quickly forgotten. Nobody saw. The principles stand. So does your superhuman reputation.

Other Food Soldiers go hand in hand with Food Academics. If that's you, you are always happy to deliver a lecture: "the theory and evidence behind my (your) food and eating choices". Don't interrupt me. I'll change your life if you listen.

Remember, if you've chosen such roles (and any other role on these pages) as an expression of the call of your soul and as your service to the world, and if it brings you overwhelming joy, which you also see light a fire in others, that's not an imbalance or dysfunction. It's a way of being you.

Test yourself for over-leaning towards 'the subtle'
Does any of the following apply to you?
- You glide through your days driven by habit, rhythms and how things have always or long been. It's hardly good or bad. It's mostly smooth, safe, familiar. Yet in the brief moments when you step out, are kicked out of your routines, you catch a glimpse of thin, transparent hooks and strings, a web of past accidents and choices. Your

past. Your accidents and choices. The web you've weaved
and caught yourself in.

- You jump from one thing to the next; struggling to find
the discipline to follow through or the courage to take a
stand. A grass to the wind and headless chicken in one.
But charming.

- You follow temptation and extreme experiences (food,
sex, substances, adventure...) as if they are always a way
to feel alive rather than, often enough, a way to kill
yourself expressly (your soul if not your body); as if they
are always a way to be You rather than, often enough,
a way of running away from it.

If one or more of the preceding bullet points described you,
check for parallels in your eating life. Do you recognise yourself
in one or more of the following eating personalities?

Emotional Eaters

You struggle to bring up vague, inchoate, often scary emotions
to the level of conscious thought. You respond to them as if they
were signals of hunger. It's not as misjudged as it may sound.
Evolutionarily speaking, situations triggering extreme emotions
required us to fight or fly. We needed our energy stores replenish-
ed. Natural then. Counterproductive today. Replenish the
emotions.

Overeaters Intuitive

You are in awe of the wisdom of the Body; the extraordinary
balancing mechanisms which underpin our choices of food as
well as our digestion. You eat accordingly—intuitively. "Your body

will always tell you what it needs." So true. It's only that when we look at you, you look at you, we see Intuition Impossible.

Surfers of Desire
(or Perfect Consumers with
a touch of Decadent Dandies)

You ride the wave of desire. In an ocean of ads, promotions, loyalty schemes, product positioning tricks, bargains, limited editions, advice from the connoisseurs....you are the dream target for marketers, advertisers, and consumerist society in general. It's not because you're simple. You can be quite complex in fact—free, refined, rich, cynical, wild....Did I say Wilde? "The only way to get rid of a temptation is to yield to it. Resist it, and your soul grows sick with longing for the things it has forbidden to itself."[2]

As is the case within any of the seven dimensions, there is far more similarity between behaviours, mindsets and personality types which we would normally consider complete opposites. Some of the people in the best and worst physical shape; some of the most disciplined and honourable people as well as some of the most impulsive, unreliable ones are as they are (and unhappy) because they have difficulty handling the unclear, half-shaped, emergent, uncertain... The difference? The former knock it, with all of its hidden promise, out of their lives. The latter are knocked out by it.

Dimension 3: The good as 'right' and the good as 'pleasurable'

Here we are talking about the dynamic or largely fixed point we fall on between doing the thing that is right v. the thing that feels

---

2 Wilde, O. *The Picture of Dorian Gray.* London: Legend Press, 2021. Kindle edition, p.24.

good when there is an apparent conflict between the two.

There is a sweet spot where what is ethical to do also feels good to do; what is seen as good by reason or spirit is also good for the body; what is good for the environment and others is also good for us; what we *think* is right is also what we *feel* is right. Such sweet spots are rarely immediately visible. They demand creativity and utmost specification of our versions of the good and the right. As a result, most of us don't even conceive of their existence. We believe we need to make a hard compromise.

Moreover, many of us take "doing the right thing" to mean "doing the thing that hurts". Often, the more it hurts, the 'gooder' it is. There are extreme situations when doing the right thing hurts indeed, yet not doing it hurts *far more*. But, overall, if we can't balance what feels right with what feels good, we haven't found the true good in a situation.

Test yourself for overdoing the 'right'

Do you see yourself in any of the patterns that follow?

- You KNOW what's right and wrong. You've lived it, you've tested it, you've breathed it, suffered from it, for it, would die for it, or Jesus already did, or if you don't care about Jesus, thousands, millions have done so! You can bet that if something is RIGHT, somebody has died for it! You have a particular dislike for those who take things too easily and lack gravity in serious matters.

- Or perhaps you won't add the above pathos, because you are not a (wo)man of pathos, you believe in equanimity and peace, but you still KNOW what's GOOD and RIGHT (even if what you know so well, earned knowing so well, is how relative and impermanent the good and the right are). You've thought about it, read a thousand and one texts about it, derived every consequence, the unintended consequence of every half-consequence, tied it all into a system of thought you've been living, testing, refining, then checked forty-eight times over and you can't be wrong. You are the living proof it's GOOD. It's only that we can't quite feel you feeling good.

- In theory, you know that your individual perspective is always incomplete and partial, that even the most ridiculous belief has a history, environment and reasoning that support it (even if not adaptive in a different context). Yet you can't help seeing those less 'refined' than you as ignorant, backward or, more compassionately, in need of education and enlightenment. How do you begin to feel what you know you must feel?

- You've always displayed exceptional ethics. Everybody believes you deserve better, far better, the best in life in fact. So do you. Yet you never get it. You may look peaceful (look closer, it's resigned). You may sound wise (listen better, chimes of bitter). Still, persistently, heroically you continue to do the right thing and not doubting enough if it is—since it hurts—wrong for you.

If one or more of the preceding bullet points described you, check for parallels in your eating life:

No Pain—No Gain

You've deserved the looks and health you've got. With blood and sweat. You feel proud! Superior? If 'they' want your body and energy, sure, please, let them do it! 90% will only talk. 'Visualise'. 'Manifest'. Flake out on day seven and moan it's too hard. Don't make me laugh (muscles ache from exercise). You have to pay for what you've got. If only there weren't those irritating creatures for whom it's so effortless and easy. 20% of your efforts for 80% of your results, sometimes 120% of them. It's maddening. Unfair. Are you missing a secret? No, they are lucky. And so are you (yes, lucky, but also missing a secret).

Moral Eater

Eating is a moral act, an act you need to perfect for the good of the animals, the environment, the workers in the long chain which brought something to your table. You bite the bullet. Full on. You dedicate disproportionate amounts of effort, time, mental space and resources to eating as a form of moral expression ('disproportionate' is only relative to other valued pursuits of yours, there is no objective measure here). You may even be compromising your health. One way or another, you end up suffering while upholding the end to the suffering of others. You are also becoming more and more judgemental of those unlike you while preaching compassion for those you like (from a safe distance, usually). Is it just ironic or self-defeating? Chew it over.

Food Spartan

You are strongly committed to a healthy and morally right diet but are also frequently flying around, waging battle after battle for some grand cause. You just can't dedicate the time, effort, mental space and resources to do it 'all' and 'perfectly', as you once did. But that's ok. There are hacks—simple solutions that are also ticking all the healthy/ morally right eating boxes. Gradually, without noticing, you strip eating to a narrow range of the simple and right. Gradually, the simple right becomes so boring that most of the joy of eating is lost. Your body becomes under-nourished too.

Finally, test yourself for the 'pleasure' extreme

Or maybe there is nothing stranger to you than human types as the above. Do they know what it is to live?! You've come to the Earth for pleasure, joy, success, luxury, brilliance, glamour.... And that's what you've been getting! You've been on top of the world so many times, for such a long time.

Not now though. Something in your luck broke. The arrows of life turned sharp. It wasn't supposed to be that way. You want yourself plugged back into pleasure again! On top of the world again! Yet the more you plug yourself in, the more you short-circuit. The more you clamber up the slopes to the top, the more you slide down their gravel.

If that's the case, you might also be willing to:
Die Young but Happy (or pretending to be).

You eat and drink as you please. You seize the day with everything! And you don't overthink anything. With food and drink, this means you are led by the initial explosion of taste and by ease and simplicity, underplaying the effect of your choices on your health, the environment and others, as well as on your ability to appreciate truly good food. A frequent aspect of your table manners is to be sarcastic of people who would rather eat healthily. Whether they pay attention to you is their problem. Yours is having a body and moods pleading for change in how and what you eat.

On this dimension, you may also be an eating personality which blends characteristics from both directions. It's when pleasure is harnessed by a strict system of rules:

Michelin Starred or Starved

You aim for the best and finest in the world of food and drink. You don't accept omissions light-heartedly. In the right environment, this is nothing but being a connoisseur true to your standards. It becomes imbalanced only if you can't move it out of the centre of your experience when it threatens that experience. It's when basic food and service in the village restaurant spoil its deep blue lake view. It's when you are so displeased with your dinner by the beach that you ignore the desire vibrating in the summer air. And, please, stay in your hotel room if you'll be sulking when luxury and privilege lose coverage. We won't have time for you. We'll be counting the stars that nobody can give or take away.

If you are keen to dig into your psyche for longer, you will be able to find the remaining four dimensions and thirteen eating personality types of this model-in-progress at *milapetrova.com*.

If you would, rather, both dig into your psyche and prepare to move out, consider the suggestions in the next section.

If you want to go straight to the pragmatics of sorting through food stocks and kitchen equipment, skip the next section and continue from ***Dealing with the excess of food supplies***.

SHIFTING THE PSYCHOLOGICAL
THROUGH THE PHYSICAL AND VICE VERSA
Stack into 'insight piles'

If you've found yourself described in any of the eating personality types discussed earlier, consider stacking your food reserves into 'insight piles'. They will tell you even more of your secrets. It will only work if you make, not imagine, the piles though. Mental maths can lead us profoundly astray. If it didn't, you would have been in your perfect shape by now.

Your first pile is for food which you love eating and, simultaneously (this is crucial), contributes to the health, energy levels and/or appearance goals that matter to you. You don't need to have the most up-to-date scientific evidence about a type of food, just your current beliefs and personal life experience. Be careful, however, to stop 'kind-ofs' from sneaking in.

If you are eating in a way that's truly good for you, you'll only have this perfect pile of 'love it and it does me good'. At the very least, it should be your biggest pile. You should also be emanating health, radiance and happiness as your default way to be. Nothing less will do. Let me remind you though—this is not because all is explained by food, but because some of the patterns of thought and behaviour that stand in the way of our happiness are also in the way of our eating.

If you come across food which you love but suspect may not be well tolerated by your body, add it to an 'to experiment' pile. Exclude it from your diet for long enough and note what happens. Include it again and note what happens.

Making robust experiments with what we eat and drink is as hard as it gets. We eat so often. We eat so many different things. We forget what we've eaten (so write it down immediately). But if the inclusion or exclusion of a product makes a dramatic difference, you won't need optimal control of other factors. And if you can't detect anything definitive, perhaps it matters little whether you eat it or not. Not necessarily, but likely.

Finally, for any food that didn't go into your perfect or experimental pile, define the task for yourself. Perhaps you need a pile for the Called and Stimuli Controlled, of things you wipe away when darkness descends upon you (although, most likely, you won't find them 'in stock'). Perhaps the Green Inquisition[3] keeps its instruments at the bottom of your fridge. If 'my' eating types don't resonate with you, formulate your own.

Find out if what you are eating is also eating you. Then throw out that food. And show that subpersonality the door.

Preferably, throw out more beliefs than food

Throw out anything which you don't genuinely enjoy eating or drinking but eat as it's a good thing to. Throw out your beliefs that you need to be eating it. Life's too short and variety of food too spectacular to necessitate eating celery, goji berries or protein bars (or whatever superfood, good-for-you food or well-advertised food you'd like to nominate for the prize of "One (wo)man's miracle is another (wo)man's trying too hard").

By the same token, throw out anything which you are eating or drinking (almost) by addiction. If you lose clarity once you go teeth deep into something, trying to squeeze the original divine pleasure from one more bite, spoon, sip, and it doesn't, doesn't, doesn't come, but you can sense it is there, you fall, fall, fall for its promise to return to you, to hit you one more time with the next bite, mouthful, sip...you are getting nowhere good.

---

3 A type from the complete model, falling on the Punishment-Rewards dimension. The Green Inquisition has you if you are eating quite healthily and loving it but, (almost) without noticing, are also using healthy eating as a way of punishing yourself. You may have messed up at work or in a relationship today; you end up eating extra healthily tonight. Your 'failure' may be one of good eating too. If it is, you don't just return to the good habits. You must first go through a period of eating excessively virtuously, a form of cleansing with a streak of self-punishment. Only after the cleansing and self-flagellation have reached respectable levels, you return to a more manageable way of applying the principles you'd broken.

Throwing out what you are having by such a compulsion rather than choice of a (guilty) pleasure won't stop you from reaching out for it in your new house. Nor do you need to stop reaching out for it if the first bites or sips still work. But you'll experience yourself breaking a pattern, even if you may need to re-affirm the breaking a hundred times more.

I hate throwing out food. I do silly things not to do it, as you'll read in the next section. Yet there are times to throw out while putting green consciousness, respect for the labour of others, and compassion for the less lucky aside. Those are the times when we are throwing out items infested with ideas that harm us. Food disintegrates quick. Patterns may need brutal symbols of destruction.

DEALING WITH THE EXCESS OF FOOD SUPPLIES
Share after the initial explosion of pleasure
and throw in a scientific experiment

If a type of food I love is believed to be 'bad' (which I now take to mean 'good in moderation'), I share it right after the initial fireworks begin to dim. At moving out, these are usually cakes I bake to clear the cupboards. In 'static life', it's mostly (non-)guilty pleasures I buy, such as chocolates, biscuits and salted peanuts. I take them to the office or leave them on benches where I know homeless people gather.

I also make behavioural experiments as I go along. The easier you make it to access such products (such as by removing the wrapping which keeps anyone's fingers two centimetres away from a biscuit) and the more attractively you arrange them, the quicker they disappear. My favourite is to experiment with treats which have been lying around in the office kitchen for days and

see them gone in less than an hour. Try it. It breaks the routine.
You'll also see what supermarkets are doing to us.

Turn into a better cook by using
all you've got and buying as little as possible

If you choose to clear your kitchen in a sustainable, responsible,
cost-effective and entertaining way, you can also choose to
become a better cook. As the rule of the game is to use as many
of the ingredients you've got and buy as little new as possible,
you will become a better cook. Your baseline is irrelevant. You
may be at the level of boiling spaghetti and grating cheese over
the shop-bought sauce. You may have a culinary blog. One way
or another, constraint is a spice for creativity unless we allow
it to make minced meat out of us.

Whenever I decide to cook something for which I don't have
a recipe, I google the ingredients or type of dish adding 'most
amazing', 'the best', 'mouth-watering', 'award-winning' or some-
thing similar. No recipe retrieved this way has ever failed me. It
used to be a moving-out and date-night hack, now it's a regular
habit.

That said, prepare for the rubbish you'll also cook. The more
'efficient' in clearing your cupboards and fridge you are trying
to be—by adding too much of what you found there to the same
meal—the more frequently it will happen. Some of it will need to
go straight into the bin. Not ideal, but at least it serves the purpose
of reducing what you've got.

Sometimes you will need to buy a new ingredient in order
to use several of those already available. Don't compromise on
essential ingredients. The most important point is not to clear the
cupboards without remains. It's to nourish and entertain yourself

(and others). Or compromise as hard as you wish. There is no failed experiment if you learn its lessons.

Generally, unless you've been preparing for a siege or lockdown, the cupboards will clear fast. It's remarkable how quickly we run out of stuff when we don't replenish supplies as per our usual routines. There is one big exception: dry herbs and spices. I often move spices from house to house. It takes time, money and ethnic shops to create a decent collection. But if I decide to leave them behind, I donate to soup kitchens.

Donate to food banks, soup kitchens or just about anyone

If you are not interested in becoming a better cook, you can donate your food supplies easily. I like the game of using up all I've got, but if I lose against time, I donate to soup kitchens, usually in local churches. I have found folk there most welcoming of used and fresh products too, such as a third of a bottle of olive oil, eggs, vegetables.

This is not an option when donating to food banks. Products donated to them (in the UK, you can find them in almost any supermarket) must be unopened and generally with a long shelf life, such as tins or dry pasta.

When soup kitchens were closed during the COVID lockdown, I posted an ad on Gumtree. A social worker picked my random collection for the families she was looking after. A Gumtree stranger congratulated me on making the effort. Sharing food can make you tearfully happy.

On a couple of occasions, I've left bags with food at bus-stops, as if forgotten, hoping that somebody would finish my work of finding the hungry or that the hungry themselves would find what longs to be found by them. I am sorry for the terror alerts they may have caused.

I recently saw wooden boxes with a sign 'Food', looking like bird houses, attached to trees in my hometown.

More in the spirit of our times, search the App Store/ Google Play for food sharing/ food waste apps in your local area. The majority are still for collecting surplus food from restaurants and supermarkets (which you may want to try too, especially towards the end of your time in a place) rather than for giving yours away, but the latter need is served too.

SORTING THROUGH YOUR
COOKING AND EATING UTENSILS
Two ways in which cooking and eating utensils
are a problematic class of objects

Even if I've grown to love cooking, I find cooking and eating utensils the epitome of characterless and soulless. Standardised, predictable objects, hard to differentiate from any other of the same type. They belong, for me, to the class of objects we wouldn't say we love, or even have much of an attitude towards, but which we use regularly, with the use improving our lives, at times majorly.

Cooking and eating utensils belong to another problematic class too—of objects for which there is no clear financial benefit of either moving them or not moving them. If we move them, we save little, possibly nothing at all, while we grant them a lot of luggage space. If we redistribute them, we buy similarly characterless replicas in our new place.

One of the paradoxes of moving well is that some of the things you'd better move on are not ones you love, but ones you don't want to be buying again. Goes vice versa too. Some of the things you love are better not moved. If you love not just having them, but seeking them, discovering them, changing them, you'd better leave more of them behind.

If you are still uncertain what to do with your cooking and eating utensils, check if some of my redistribution experiences and suggestions, coming next, can help you decide.

Contexts which have welcomed my cooking and eating utensils

Freecycle has been an unfailing platform for cooking and eating utensils and strange combinations of them.

Many UK charity shops accept crockery, china and glassware (but not pots, pans and baking trays). Tea and coffee sets seem particularly welcome or frequently donated.

In one of my universities, during induction week, there were stalls where crockery, cutlery and other kitchen equipment abandoned in residences by last year students were offered to the freshers. If you have a university nearby, you can always send an email to Student Services or student societies.

If you have an excess of little spoons, consider bequeathing them to an office. If you've ever worked in one, you'll know there is a little spoon eating monster in every office building.

Difficult items or wrong contexts?

Of all kitchen equipment, I've only tried selling high-quality, expensive cutlery. I failed.

I have come across only one charity shop that accepted pots, pans, trays and similar accessories prone to scratching and charring. There must be health and safety risks associated with re-using them. Just as likely, used cooking equipment doesn't

make an attractive display while taking up much space.
Or it might be a niche in the charity business.

Contexts in which I didn't ask,
but you might try (during the day)

The fine cutlery I couldn't sell ended up in a bag in front of a
church, at around 3 a.m. on the morning I was supposed to vacate
my flat and fly out of the country. It was one of four bags I left to
God's sleeping servants that night, trip by trip in the pitch dark.
I despise 'just leaving' solutions, even if they are mine, even if
the recipients are likely to perceive God's plan in them. You can,
however, legitimately offer your crockery and cutlery to churches
that run soup kitchens.

Plastic post-fantastic

I do not pass on any plastic containers, such as lunch boxes or
mixing bowls. Even after a few months of use, most look pathetic.
They can also be bought too cheaply to be of interest to any buyer
or donation beneficiary. I've been recycling plastic containers and
recently stopped buying any altogether.

I keep, however, one tightly closing plastic box for my leaving
day luggage. The latter always has something, typically cosmetics,
which is either fragile or in danger of leaking.

Once-in-a-blue-moon kitchen gadgets
and the inconclusiveness of 'very rare use'

Do you have any clever super-specialised kitchen gadgets? Think
egg slicers, pineapple corers, apple dividers, toast tongs, tea bag
squeezers, whisks, meat tenderizers, skewers, pasta making
utensils, kitchen timers....Which of them do you use once in a

blue moon? Can you do what they do without their aid, be it more slowly and less uniformly? Will you miss them?

Very rare use is not, in itself, a reason to leave an item behind. I carry on a manual walnut mill, a family possession at least as old as I am, even though I use it only once or twice a year. There is no walnut flour like the one it mills, coarse and crunchy yet still having the consistency of flour rather than finely chopped nuts. I wouldn't sell it for a small fortune. More accurately, my commitment to this piece of green plastic with metal parts going rusty begins to waver at the £4,000 mark (previous draft had £7,000). I don't have a sentimental attachment to it. It's only that its function is unique and valuable to me.

Bequeathing that which no-one else was allowed to drink from

If you have a favourite coffee/ tea mug or breakfast bowl, of the type only you are allowed to touch, I'd say you owe it special arrangements. I either ask for mine to be adopted by friends or leave them as part of a good team's office collection. A mug to feel as yours always helps a newcomer.

Smoothing the sharp edges of life

I have a robust observation that even the best equipped houses need a high-quality can opener, grater and/or scissors. If I am leaving a furnished place, I typically leave mine behind. I am obviously on a mission of protecting tenants from the sharp edges of life.

Chapter 15, *Chapter 13* and *Chapter 20* can help, respectively, with electrical appliances, kitchen textiles (such as tablecloths and tea towels) and sentimental items found in the kitchen, if any.

Whenever I see a well-equipped, inviting kitchen, I think of one of my aunts I haven't so far mentioned and who, unlike any of the others, would have been seriously offended if I didn't.

Aunt Bianca was a laughing stock, yet received all the respect, even veneration, she commanded. She wore dresses with gigantic flowers and bedsheet lace lining; dreamed of plastic surgery; was writing an epic semi-biographical, semi-political book for decades; and farted profusely, often announcing it was her slipper that screeched.

She had been a beauty in her youth. (I never quite saw it in photos, but delicate features, red hair to green-grey eyes, thin ankles and bra cups from the middle of the alphabet get you the attention of one.) She never married. Apparently, the love of her life was made to choose between her and his army career. 'They' feared she might be a Mata Hari of sorts: apart from her charms, she had two sisters in the U.S. and a brother from the suppressed opposition. She denounced 'them' as idiots: she was such a scaredy-cat that she even slept with her night lamp on. How on earth could 'they' fear her a spy?!

A journalist who reported on the achievements of communism wherever they happened, she'd lived out of a suitcase for decades. She got her first independent flat well into her fifties. And while I'm still taking her self-propagated legends of beauty and connections with the political elite with a pinch of salt, I've also come to believe she was one of the most independent, adventurous, self-determined and brave women of my family and the world she lived in.

I often visited her as a student. Belying her image, she was a fabulous cook. One had, however, to hear the same old tales of how having a kitchen to herself changed her life; how extra finely she'd diced the carrots; and how she'd been 'the living devil' again, making something out of nothing.

I'll never be talking of diced vegetables.
My life will always be changing for the better.
By a kitchen?! I said 'life'.
I'll never be repeating my stories.

For fifteen more years, I continued to think what I was thinking back then, when I was eating opposite her and nodding to what I was so fed up of hearing. I cooked occasionally, depending on how well-equipped the kitchen of a particular house was and how many housemates I shared it with. I *could* cook. I prepared food every day. I loved baking. I only belonged to the tribe who always have 'more important' things to do and think about and who find no spirit in cooking.

This lasted until my first move for no respectable reason. In it, I also chanced upon a magnificent kitchen.

I had moved 'to think differently'. In the summer preceding that winter by the seaside, I had admitted to myself that my life looked far better than it felt—a pretty polished little maddening prison of an averagely successful academic existence. You don't leave a prison, let alone the pretty ones, without thinking differently. This meant:

1. Thinking without the interference of too many thoughts from my usual circles. Until we check properly, too many of our thoughts are neither truly thought, nor ours, just soaked up from around and stuck on repeat.
2. Thinking less of the small things, with too many of them coming from a world of social expectations—

always lower in a new place.

3. Thinking more of the biggest of things, which rarely happens through thinking intently and more through floating, dreaming and surfacing from non-thinking.

The kitchen of this period of life transformations (part of it but not caused by it, as I had promised myself, but wasn't that what my aunt also meant?) was, indeed, an accident. I had tripled my budget for staying at a B&B while house hunting. I had to find a more sustainable solution. *Tomorrow.* So when tomorrow came, I left with no roof for the night, a single viewing for the day, and my perfect cool—youthfully naive—*I'm a little spoilt and will say NO to anything that doesn't please me* face on. Ten minutes after my only viewing, I was unpacking in a luxury seaside flat for the rest of the winter. My back-against-the-wall solutions are pure magic.

So was cooking in my winter kitchen, which also happened to help with thinking differently. On moving out of that flat, my muffin trays, blender, ceramic beans (for blind baking), cookie cutters and other kitchen utensils took more space than my clothes did.

Aunt Bianca and my own kitchen-associated life transformation are also behind my farewell dinner ritual at leaving a place. Statistically, you won't have time for a celebratory dinner on the night before you go. Until you crack your own house moving code (and reading of mine may help immensely, but can never be enough), you'll be needing 'one more day' as if by law. You'll take it from the night.

But should you have that last supper, consider adding three things to it: a pie, a glass of champagne and a candle.

The pie is humble. For all the times you've moved in ways you've said you never would. For all the times you've found yourself living, from one house to the next, in ways you've sworn inadmissible (ever, any longer). For all the times you've raised eyebrows at people who've opened their homes and hearts for you, set a table for you. For all the times you've nodded—disagreeing, disconnected—without finding the courage to spit out what needed to be spat.

The champagne is expensive. For when you've made a leap far bigger than the book of smooth transitions has ordained. For when you've turned a grey lead ball in the azure sky, wings malfunctioning from the moment you set off. It doesn't matter if you flew in the end—as most times you would have done, that's the nature of leaps—or fallen flat on your face. You've moved the inner scale of what's to be tried and how's to be flied. Champagne is for victory, champagne's for defeat.

The candle is for courage. For dispersing the fear which has once, ever stopped you from making a move. Which may now be stopping you from making a move. Not of a house. Of love. Of freedom. Growth. Whatever. The moves that truly matter.

You don't need a candle?
Wait, I see...
a scarlet letter
on your chest:
R
for
REGRET
burning you
alive.

Alive?

It's never over until you're fully over.

You burn to ashes

and they read

R

for

READY.

Now you

LEAP.

PART IV
BOUNDARY-CROSSING
THINGS

There is an objective boundary which the types of objects discussed in this part are enabling us to cross. It is often a form of the *home – outside world* boundary.

We may be crossing it in physical reality, as made possible by the documents and identifiers which prove our right to be in a particular space (*Chapter 17*).

We may be crossing it in our imagination, as through books (*Chapter 19*).

Perhaps most defining of our times, we may be moving in and out of realities and spaces in the virtual world, often in parallel to moving in the physical world (electronic devices discussed in *Chapter 15*).

Nevertheless, what brings these chapters most strongly together is something about the inner psychological boundary they are illuminating. Usually, it's one I've found particularly hard to cross. It often took me decades to, even if, when it happened, it may have been in a snap, from one day to the next in the wake of an insight. Those difficult-to-cross thresholds are linked to:

- **Attention, lack of attention and being taken for granted**, discussed in the context of **technology** (*Chapter 15*).
- Culturally inherited beliefs about what it means to be a **true woman (or man)**, discussed in the **context of DIY equipment** (*Chapter 16*).
- The **glorious visions we have (had) for our lives v. the lacklustre of the everyday**, as seen from the perspective of the **paperwork** we accumulate (*Chapter 17*).
- Our **guilty pleasures**, escapes and **superpowers** and the grey zones between them, as seen through the prism of **cosmetics** (*Chapter 18*).

- The challenges of **self-destruction, self-creation** and **self-salvation** as handled through **books** (*Chapter 19*).
- The **myths of letting go** as associated with the 'sentimental items' we hold onto (*Chapter 20*).

I don't think it's possible to gradate precisely the types of objects we own in terms of the psychological mess they can re-awake. Yet to the degree to which we can expect it, it makes sense to move from the psychologically easiest to the psychologically most difficult.

Here comes the most difficult part of this book.

CHAPTER 15

YOUR AMAZING TECHNICOLOUR DREAMHOUSE
AND THE TAKEN-FOR-GRANTED

I've been closest to undressing in public – sober, brightly
illuminated, pressure cooker-like simmering – at an airport café,
in full view of at least forty potential spectators and to a broader
departure lounge audience of at least ten times more. I was
failing to get the man I was parting with to look at me, let alone
talk to me. A tantrum was bursting bubbles quietly, about to tip
into boiling. I took out pen and paper and started brainstorming
*Ten ideas[1] for making a man lift his eyes off his phone other than a
dramatic "I'll wait by myself then, farewell" exit.*

No 1: Undress.

I shared the list with him before I began its execution. His
smile was naughty. But his stories of why he disconnected from
his nearest and dearest before a trip (trips from which it was
possible not to return) were serious. If you have a desperate need

---

1 The ten ideas idea, which I apply most consistently when my back's against the wall, is again an
idea of James Altucher. It is all over James's writing but perhaps try Altucher, J. *"The Ultimate Guide
for Becoming an Idea Machine"*. jamesaltucher.com/blog/the-ultimate-guide-for-becoming-an-idea-
machine. Undated, possibly 2018. Last accessed Aug 2022.

to be distracted, there is likely to be a dark(ish) reason why. I no longer minded his scrolling. He reconnected. With me.

The slow and certain erosion of attention resulting from the overuse of technology often has a darker foundation outside of technology. This insight was one of the main reasons why I stopped urging others to re-own their attention, something I was generally doing out of motivations far nobler than wanting that attention for myself. The other main reason for stopping was the futility of my attempts, which were at their most earnest, creative, annoying and useless with my mum. I've spent the summer holidays of at least four years trying to persuade her to stay less on Facebook, the Chronophage ('chronophage' = 'time-eater').[2] Exhortation, logic, nagging, threats and refined psychology achieved nothing.

I used to find attention the most boring of all processes on the Cognitive Psychology curriculum. A shape bereft of content, a nothing without its stuffing, a light switch which we have enough control of apart from when we don't. Now I can't have enough of it. It's the most secret of my secrets, of our secrets, and those of you who have the same secret are now smiling, will soon smile. Attention is an almost universally underappreciated key to mastery, creativity, achievement, extraordinary character, extraordinary relationships, courage, sustained well-being, happiness....Hone to extremes and choose, with utmost awareness, how to direct your attention and you are on the surest path to all of the above. That's what I wanted for those I love.

The laser focus of your attention won't grow, however, out

---

2 A name I borrowed from the ominous Grasshopper Clock at Corpus Christi College in Cambridge: johnctaylor.com/the-chronophage.

of alerts for every incoming message, tapping your phone 2,617 times a day[3] or staying Y-times-a-day-current with the moods and movements of your social media contacts. Yet if the last few lines apply to you (and self-serving biases will tell you you are not that bad), you'll soon find yourself distracted by a pinging message or a sudden urge to check your emails rather than pay attention to what I can suggest about reclaiming your attention.

I don't intend to suggest anything though. I now leave your hijacked attention to you (and the Creators of both you and the device that controls you). Unless I'm off-centre, I refocus my attention away from the task of being a guardian of your attention. Sometimes, the researcher in me studies you: the anxiety; the dependence on field stimuli; the breaking of social convention or the creation of a new one; the paintings at MOMA you didn't see in any other way than through your phone camera. Sometimes it's the sage who seeks your light against the glare of your screen. Sometimes the pragmatist-cum-cynic rejoices that those of us who control our attention, a dwindling minority, will rule our well-being, our lives, our world and more of *your* world than is good for you. It serves me well. It serves me less well than having people who are fully present to themselves, to our communication and occasionally—to me, but I've given up the fight of saving anyone's attention from technological disintegration.

Instead, I'll only try to sharpen yours to the invisible technology you own and thus facilitate your move. Scan the fifteen categories of technology in *Box 9*. If you'd like to invite even more complexity, take a look at *Box 10* on the grey zone between *use–don't use*.

---

3 Winnick, M. "Putting a Finger on Our Phone Obsession. Mobile touches: a study of how humans use technology." Dscout blog, 16 Jun 2016. *dscout.com/people-nerds/mobile-touches*. Last accessed Aug 2022.

BOX 9

TECHNOLOGY ON THE MOVE[1]

1. **'Can't live without you'/ 'lifeline technology'**: that which you can't possibly leave behind, unless you are moving to an ashram, unless you've been living on the fringes of modern society in the first place−mobile phone, computer (desktop, screen, keyboard, mouse and all) and/or laptop and/or tablet, associated chargers and cables, memory sticks, external hard drive...

2. **Extras and peripherals to 1**: these are often integral to the set-up of your 'lifeline technology', but easier to leave behind as they don't carry information−router, printer, portable keyboard, second screen, external camera...

3. **Audio-visual technology**: TV and sound systems; headphones, microphones, headsets, sound amplifiers, remotes; the external carriers of the contents which you watch/ listen to (DVDs, CDs, let's not go further back in time)...

4. **Professional or hobby-related technology**, perhaps:
   a. DIY equipment
   b. Electronic devices that optimise your exercising
   c. Photographic equipment
   d. Gardening equipment
   e. Computer games equipment

---

1 I may need to mention again that here, as in most of the book, you won't find a serious, neat, scientifically respectful classification. The main goal of my technology classification is to help you 'see' as much as possible of the technology you own. At times, it also tries to identify and group objects which need identical house moving decisions. For instance, I find it more useful to have 'computer screens' in three different categories—'lifeline', 'obsolete' and 'excesses'—rather than in one of 'computer equipment'. The former hint at our future actions. The latter doesn't, even if it's more respectable and formal. You may also find that you won't call 'technology' some of what I call 'technology' and prefer, instead, something room-specific, such as 'kitchen equipment'.

The lack of examples is treacherous. My brother counted for me, amongst his DIY equipment, fifteen electrical tools of his own, three of shared ownership with our cousin, five sets of fittings and thirty or so individual drill bits.

5. **Electrical fixtures (white goods)**: they often come with the house if rented, but may be yours and in need of moving (not that you've forgotten)—fridge, cooker, washing machine, dishwasher...

6. **Portable kitchen equipment**: kettle, microwave, coffee machine, toaster, juicer, smoothie maker, blender, mixer, sandwich maker....Particularly invisible.

7. **Portable housework technology**: vacuum cleaner, iron, steam cleaner...

8. **Health, beauty and pleasure technology**: epilator (first in line because my Braun epilator has served me since 1998), shaver, electric toothbrush, electric face brush, hair dryer, hair straightener, electric massager, electronic scales....Then you may have a vibrator and other sex toys (one of the rare occasions a person makes life easier). Or, more sadly, you may own a blood pressure monitor, a glucometer or other medical devices. Electronic cigarettes and their chargers come here too (you decide if it goes under 'pleasure' or 'health', as in 'health concerns').

9. **Existential technology**: wall clocks, portable lights and lamps, and portable heaters. Of course time is an existential matter. So are light and darkness and the home fire. In my rough definition, 'existential

technology' carries a rich, even heavy, symbolism apart from having pragmatic daily functions. Maybe you need to add bathroom scales? An air quality monitor?

10. **Genies and their lamps**: Echo, which runs Alexa, and suchlike devices that serve as your personal assistants and respond to your voice, talk back, control your smart home, etc. (the Brave New World version of the genie in the lamp).

11. **Obsolete technology**: gramophone, cassette recorder, old radios, answer phone machine, i-pod, black-and-white TV, non-digital camera, non-smart phones, non-flat computer screen, floppy disks, CDs with information on while you no longer have a CD/DVD slot...

12. **Broken, senile and/or dying technology**: a juicer that gives off a whiff of a burnt engine when you are using it, an old laptop that is unbearably slow but still working...

13. **Excesses**: typically of cables, chargers and basic earphones that come with every new phone, but perhaps also the phones themselves; old laptops, tablets, screens which may not be fancy but are all working and usable...

14. **Support infrastructure** (that may itself be a form of technology but not necessarily): extension cords, travel adaptors, laptop bags, protective covers, mousepads, beautiful and sturdy boxes in which the appliances came, stands on which they reside or are used (TV table, ironing board); spares (of light bulbs, brushes for the electric toothbrush, batteries)...

15. **Enigmas**: 'things' and parts thereof whose name, nature and function you have no idea of.

16. **Any other category?**

BOX 10

'I USE'/ 'I DON'T USE' IS NOT A 1 OR 0 MATTER

There is 'I use' and 'I don't use'. But there is also:

First I used daily, several times a day, now hardly ever, but it'll do me good to revive the habit (juicer).

It's broken from use, so I don't use, but would use if repaired (blender).

It doesn't feel like I'm using it, as I use it without touching it, without even seeing it, but I use it for most of my waking hours (wi-fi router).

I use it but need to buy a new one as this one is crumbling (headset). I want to buy Bose though, so it will be some time (ten years so far), so I'll need this one for a little longer.

I use it but soon I won't (epilator, I'm finishing my laser treatments). I used to want to stop using it, stop needing it entirely, but now I wonder. I may miss the tingling, the skin awakening.

I use it, and I use it with fear that its battery will die right when I'm setting up a payment for my next house. Yet I can't order a replacement from the bank because I've not changed my address with them and I'm moving out of this one too (bank card reader).

I don't use but may need one day, although, most likely, I won't (old memory sticks with information on).

I don't use it and hardly anyone does, so I can't find how to redistribute it lovingly and respectfully to acknowledge its faithful service (old but working digital camera).

I don't use but may need to use as they may be parts of what I use (enigmas).

I don't use but will need again when I visit the U.S. again (travel adaptor).

I've hardly ever used but intend to begin to use or have to begin to use because I've paid money for it (that's not me!).

Heidegger writes that technology becomes visible when it breaks. He can't have moved enough if he'd missed 'when moving house'.

DEALING WITH THE PHYSICAL CHAOS

As I've often moved with one suitcase, my own journey through the mountains of technology has been of radical minimisation and outsourcing of ownership. This may make my suggestions too extreme for most of you. See what you think.

Re-evaluate owning v. outsourcing to the professionals (and tapping into their mastery more regularly)

I outsource the ownership of certain types of technology I use rarely or, just the opposite, daily, to the professionals.

Unthinkable for many women (mostly), I don't own a hairdryer. Twelve years ago I realised I was using it only slightly more often than I was packing it to move out. I sold it. I've never missed it. It's not because I don't care about my appearance. I do. I had reduced the frequency with which I heat-dried my hair to keep it healthier, that's why I needed a hairdryer so rarely. Since selling mine, I go to the hairdresser's slightly more often. I doubt it's more expensive. You buy far fewer products for protecting/ restoring your hair from heat damage.

I've similarly outsourced owning a coffee machine and coffee making gadgets, such as a milk frother. I drink coffee every morning. I'm fussy about it. I've decided that the complexity of moving a coffee machine is yet another, even if not a major, reason to have my coffee in a café. I only own a stovetop espresso maker for emergencies. And yes, it's times more expensive. The joy is worth every penny. I am also supporting independent businesses.

See the bigger picture around
high-tech/ low-tech solutions

In contrast, I've gone back to several low-tech personal hygiene solutions after having had high-tech, semi-professional alternatives for years.

When I first had an electric toothbrush and an electric face brush, I would have requested them laid down by my side in my coffin, available for all possible worlds. Recently, I separated from them just as whole-heartedly. The novelty had worn off. The appliances had become yellowish and limescaled, although perfectly functioning. The negatives of using them—side effects, cost of replacement brushes, environmental impact, opportunity costs—had accumulated.

A dentist commented he observed far more enamel erosion in people using electric toothbrushes. I didn't want more of that. I've already had my teeth rebuilt partly because of enamel erosion. I know it's a matter of correct use, but normal human not-always-mindful use (mine) is part of the equation.

The replacement heads for my face brush had soon out-cost the appliance (a brilliant commercial model, of course). They were non-recyclable plastic that needed to be changed (thrown out) every three months. I also missed using and testing new fragrant, textured, luxurious exfoliators.

Alternative candidates for coffin contents also entered my life. One was a brand of Swiss toothbrushes, simplicity incarnate (Curaprox, if you are interested; Amazon rating of 4.8 out of 13,000 reviews, Aug 2022). I also became a fan of Konjac sponges. They are compostable and shrivel to a third of their wet size when dry, also becoming feather-light. (Konjac is a potato growing in high altitudes, for those of you who are thinking of misspelt and misused 'cognac'!)

If you'd argue that your new high-tech personal hygiene (or other) gadget has changed your life, keep it, move it, let us try it! But if you are no longer that certain, check the bigger picture of side effects, recurrent costs, environmental impact, missed opportunities and move complexity. You may find the numbers not adding up.

Make time for yesterday's objects (and data)

If you have **carriers of information bigger than your finger** or using old standards (such as CDs or floppy disks), either dispose of them directly (and responsibly) or bite the bullet of transferring the files.

If you choose to transfer the files, in 98% of cases it will be pragmatically irrational. You'll never look at them again. But it's a ritual of closure and those are 'emotionally rational'. Closure is never secondary to use.

If you have **ridiculously old, even broken, technology**, don't write it off too quickly. My family has found new homes for a maddeningly slow laptop, a broken Kindle, and even a non-flat computer screen (though that was some time ago), amongst others. All of them were transparently advertised. "I should have paid the buyer, not the other way round" is one of the sweetest feelings in house-moving commerce.

If you are working for a bigger organisation, you may be able to access your **employer's processes for the safe disposal of electrical equipment**, even when it's your own. The universities where I've studied or worked have always enabled that. We could also ask for the hard disks of our personal machines to be erased. Having sensitive data handled appropriately is no small matter in redistributing technology.

Prior to the pandemic, I've been dropping **irreparably broken phones** (those whose screen doesn't light up) for responsible disposal in the shops of my mobile operator. It's no longer, or at least not currently, allowed for health and safety reasons. My techno-rubbish was, instead, welcomed by a small independent phone shop on the high street.

None of my **old phones** has passed the checks for trading in or donating (broken phones are fine, by the way, as long as they can be switched on). If you want to check your old phone(s) and don't have a go-to service, a simple search ('trade phone', 'cash for phone', 'donate phone', etc.) will return numerous options, both local and over-the-post.

Invite randomness to co-create electric dreams

As with any type of possession, my favourite way of donating technology is through the randomness of Freecycle, or any other way in which I'll meet perfect strangers.

My bitter-sweetest memory of freecycling technology is of giving a keyboard to a woman with serious mental health issues. On a dry day of perfectly still air, she had glued herself to the wall of the apartment building. She emitted levels of goodness and vulnerability which, if unsupported by a thread of steel in your spine, knock you out of normal society.

I could have turned into her rather than me.

I passed on the keyboard. I dreamt it held quanta of the steel of me which would seep into her fingers and into her spine and brain while she keeps her soft heart and goodness. Then one day she would need no wall to stand by, no matter how wild the storms of life bashing against her. I dreamt and I knew that, realistically, that was only a computer game future for her.

My blender (along with other kitchen utensils I had posted on Freecycle) went to the mum of a six-week-old, with the family only just arrived from South Africa. She asked about my plans. I told her. She said the world was my oyster and shone her blue eyes. And so the world became and still is. A blender for a blessing.

Less dreamily, I gave my juicer to a friend whose son tried to vomit when I told him of my vampire (beetroot) juice. I was reassured by my friend that this was attention seeking, not a bad omen for my juicer.

Venture into the realm of the unknown
(or find out why you wouldn't)

If you've got some time for the non-essential in this move, you may want to attend to technological enigmas. The homes of many of us with no meaningful technical knowledge have plenty of these — parts with a function we have (almost) no idea of.

We keep such enigmas in case something breaks down or short-circuits and the shops of the whole town are out of stock or it's Christmas and the replacement fuse, now fully recognisable, turns out to be right there in the cupboard under the sink. More realistically, we find it difficult to make decisions about the unknown.

If I have such unknowns in the house, I ask a technically competent friend to identify them. They are usually objects that remain from previous tenants or perhaps the landlord. Somebody needs to break the cycle of inheriting rubbish. It's one of the ways in which I leave things and places in better shape than I'd found them in — unburdening houses of stuck objects and/or liberating imprisoned objects.

If neither I, nor my advisor can use the objects we've now named, I redistribute or throw them out. It's far easier to throw something out when you know what that something is.

Is it though? Would you rather know or not know that which you are throwing?

If you would rather know, go to the next section. You're (mostly) ok on this count.

If you would rather throw out the unknown rather than first make it known and then decide more informedly, it's highly likely you do the same with strange ideas and people.

Is it because you find them suspicious? Not knowing is keeping safe.

Or is because you can't face caring for them? The Wonderland Alice in you cannot eat the ham she's been introduced to, cannot ignore a person whose pain she's witnessed, and cannot throw out a part if she knows the body it belongs to.

Until a moment ago, we were only talking about random, unimportant parts.

Now it's about the walls or porous boundaries of you.

Turn the techno-light discomfort
of the last few days on its head

I've mentioned more than once the inconveniences of the last few days in a place you need to return to its unfurnished state. I am repeating myself. I may do it again. I want your brain to prepare. Such inconveniences are far easier to put up with in theory than in practice. I also want to imprint the idea that discomfort and stoicism in a house move are optional, even if natural. Importantly, if they are natural for you in general, one of the best things you can do for yourself is to blow them to pieces in your last days in a place.

If your microwave's gone, please don't dine on cold lasagne but take yourself out to dinner. If you've donated your kettle, please don't make instant coffee with hot water from the tap but try out a new café. If your TV's in a box, please invite yourself to the movies.

And if you are telling me that you can't because this move has drained your accounts, please think again. Most likely, you are trying to control the grand expenses of moving house by controlling that which makes no meaningful difference but is controllable. I've done it for too many years and with too deep a conviction. It's pointless.

Yet if you are telling me you can't, I'm sure you are right.

EXPLORE YOUR TECHNOLOGICAL ADDICTIONS

Finally, while I've given up the fight of saving and protecting your attention, I hope you haven't. Below are two suggestions for reclaiming (even more of) it, especially if you've never thought of it as the most under-rated key to all you've ever wanted.

1. Collect the baseline data

Make a week's audit of how you use your lifeline technology, for anything other than work or creativity. You don't need more than a sheet of paper, real or virtual, although a clicker counter can help too. Note the number of times you pulled out your phone, checked your email, checked your Facebook account, interrupted a face-to-face conversation for a message or phone call, whatever, as well as the number of times you felt like doing it but refrained. If you go to "Digital wellbeing and parental controls" (under Settings) on your phone, you can find most of this information for your phone apps there. The act of observation will influence your actions but not that quickly to invalidate the observations.

Record how much time you'd spent in each interaction or note down the system information. This is how I stopped using messengers while working, way back in the dark ages of ICQ. What felt like DEFINITELY no more than five-minute breaks for a quick chat were consistently fifteen- to twenty-minute ones.

Record how you felt before and after.

Do the sums. Compare with the time you need per day to move on with one dream (exclude the time you are helping that dream, some of those apparent distractions may be achieving that). See what you like and what you don't.

If you like all of what you find—how fabulous! And how improbable.

If you are terrified by the microscopic tears or straightforward fractures to your attention or by the amount of time eaten by your pet chronophages, I'm not suggesting you donate your addictive technology when moving.

But any big change—and a house move is a big change—facilitates any other change.

2. See it as a solution so that you can find the problem

The second suggestion for self-study requires much finer detective work. It is, however, one of the royal roads of stabilising your attention while working out what destabilises you in ways far broader than attention.

Every time you reach out for your phone, email or social media feed without a real need to check what's on, inspect your thoughts, feelings and the contextual stimuli. If you pay close attention, you'll catch something, internal or external, which has triggered your anxiety. You will see that those little triggers are hundreds, even thousands, within a day, especially in unfamiliar environments.

Most of them will be ridiculously unimportant or low-level: entering the space of a bus stop, one of many social spaces which tend to register a newcomer (you); receiving a mildly disturbing email; seeing that the family who asked for their bill in the restaurant after you are already receiving it, while you continue waiting; catching a glimpse of a confident, attractive woman/ man, while you are anything but it today or any day....

Often, you can appreciate that there was a trigger in such apparently innocuous situations only by noticing yourself grasp at your phone, not by the way you thought about what you saw. In your conscious world, that little negative thing deserves NO attention as a potential threat and never deserved it. Alternatively, it used to have your attention, but you've worked through the 'issues' and it no longer matters.

Yet your reactivity tells a different story if you allow it to. If you take your reaction as an unconscious attempt at a solution (your phone or inbox are spaces of safety and potential positive stimulation) and work back from it, you may be able to reach the problem, even if your consciousness doesn't register its presence or denies it the status of a problem. If you regularly work back from such low-level solutions (it needn't be reaching out for technology, it may be, for instance, taking a sip from the mug next to you), you will find that we react to our environment at far more miniature levels than we are typically aware.

If you continue asking why you needed a solution (comfort, reassurance), you will begin to reach some hairy-scary deep issues. Then you may choose to address more of the roots of the anxiety rather than dope yourself against it.[4]

I'll love it if you are checking your phone this way.

There are many other reasons apart from the hijacking of attention why I lose my warmth around technology, even if I do my best to appreciate it.

It weighs me down when moving.

I can't repair it if it breaks.

I know so little about it that I cannot admire the huge complexity behind it.

I'm in awe of it, thrilled by it when it's new, but it becomes invisible in days, and now it wants attention.

It creates so much waste.

It makes us miss the sunrise from the train, the love birds, real birds, playing on the train tracks.

It's faceless.

It's everywhere.

I don't like it when I stay cold. I don't trust myself when I don't feel a valid duality.

Maybe I deserve to be sent away from civilisation again. It always fills me with deep appreciation.

Maybe I'd better remember more often how, when my grandma was calling her sister in America in the 70s, she paid a third of

___

4 If you overeat or smoke, the mechanism of using food or cigarettes to suppress both high- and low-level anxiety is the same.

her salary for a minute of conversation and had to run out of the bathroom naked and dripping. You couldn't predict when they'd connect you through the post office. You couldn't take your phone to the bathroom.

Maybe I'd better remember that my longest held address has been my main email address. I've had it for twenty-three years. I've had about twenty-three postal addresses in that period.

No, it's not even that.

I know what I need to remember.

It's the times when I, like you,
boring black, white, grey machine
have been taken for granted–
reliable, undemanding, loyal, easy to replace.
Obsolete, old, scratched.
The times when I, like you,
have been switched off
while crying for them to help me come to light.
Dark and short-circuited on the inside,
screen as if asleep,
mis-pixelated only for those
who read energy.

I promise I'll try to read yours.

CHAPTER 16

DO IT YOURSELF. NEVERMORE

You can't be hard on yourself while wiping lubricant off your
bright red fingernails (lubricant for bikes, I mean; otherwise, sure,
interpret 'hard' and 'yourself' and join them up as you please).
Nor can you lying on your back under the kitchen sink, only short
skirt and toned legs visible outside the cupboard yet relaying
the rhythm of hands, arms, face tensing-relaxing in the semi-
darkness, responding to your efforts to screw the nut of the loose
tap above. No one can feel sorry for you. No one can shame you for
being an unattractive woman (no man keen to help), a cliché of a
woman (helpless with anything that breaks down), or both.

Welcome to the Queen's way of Doing it Yourself (QDIY).

Most people DIY for one of three reasons: 1) they have the skills,
enjoy the occasional tinkering and it 'just' falls upon them to do it;
2) they aim to save money; or 3) they (the blessed ones) have found
how to fly high and away into other worlds and dissolve into bliss
on the wings of a drill, hammer or chainsaw.

Some of us though—rarer birds but not that rare—are DIY-ing

because we are ashamed to be single. I didn't know it of myself.
It's been safely camouflaged by some joy at tinkering (genuine,
intense; but since I know so little about mechanisms, rare) and
by unwillingness to pay money I could spend on, say, cosmetics,
travel or training courses. Yet the real reason I was doing DIY, I
came to realise, was to avoid feeling a terrible person and a failure
of femininity. Hence the Queen's way to neutralise the spell.

REAL MEN, REAL WOMEN AND
REPAIRING BROKEN LIVES IN THEIR ABSENCE

At the time and place I was born, every proper man could do DIY.
If you had to call a plumber, an electrician or a carpenter, it was
not because you had a problem around the house. It was because
you had a problem with the man of the house – either there wasn't
one or he had "his hands shoved up his ass", as the saying went.
This was still OK if you had a string of 'candidates', hoping for the
electrics of your home (heart) to short-circuit. It was even ok if you
had good male friends.

When I left home home, I no longer had the men of the house
around – my dad, brother and granddad, as well as all the male
neighbours and friends of the family – to fix daily life. ('Female
DIY', like basic sewing, I can do and don't usually count as DIY.)
As far as boyfriends went, they were typically skilled (though I fell
for things other than DIY abilities) but were friends for far longer
than they were boyfriends. So, technically though less so mentally,
I've had long periods of not having a boyfriend. 'Candidates' and
male friends I've somehow always had but would never ask for
their help.

In those times I wouldn't tell it to myself with the clarity that
follows (aren't such 'truths' far harsher and darker when vaguely

admitted?) but I wouldn't ask for help because I didn't think I was likeable enough. Then if somebody didn't like me enough, they would help me not because they wanted to, but because they felt obliged. And I never, ever want you to do anything for me which you don't want to do anyway. Refusing is quite all right. Doing it for me while not wanting to do it is terrifying. And before I've weaselled out of the admission and shown myself as better than I was – only scared and principled rather than scared, principled and cruel – I sometimes wouldn't ask men who would willingly, madly happily help me to help me as some of them were losers who had a crush on me and I wouldn't want to explain that I've been helped by and might owe a loser. (I am genuinely sorry, guys.)

When I stopped fearing that all that was good in me was rotten deep down, rickety social structure that would collapse in extreme circumstances with no chance of repair (I have no illusion that it may, that it's even highly likely, but my faith in the True Good has become unbreakable), I also gave myself credit for resisting to use men and people overall:

Since the time of high-school Kant, a person could only be a goal, never a means. Even before the Kantian distinction, a man was there to be loved as a quintessential Other, end of story, not loved and expected to build you a house, pay for your lifestyle, 'give' you a child, or repair your oven. You may be thrilled if some or all of that comes through him but you can't place it on him.

Since I could have a vision for my life (from around the time I could read grown-up books), I was also adamant that love, friendship, freedom, truth and purity of heart will be present at their best in my life. This determination didn't always shine. If anything, it often felt like a disease of grave naivety I had to find a cure for or a disability whose hiding I had to refine, but it has nonetheless guided every important choice in my life. A resistance to 'burden' love, relationships and friendships with requests for help was one such choice. It took me decades to work out that requests for help can also solidify the love, relationships and friendships, not primarily undermine them.

The upshot of not wanting to ask men I knew for help meant that I would attempt plenty of DIY myself. And if you haven't worked it out, I wouldn't call in professionals not so much because I minded paying, though at times I did, but mostly because they would conclude I was a terrible woman who had no boyfriend, no men interested in her and no male friends. The better they thought I looked (I am one of those women who fluctuate depending on the eyes of the perceiver and the day), the more they would believe I was unbearable. Not only *they* would believe that and start drilling holes in the covers of my psyche, but so would anyone who asks who's helped me with the gas bottle I couldn't connect or the shelf that fell under the weight of the books. Obviously, half the town is regularly asking for a written, signed and peer reviewed report on my home maintenance. I'm also required by law to supply it.

So I would make up my mind that something was within the zone of my DIY development. I would read manuals and/or watch YouTube videos. I would buy new tools. I would set up an orderly process and a working space. I would start with a thrill that far exceeded the anxiety.

Sometimes, I'll work it out. Then I'll lift arms, hands in fists, and whisper, say, shout, 'Ninja! Ninja! Ninja!' More often, however, I would go through trial and error without being able to break out of the cycle. Narrowing of consciousness. Hands beginning to shake. Movements with no thought behind, just a panicky need to try something else, *now*. Instructions that don't match what I am seeing in front of me. More trial and error in half mental darkness. Ultimately, I would break down crying and call for help (though never while crying, of course).

The tears are not necessarily from failing to achieve a functioning outcome.

They may be because what I've created works but is UGLY. Do you know the feeling? You can't tolerate ugly thorns in your energetic field, even if they are usable objects, even if you don't see them most of the time. They are there. They vibrate. They must be changed. They must be fixed, gone, erased out of perception and memory.

Sometimes the drama arises in philosophical investigations of elusive concepts and substances. How do I know if I've cleaned *all* the degreaser, which would otherwise damage the chain, since it is *colourless*? How do I know what 'a little oil' means?

Or it can be the doubt of the easy fit or hard press.

It fitted so easily, which makes it highly likely that it's right, but how can I be sure it's not the Devil? The same that had me cycle, for a month, with handlebars fitted in the opposite direction?!

If it requires so much force, am I not more likely to break it rather than fit it/ remove it?

Whatever the pattern, the balance of my DIY-ing was heavily skewed towards anxiety and crying.

IF YOU ARE NOT GOOD ENOUGH AT DIY, IS DIY GOOD ENOUGH FOR YOU?

As with more than one of the sources of garden-variety suffering I am writing about, I didn't know I was suffering until I found myself not suffering any longer. I can, however, remember some of the steppingstones on the path to peace.

First, I was told I shouldn't be crying while doing DIY. It was said with so much warmth and compassion that I had to think deeply about it and agree after the deep thinking. I've long done things crying. I see your suffering as mine. I've had plenty of reasons to cry out of fear and anxiety when younger. When old trauma shifts, I cry. I cry when I see beauty and humanity where you expect none. I cry at books and at movies. I have my chin shaking when you are rude to me, unfair to me, dismissive of me, although I'll do all within my power to cry when you can't see me. There are often weekly reasons to cry, in some periods daily. That it is unnecessary and/or avoidable to cry because of DIY is not self-evident.

The young man who told me I shouldn't have been crying while assembling a desk (as the case was) also offered to do it for me. Two hours and four pints after the topic arose, he offered again. This didn't feel like 'obliged' to me. It felt like 'will be happy to'. I accepted. He didn't come.[1] But while waiting for him to come, I figured out that a) a desk is too important in my life to wobble, so I shall buy that beautiful solid *assembled* oak writing table which cost five times more than what I had bought; and b) indeed, I shouldn't be crying while doing DIY.

(Tears + DIY) x (from now onwards) = NEVERMORE.

I had also started earning better money. It coincided with living in agency-managed places. They always had a reliable workman to call. I hardly needed to pay. When I did, it was with deep gratitude for the division of labour and my earning capacity. This is when,

1 For the record, this absent-minded man then became and continues to be one of my closest friends!

during a move, I donated most of my tools.

Perhaps most importantly, I realised that even for the things I was truly keen on learning, like maintaining my bike, I would never dedicate the time it takes to learn it properly. I still end up with my chain in a ribbon or parts fixed in the opposite direction, no matter the earnestness with which I try and the careful instructions I've been given. I still have a long road to go. And I won't take the time to walk most of it.

I won't take the time because I've been following the advice of Warren Buffett. Write twenty-five things you love doing, choose the five you love the most, and forget about all the remaining twenty for the rest of your life. I won't prioritise that brutally. I don't want a life resembling Warren Buffet's. Let alone, it turns out, it's nothing that the Man said.[2] I still take it as wise advice for the limited time we've got on Earth.

Top five, in variable order: write all the books and non-books I have in me; move, explore, enjoy my body; connect deeply with people and bring out more of their and my own light in the process; do girly things; tune into my Soul and touch the Eternal.

Some of the twenty: learn to dance tango, flamenco and Charleston (and more, as long as it counts as one 'thing'); teach research methods and academic writing at universities in fragile and conflict-affected countries; walk the South West Coast Path; sing; be a wizard of conflict resolution; work with trauma and feel it release its grip on souls and bodies; train as a masseuse though only practise on my own folk....

You don't need the rest of my list. Write down yours. Remember

---

2 Schwantes, M. "Warren Buffett's 25/5 Rule Has Been Debunked. Here's What You Should Do Instead". Inc. 29 Jul 2020. *inc.com/marcel-schwantes/warren-buffett-25-5-rule-career-goals.html*. Last accessed Aug 2022.

yours. Is all or any of the DIY you are doing, or whatever psychological equivalent of it you've thought about while reading, in the top five, even the top fifteen, of the things you love the most? (You should know straight away but check against the ideas in *Box 11* if not.) What on your list remains persistently undone, unstarted even? How many more years are you hoping to live?

Will you have Done *Your Life* Yourself by the end of it?

FOUR IDEAS FOR REDUCING THE PHYSICAL CHAOS

Here are my rather simple redistribution experiences around DIY:

- I gave the fancier amongst my tools to an army medic training to be a proper doctor. He had come to collect cushions and cleaning utensils. He left with hex keys, screwdrivers, hammer, whatever branded tools I had, on top. You 'capitalise' on people who come across as potential ace owners of your possessions (though you also always, always go through due diligence to check if they want and need what you are offering).
- The tools I didn't think well of, such as some cheap screwdrivers for my laptop, I dropped in a container for metal-plastics recycling. It would have been eco-friendlier to increase their chances of re-use. But I don't redistribute what I've never felt remotely good enough while mine.
- My bike maintenance tools I still own. They are staying. Some basic tasks are a matter of love and care, not DIY.
- The excess of needles and threads I had, I dropped, with a note, through the letter box of a local seamstress. She had given new life to my trousers and an old friend's warmth to me. She was on holiday, otherwise I take it

as bad form to avoid the face-to-face conversation (as I've written more than once by now). I'm not saying it's always easy. But it's the ethical thing to do. It helps in passing on opportunities, not tasks. It's good practice in having the limits of your comfort zone blasted out.

Those of you who will be cleaning and arranging tools in meditative abandon while preparing for a move, designing functional, space-optimising yet aesthetic compositions of oddities—I salute thee.

During the time I was learning to do less of what makes me cry, beginning to earn better money and applying not-quite-Warren-Buffet's advice, something far less visible has been happening in the background.

I grew to feel, worked to feel, fought to feel, was graced to feel a good person and a good woman.

I had DIY-ed myself.

From Unbroken.

BOX 11

WHAT DIY-ER ARE YOU
AND ARE YOU IN NEED OF REPAIR?

I'll suggest that if you are anything but a blessed one, it's you who needs repair first, not your things (doesn't mean that the blessed don't need repair but DIY-ing can do it for them).

The 'blessed ones'–who turn DIY-ing
into a quest, an art and self-therapy

You enjoy tinkering. You get a thrill from turning things back from the brink of death. You restore the vibrant selves of objects, even make them higher versions of what they once were, energy surging from within, your own vibrant Self coming forth too. You repair what somebody broke or neglected in things while hum-hum-brrrrr-brrrrr repairing what life broke or neglected in you. You fly high and away into a world of DIY peace and flow, even if occasionally getting lost in obsession land–finger bruised here, knee needing stitches there.

Too capable for their own good

You have the skills. You get down to it. There are other things you'd rather do, but it's prudent. It's independent. It's simpler in the arrangements. You enjoy the occasional tinkering. You may even find peace of mind descending upon you while doing DIY, though you mostly want the job done.

If that's you, what needs to be repaired is less your garden fence than your relationship to pleasure, joy, duty and truly feeling what you are feeling.

Money-wise and soul-foolish

You are DIY-ing to save money. It's another life chore amongst many. But what do you do. No money in excess. No other meaningful source of help. You have to rely on yourself as you've always done. And you are strong and competent and not to be defeated. And you've done it again.

If that's you, it's less your electrics or plumbing that needs to be worked upon, but your relationship to money, receiving and self-care.

CHAPTER 17

YOU ARE NOT JUST A NUMBER

I was preparing to die young, in my late thirties at the latest.
I was less certain how I would die, but since I was about eleven,
I thought it would be in a concentration camp, a prison or a fight
for freedom.

There is no family history there. My family is lucky. I am lucky.
Rather, it's been literary influences (the likes of *Uncle Tom's Cabin*,
The Count of Monte Cristo and *Remember Their Childhood*, a book
of stories about children from communist families killed by the
fascists, propagandist but still heart-breaking); cinematic ones
(*Schindler's List* and *Life is Beautiful* are later years, but decisively
formative) and random comments of my parents (as of my mum,
furious to learn that, in kindergarten, we were being hosed with
buckets on our heads to wash off the beach sand). Whatever the
specifics of my life path though, I had to be able to stand up for
the weaker, uphold what I believed in, and never betray anyone.
Whatever my ultimate end, it had to be one of dignity, courage
and true freedom. I had to prepare for extremes. If you are not

prepared for the worst, you are not prepared.

When I'm scared or overexerting physically, I shake more than anyone I've seen shake. I cry all over the place, as you know all too well by now. I gradually abandoned the hope I can train my body's physiology. I focused on training my mind, accepting and transcending pain, and designing psychologically paradoxical responses to confuse my captors. I've crossed the threshold of forty. I've not been tested on dignity, courage and true freedom in extremes as the above. I sincerely hope I'm spared them. I hope I am spared, but I also suspect I'll find myself in an emotionally equivalent alternative. A part of us yearns to be tested, will only believe we've lived if we've been tested on what we've been preparing for.

Still, my current visions of carrying chains would have been far rarer if I didn't have to supply so regularly so many of the numbers of my life—single citizen number, identity card number, passport number, National Insurance number, National Health Service number, permanent residence card number, settled status number (which I almost missed on, as I thought that's the role of a permanent residence number), student number, diploma(s) number(s), alumna number(s), employee number, payroll number, pension scheme number, bank account number (and sort code)…. Of course you matter to us and are not just a number. You are at least twenty key numbers and several hundred less important ones.

THE BEAST, THE BEAUTY
AND THE BATTLES OF PAPERLAND

In our day and age, our personal numbers remain mostly immaterial. But once upon a time, numbers came on paperwork.

Paperwork accumulated. It occupied, crept into a growing number of drawers, shelves, cabinets, boxes, even rooms. If you, like me, remember learning to use a computer (rather than emerging from childhood mostly knowing how to), you either have a Kafka-esque Beast to face during your move, or have previously spent soul-drying days chopping its heads off. Other than it's not a Beast, but the Beauty and the Beast. It terrifies you with its size. It weighs you down with boredom and irrelevance. But it also unravels you through the beautifully shaped squiggles of your childhood handwriting, your full name in silver letters, or a youthful photo of you. It breaks your heart, and you can't chop its heads off:

- Heads (paper piles) of the duly numbered and bureaucratic.
- Heads (paper piles) of the quintessentially emotional and personal—the likes of old love letters, postcards, journals, random sheets of paper with your heart poured over them.
- Heads (paper piles) of what was once knowledge- and information-rich and/or a record of your learning, and which, after so many years, you have massively improved upon (your learning) or can find in massively improved ways (the knowledge). Yet it feels curious, and it carries a touch of sentiment, and it is a record of past times and you in them, and it holds your hesitant, childish, beautiful, careful, messy, moody writing, drawing, doodling—that which you find in old telephone and address books, school notebooks, lecture notes, work diaries...
- Heads (paper piles) of what is still knowledge- and information-rich (think printed articles, copied book

pages or old data) and which is perched on the keep-discard edge because:

1. it is too heavy and takes too much space (discard);
2. you may never use it again (discard);
3. you can usually find it in other ways (discard) BUT
4. it will take crazy amounts of time to review (avoid the task);
5. will take even more time to find or save in alternative formats (avoid the task); and
6. has added value in this format, such as your notes and highlighting (keep).

Welcome to Paperland.

The older you are, the vaster it is.

No one of the last century's generations can move paper-free by accident. We used to live through paper. This is what held our information. Knowledge. MEMORIES. This is how we curated a self too—amassing, displaying and protecting our identity and seeing it unfold over time.

The stranger you've been, the harder you'll leave it behind too. Those of us who've moved countries and thus lost the social and political certainty of who we were, constantly needing to prove we are we and have the right to be here, are even more attached to paperwork. It's safety. It's new roots.

SHRINKING IT TO TWO FOLDERS AND A PURSE

Attenuating my paperwork—to about 5% of what it once was—was a cross-moves experience. For about half a year of static life, thirteen years ago now, I spent the mornings of every Friday going through my collection—skimming, reading, discarding, shredding, transferring into electronic format, occasionally burning, rarely keeping....

The decisive battle against old paperwork has been won. My and the world's habits of using paper have changed unrecognisably too. Yet culling paperwork is still a part of each and every move. There is no finality there. The little that ends up surviving across moves is my growing number of numbers (mostly kept in electronic format); timeless or current credentials of identity and ownership (also carrying numbers, but until we have microchips implanted in our bodies, we will need old-fashioned birth certificates or diplomas, for instance); and a collection of sentimental items.

This chapter is about numbers and credentials – that is, the duly numbered and bureaucratic as per the bullet points above. For ideas on what to do with the other heads of the Beast and occasional Beauty, see **Chapter 20** on sentimental items and **Chapter 19** on books.

Paperwork divides are not as clear as the above may suggest though. Duly numbered and bureaucratic doesn't mean sentiment-free, for instance. When I first started saving my numbers and discarding their paper, I let go of the likes of:

- Ten-year-old payslips I've kept so as to appreciate and celebrate the upward trajectory of my salary.
- Letters from the Inland Revenue (the UK tax office) informing me of overpaid taxes for which a cheque had been issued. Keeping the letters was supposed to attract magically more of the same.
- Job contracts (twenty-one contracts for nine years at two universities), which I wanted to count with a vengeance against the academic system of short-term employment.

Apparently, the UK academic sector is only second to hospitality in terms of work casualisation.[1] I did, indeed, count them for a blog in Nature.[2] I had my vengeance. I found peace. They were shredded.

- The confirmation that the jobs of an impostor were removed from my National Insurance record. If it's happened once, it could happen again. And this time they'll persuade everybody that they are the Person and I am the Shadow. And then they'll be celebrating their wedding, and fireworks will be illuminating the night sky, but I won't hear anything as I will have just been executed. (This is not my sick imagination, it's Andersen's "The Shadow".)
- Records of exams where I've smashed the ceiling.
- Old student cards where I am "oh so young, oh so pure-hearted, oh so intense!" in the photo.

We all have good reasons to keep clutter. Until one day we begin to notice the clutter rather than the good reasons.

My key numbers are spread across emails and files. They are not particularly well organised. Partly, it would require more effort than I want to invest in enumerating myself. More strategically, relative filing chaos which has further organising principles held solely in one's mind is a form of data protection.

This is the paper- and plastic-work I currently keep:

---

1 "My university plans to lose 500 casual staff—so I'm refusing to mark exams". *The Guardian*, 01 Jul 2020. *https://theguardian.com/commentisfree/2020/jul/01/goldsmiths-sack-casual-staff-examsuniversities-covid-19*, referring to Careersmart. "Casualisation of the professional workforce". Last accessed Aug 2022.

2 Petrova, M. "On academic job insecurity and the ultimate tenure. Thoughts from contract No. 17". Naturejobs blog, 22 Mar 2017. *https://blogs.nature.com/naturejobs/2017/03/22/on-academic-job-insecurity-and-the-ultimate-tenure/*. Last accessed Aug 2022.

Identity documents–passport, national ID card, birth certificate and permanent residence card. Even my permanent residence card has become superfluous since I wrote this. There are now versions of settled status in the UK and you prove settled status only electronically. I have let go of any old application forms, e.g. for visas or residence, or letters accompanying their receipt.

'Right to be here' credentials–cards which demonstrate where I belong as an employee or a member, such as to my university, library or gym, and grant me access to their spaces.

Financial affairs means and ends–bank cards (obviously) and some random letters from the bank, tax office, utility companies and pension scheme (though I often wonder why I pay into a pension, the system will fall apart by the time it's my generation's turn).

I opted out of paper bank statements and payslips the moment they became available electronically. When printed, they have the evidential status of their printed counterparts (though bank statements, for instance, may need to be stamped at the bank). Some paperwork I still prefer to be able to stick in front of my eyes–such as tax letters and utility bills–but I only keep the latest ones. They are ready proofs of address and identity and of having my key financial affairs in order.

Receipts for purchases I now decline for anything other than items I can envisage returning or showing a fault. I've been playing catch-up. The steady rise of cashless payments and online banking, further expedited by fears of contagion during the pandemic, decimated the religious receipt takers amongst us. I was one of them. If that's ever been you too, prepare to find a fine collection of (unprocessed) receipts in the drawers you'll be clearing.

Until a couple of years ago, I took each receipt that was issued and made a mental note of each that was not. I kept an Excel record of all my spending. I've tracked the patterns. Approved most of them. Was proud of many. Changed several. I did it for fourteen years. I had a receipts-task for every weekend and every move.

Until I didn't. One fine day I was struck by the realisation that top-notch accounting affects neither my financial decisions, nor my money flow, even if it adds specifics to what I know, gives me a sense of control, and helps me fall asleep on sleepless nights. I also concluded that I was dumb that it took me a decade and a half to realise it. I am still grateful that I know, for instance, how much my typical move costs or what's the total of my non-negotiables but, after the first one to two years of sublime personal accounting, I've reached no dramatic revelations or shifts in spending habits through it.

This doesn't mean you can't reach them. We all have unique paths to revelations. But if you find piles of receipts to handle before a move, check with yourself if even inspecting them makes a worthwhile difference (collecting them doesn't). It now feels blindingly obvious that the way to financial abundance is through inspecting and healing our relationship to money, receiving and spending/ giving, but it's also me who insisted on reviewing all my purchases for fourteen years. I won't insist that you think again. You may have your own decades of accounting duty to serve.

Education credentials – diplomas and transcripts from my degree studies. I'm still finding semi-official printouts of exam results I was super proud of, sentimental letters granting me a coveted scholarship, or certificates from brief training courses, but the collection has been minimised beyond recognition. No-one has ever asked me of evidence of short-term courses I'd said I'd taken. In turn, most of the pride-worthy paperwork felt like an over-chewed chewing gum when I last flicked through it. It no longer moved me, so it's now gone. Just as most of the knowledge and skills it certified.

Healthcare records—the original document granting me a National Health Service number and, if I've been to the doctor's recently, the latest letters and test results. I shred those (or cut the X-rays) and dispose of them once the period of care has passed.

Again, this attitude to health documentation is new to me. I was taught to hold on to health-related documents obsessively. I still have my paper records, from a new-born to university student, at home home. But UK general practice has had electronic records for over twenty years. I am duly filed. I trust enough the record keeping of the health service.

Because, knock on wood, I rarely need it.

If you, however, have a chronic condition and/or are using a broad range of health services, don't ever think of recycling your health-related paperwork, especially if you are moving! Trust me, I've worked on a study of electronic patient records and their sharing.[3] You need your personal records. Unless you live in a country I've not read about and one which hasn't shouted to the skies about its digital health achievements, there isn't a complete and unified patient record out there in the Cloud of you. Your single record (and not every country has them) is a rather

---

3 Prepared to Share? Study of patient data sharing in complex conditions and at the end of life. *phpc.cam.ac.uk/pcu/research/research-projects-list/prepared-to-share/*. Last accessed Aug 2022.

basic summary. Every healthcare organisation, sometimes every department within it, keeps its own record for you, which can't be easily sent back and forth. Clinical IT systems are not interoperable as a rule. They won't be soon. Data protection rules are complex. Keep your personal healthcare folders. Never let them go.

Legal documents—such as for my phone or current house lease (which I always keep until the final confirmation by the agency or landlord that "all is fine, all the best for the future"). I only keep the first page of my current work contract, detailed terms and conditions removed. I either live them or have discovered they are puffed air.

Loyalty or gift cards—I have a bare minimum of loyalty cards. I don't want them to be skewing my true needs and desires. I don't want the tenants after me to be receiving irrelevant letters, as no loyalty scheme can keep up with my changes of address. I also refuse to spend time tracking points and deals and participating in games somebody else has devised for me. I have my own games. I do have cards preloaded with money though—such as for travel on the tube or gift cards for cafés.

Whether we agree or disagree about the overall benefit of participating in loyalty schemes, their cards and associated paperwork will most likely stop being a moving house issue any time now. The ways of paying, gifting and collecting brownie points are turning more and more immaterial. It helps with a house move. It doesn't help with moving away from past choices.

Warranty cards—purged at each house move for items which have gone out of warranty. I recently threw out all instruction manuals I had, taking the advice of Marie Kondo.[4] I read and even highlight instruction manuals, but the only manual I've opened after getting used to an appliance was for a digital camera I no longer use. Normal people don't read instruction manuals. If you are a normal person, it's extra irrational to keep them. The professionals will find a way to repair an item with or without a manual.

Key and random letters from the preceding categories – I keep those for easy access to my numbers. I also keep them for when a Big Black Hole eats all records of all organisations of all times or when another imposter challenges me.

I've always had a shredder or a locked container for confidential data (professionally shredded after) at work. If you have no access to one, look out for public services for confidential waste destruction. Some libraries, community centres and even commercial companies offer them for free or at minimal charges. These can be regular services or shredding events ('shred fests', 'shredathons').[5] Search for variants of 'free shredding', 'public shredding', 'community shredding', 'one-off shredding'....

My life admin is now down to two thin folders and my purse. The grand total is no thicker than 4-5 centimetres. All goes in my personal bag on moving out. I can also pack it in seconds. Don't underestimate the value of organised paperwork in running for your life.

---

4 Kondo, M. The Life-changing magic of tidying: A simple, effective way to banish clutter forever. London: Vermilion, 2014, p.119.

5 R.K. Black, Inc. "Shredding event basics: What they are, how to find them and how to host one". Company website blogpost, 7 Sep 2017. rkblack.com/blog/posts/view/52/shredding-event-basics-whatthey-are-how-to-find-them-and-how-to-host-one. Last accessed Aug 2022.

Though, can I tell you of a suspicion you may harbour too, dear reader?

Our most difficult fights and flights may have nothing to do with concentration camps, stone walled prisons or the scenes of a terrorist attack.

They may be quite the opposite in fact—banal, unspectacular and bloodless. They may be as-if unimportant decisions at as-if unimportant crossroads, disallowing comforts and conveniences, approvals and disapprovals, furrowed foreheads and golden stars, mortgages and stable salaries, kind-of-good average marriages and love affair rounds, one-hundred-things-to-do-before-you-die, number after number after number after number to lock you up in a safe enumerated life. They may be as-if minor refusals to let the watered-down, drop by drop, corrode the noble metals of your soul.

You are not just a number, I heard that.

Are you the living proof?

CHAPTER 18

HOME IN A BOTTLE OF FACE WASH

Your toilet's blocked. As if your life wasn't enough. You pour in quarter of a bottle of shampoo, then half a bucket of hot water. You watch. Faeces and drags of toilet paper rise. You wait. You pour in hot water again. Three, two fingers to the rim and rising. It's Sunday morning in an icy January and you are deep into your overdraft. Shit, please, move. Nothing. Then—POOOOF....

One of the most useful things I learnt in 'my' eighteen-room mansion, with its centuries-old plumbing, was to unblock a toilet. There are times when shampoo down the drain clears the way. And while a house move shouldn't be one of them, if your bathroom is like 95% of those I've seen, you will be tempted to pour down the drain dozens of bottles, tubes, pots of products you've tried, were disappointed with, underwhelmed by, have almost finished, then left aside when you bought something new, got bored with, bought as get-one-get-one-half-price, received as a present but didn't like...."I can at least recycle the containers", you might say. No. Try better.

Before I suggest how, a minor clarification: it may be a Humpty-Dumpty-style distinction ("When I use a word," Humpty Dumpty said in rather a scornful tone, "it means just what I choose it to mean—neither more nor less."[1]) but I use 'cosmetics' for products that are supposed to make us more attractive and tend to be more expensive, and 'toiletries' for products that enable basic hygiene and cost relatively little.

(THE PSYCHOLOGICAL EQUIVALENT OF) COSMETICS IS WHAT YOU START YOUR HOUSE-MOVE PLANNING WITH
Toiletries and cosmetics are the first thing I register on my 'transition time' radar. They are 'my precious'. I can find home in a bottle of face wash. I can live anywhere if I have running hot water and high-quality cosmetics. It's only half a joke.

If this sounds incomprehensible, you need to identify their psychological equivalent in your life. It may be shoes, fine wine, sports gear, photography equipment, jewellery, antiques, art, cars....It may also be a passion which doesn't translate into possessions, such as travelling, having a daily coffee out or personal development. In the latter type of cases, it's less relevant to the pragmatics of a house move but, as ever, thinking through the associated issues may help you move.

It's a type of possession which meets most of the criteria below:
- It feels like peace, me-time, personal space, replenishment, protection, adventure, empowerment... sometimes practically the only context where you are finding these.
- It sucks in more than a sensible proportion of your

1 Carroll, L. *Alice in Wonderland* illustrated & *Through the Looking-Glass*. Independently published, 2013. Kindle edition location: 2647.

money, time and mental space, where it leaves other needs under pressure, even 'threatened'. You may even be unwilling to 'confess' how much money or time you spend on it.

- It lifts your mood noticeably and reliably, as few other things can do.
- You are anxious or frustrated when you don't have it or don't have it of the quality you are used to.
- If you haven't had access to it for a long time, your body is vibrating when you are about to touch it.
- Yet it's not considered addictive or harmful to your health, often to the contrary. It goes with a significant level of social prestige.
- You are a subject specialist in it.
- You are more porous to marketing and advertising manipulation and excellent customer service with respect to it than you are willing to admit.
- You accumulate more 'units' than you need or can use.
- The fact that 95% of the time promises (of the stars) don't match reality (possibly wonderful, but not the stars) doesn't make you much more sensible in buying it. This time it's the thing.

If you've identified your psychological equivalent of my cosmetics, then it may make more sense if I say:

When life was running four times faster than I could, cleansing my face was the only time I remembered to be slow.

In the decades when I've shared a house, bathrooms were the only space where solitude was guaranteed. No housemate would invade it. No-one would bang on the door until an emergency.

When I hardly knew what self-love and self-care meant, massaging my body with lotions and potions—slowly, gently, caringly—was the closest to these I could give myself.

When I was a teenager, which seems to have lasted decades if problem skin is the measure, a product that worked on my skin transformed my life.

When almost everything I had, I had to share, cosmetics was MINE. It was untouchable so as not to exchange bacteria. Long live bacteria.

When I felt guilty for spending any money on myself, this was money I felt justified to spend. I would feel a tinge of guilt. I would hide either the cost or the jars. But I would also believe it was my best spent money.

Notice the fears and sadness, even if cosmetics was the salvation. This is one of the ways in which 'that thing' is different from your superpowers and their attributes.

Many of the practicalities of handling cosmetics in a move will not work for its psychological equivalents (you can't 'finish' your earrings, mountaineering equipment or bikes, for instance). Some will, however, work at a higher level of abstraction. The section headings below point towards that level.

INVENT A GAME TO RECONNECT TO THE ORIGINAL JOY

I have a game for finishing my lotions and potions. The goal is to move out with the tiniest bag of cosmetics and toiletries as possible; throw nothing of what you find at home; and buy as little as possible (towards the very end, only travel sizes). It turns your move light, green and cost-effective. It gives you (or me) a progressively growing sense of liberation. When a bottle or a pot which has been on the shelves for months, even years, is suddenly gone, it doesn't feel like an empty place. It feels like breathing space.

Mostly, however, the goal is to feel the ecstasy of abundance when faced with misery and fear. You cut the tube of a moisturiser in half and discover a three-day supply. You run out of body lotion and find the sun protection cream from last summer. You thought you had no toothpaste and remember the terrible herbal one you couldn't throw away.

I'm as happy as once upon a time. Once upon a time, I bought a toothpaste with three coloured stripes, a legend from the West, the moment it arrived on the markets of Eastern Europe (even if part of the legend was that 'the rich' were brushing their dogs' teeth with it). Once upon a time, I paid a quarter of one of my first salaries for an Estée Lauder serum. It was nothing short of bottled magic (now it's about one-sixtieth of my rather average UK academic salary, with a proportionate reduction of magic effect). Once upon a time, I kept a transparent Magnolia soap—a birthday present—in between the bedsheets for years and took it out to celebrate finishing high school.

Thank goodness those times are gone. But when, at moving out, I squeeze final drops of a moisturiser, toothpaste, body lotion...there flows liquid gold. I'm ecstatic in the midst of misery.

GO OVER-THE-TOP

If you have frills of beauty care such as face masks, hair wraps, massage oils, eye patches, nose stickers to remove blackheads, foot socks for exfoliating dry skin...commit to using them. It won't minimise your luggage size by any meaningful measure. But it will minimise your pores. It will add glow to your skin. Bounce to your hair. It feels far better to be asked, while preparing to move, if you've been on holiday than if you are really ok (yeah, why, no, nothing, you look a bit tired).

REPURPOSE WHILE REFUSING
TO COMPROMISE ON STANDARDS

You can downgrade products while upgrading body (or house) parts. A mediocre facial scrub is a decadent leg exfoliator. A shampoo which doesn't foam enough but smells divine can become a body wash or liquid soap (or floor cleaner; I hope I don't need to remind you to be careful with wooden floors). An eye cream that made your eyes sting can brighten up your décolletage, and so on.

If you are running out of products, check for substitutes in your kitchen. If I run out of body lotions towards the end of a move, I switch to olive oil. Massage it over your body before a shower and you won't need a lotion after. (Take the bottle to the bathroom if it's far from the kitchen, otherwise you'll leave too many sticky traces.)

Most cosmetic products have a lifespan of six to twelve months after they've been opened (you can see a small cap with a *number M* – number of months – indication on the tube, bottle, etc.). Samples tend to last from a few weeks to a year.[2] You can argue that unless it stinks, it is not a real best-before date, but the interests of cosmetic companies wanting you to buy again. This is my mum's philosophy. My own is that even if that's true, I don't want my body to soak up ingredients that can mummify it. Choose your point on the continuum.

---

2 Kondo, M. The Life-changing magic of tidying: A simple, effective way to banish clutter forever. London: Vermilion, 2014, p.131.

REDISTRIBUTE TO MAXIMUM APPRECIATION, EVEN IF NOT MAXIMUM GAIN

I've seen unopened products accepted in some charity shops, food banks with broader 'inclusion criteria', pharmacies and even in my local yoga studio, which is a drop-off point for the Hygiene Bank (*thehygienebank.com* – as of January 2022, the Hygiene Bank has 885 drop-off points in the UK).

Opened, even barely used cosmetics and toiletries are difficult to redistribute, including to donate. There are health and safety issues, and some claim 'dignity' ones. My favourite ways of redistributing opened products are by leaving them in youth hostels or offering them on Freecycle.

Almost invariably, youth hostels have spaces for what some travellers leave behind and what other travellers may be short on. If you've ever travelled with a single rucksack, you'll know the experience of running out of shampoo or toothpaste in the middle of nowhere or in the middle of the night. You'll also know the brutal selectivity against non-essentials. I, for one, have cried with gratitude for a conditioner I found in a youth hostel, left behind by "an American girl who flew home last night".

The last time I Freecycled cosmetics (Guinot products, some of which were down to only a quarter of the bottle), I met a beautiful soul, a shy mum of a little boy with another child on the way. Her growing family didn't have the money for such luxuries. She was overflowing with excitement and gratitude. I was doubly happy for seeing her happy and for being 3 x 500 ml bottles down.

Box 12 has further suggestions on what to do with opened products.

BOX 12

THE CHALLENGE OF USED COSMETICS

- **Little used expensive cosmetics** I offer to friends and family. I do it cautiously. Our skin and tastes need to be similar enough to make my products suitable (think foundation), yet different enough to be worth testing on a different person.

- If I know that a product isn't for me at first use, I **sell under the 'almost new' category** on eBay. I treat such mis-buys mostly as an opportunity to connect things and people and maintain high seller ratings. I copy some of the reviews which inspired me to buy it. I also describe my skin so that buyers with similar pain points can avoid it.

  I've not been able to recuperate a meaningful proportion of the costs of opened cosmetics, even if 'use' had reduced it by three drops. But I've had five-star reviews.

- **Toiletries Amnesty** has a sizable **directory** of organisations accepting donations of toiletries, cosmetics and other sanitary, hygiene and first aid products: *toiletries-amnesty.org/directory/*.

  The majority are in the UK (427 as of Aug 2022), but there are also worldwide locations (27). The profile of each organisation contains an 'Accept part-used products?' field. You can also limit searches by an identical filter.

  The lady at the local charity I found through Toiletries Amnesty commented that what I was donating (part-used cosmetics) was extra helpful for their clients—women with a history of addiction, often unused to self-care. Luxurious products make self-care far more likely.

- I've come across a range of **projects and charities** which would accept part-used toiletries, cosmetics and similar products and then run out of capacity, becoming victims of their own success. My favourite was Give and Makeup, which supported women affected by domestic violence. Even if you can't use the routes of an organisation, you can borrow their ideas on settings and groups in need.

- **Make-up and beauty empties recycling** is becoming a common high street practice. It may be an initiative of a particular company (such as Maybelline boxes for make-up in UK drugstores and supermarkets) or offered in a company's shop (I first saw containers for beauty empties in L'Occitane), but most companies are not limiting recycling to their own products. They may, however, be limiting the number of empties you can bring in at a time.

- I recently saw **recycling boxes for dental hygiene products** – such as empty toothpaste tubes or used toothbrushes – in the waiting room of a dental clinic.

- **First aid products** (problematic belonging to this chapter but, in my homes, they sit alongside cosmetics and toiletries) I've left with first aiders in my office buildings. I am not sure if all are that receptive though, again for health and safety reasons.

When I was last editing this chapter, two young women on the train seats opposite were experiencing a fallen false eyelash drama. "Oh, My God!!!! Oh, My God!!!!! Oh, My God!!!!!!" Shouting, embarrassed laugher, mirror checks, "I told you!" and all.

Apart from trying hard to keep a Botox-like non-Botoxed face of minding my own business, I was struck by the thought that maybe, in this chapter, I sounded just like them, even if I'm decisively not (no false eyelashes here; a total taboo on taking a mirror out in public; and visceral dislike for speaking on public transport, let alone so loudly. And yes, I am allergic to the OMG expression, especially abbreviated). How do you write about cosmetics and your love for it without being mistaken for the eyelash-fluttering-falling type?

Some of you have had the red light flashing already. When you (I) have a knee-jerk reaction to a type of personality or behaviour, it's highly likely it's your (my) own. Maybe in a more refined, educated, polished way that belies the similarity, but still there. After all, what's quintessentially different between stating that you (I) can find home in a bottle of face wash and raising hell on a train for a fallen eyelash?

Nothing.

Nothing's different unless you KNOW, unless you FEEL that a bottle of luxurious face wash, an eyelash, a vintage year wine, fancy new bike gear, fancy new car, [add your own psychological equivalent] can be rather good things but they are only a train to a destination. Moreover, there are countless other trains that can get you there.

It's not that long ago that I *was* those girls, or what I saw of them on that day, even if my daily make-up was nothing more than mascara and lip gloss and even if I'd never announce a beauty malfunction to all the passengers on a train carriage. I too would have been terrified to lose my lotions and potions. I too wasn't aware they were only one train to destinations which can be reached in hundreds, if not thousands, of alternative ways.

Why did it take me so long though, until around I turned forty, to have the fetish of cosmetics fade away? Why is it something I never doubted my choices about, even if I would doubt myself about almost anything? Why, even when a part of us will agree that something is superficial and excessive and we can do without it, we are spellbound to have it?

Notice I'm talking of something different to choosing, clear-sightedly and light-heartedly, to have such things. Enjoying the abundance of life beyond the basics is a marvellous thing. This is not a point against having that we can objectively do without. It's about choosing to have what we can objectively do without from a place of joy and expansion, not responding to a compulsion, fear or the need for immediate salvation.

HEALTHY CORE AND ROTTEN LAYERS

Many of us can't see the rotten layers of our loves for certain types of possessions because there is something undeniably healthy, joyous, vibrant, exuberant, curious, ecstatic at the core. Then, whatever arguments about what's 'rotten' reach us, from the outside or from other parts of our psyche (such as something being superficial, exorbitantly expensive, unnecessary, vain, manipu-lative, etc.), they are repelled from that solid, luminous, truthful core. There is dirty bath water around the baby we can easily, or not so easily, throw out but we only feel the baby threatened.

High-quality cosmetics stood, in my life, for personal space, blissful solitude, (semblance of) free time, peace, self-care, generosity to myself, luxury from a world of abundance when the whole of life was at the level of the basic. I would have electrified the air if anyone had challenged me for paying more than was sensible relative to my means or for the vanity, emptiness, futility or non-feminism of my love for lotions and potions. I'd fight against judgements floating in social air, even if they'd never been addressed directly at me:

No. No. Don't even think of giving me your wise counsel. Do you know that I don't stop? In trying to be good to others, to be true to what I find out to be true, to do work that's meaningful, to take care of those who need care, to grow, to learn, to fight, to stand, to seek, to feel suppressed pain, to heal pain?

I'm not giving up on what's my only stupid, easy love. My only moments of peace. My only time of lightness. My only certain daily time of distraction from all that I need to think about, resolve, repair in my own life and yes, I'm sorry for the romantic fantasy, or I'm not sorry at all, in other lives, in our world. Yes, I'm one of those who can't feel that all is perfect, as it's meant to be, and we weep and we try and we mostly fail but sometimes succeed.

I'll have as many bubbles on my nose as I want to. The seaside in my wash basin. The scent of the forest down my body. The touch of me to me. Get lost. I've deserved every penny of those I'm spending, any moment of time I waste, any level of being superficial.

In the times when high-quality cosmetics mattered that much to me, I've never read or heard or thought three things that are blindingly obvious to me now.

The first is that enjoying good cosmetics (or whatever your psychological equivalent) is a beautiful way to awaken the senses, return to your body, be generous to yourself, recentre from your scatteredness, find lightness in the everyday, relish in the geeky knowledge of something concrete, material, tangible....But it's only one way of an infinite set. Most of us have made something so sanctuary-like, so precious, so non-negotiable because we've denied ourselves too many of the other ways to reach the same experiences.

The second is that the harmful kind of tinkering with one's face—whether popping a pimple or squeezing blackheads out— is for some people, for most people who tinker with their faces, for the me-person, an anti-anxiety technique. I've never self-harmed physically (other than self-harming my skin in the above way) but I'm pretty sure that's what happens to many people who cut themselves. Your attention's laser-sharp focused. How else do you squeeze out the contents of a tiny pore? How else do you use a razor on your skin? Your whole mind is in this tiny pore, this narrow cut and in that same deliberate, repetitive, half-conscious stroke, with which you've become one, you are squeezing out, cutting off any thought or feeling that's made you anxious.

Then, when you've made a good mess of your face or when you have your arm dripping blood, you have a far more tangible thing to deal with than whatever spiked your anxiety in the first place. Harder to explain perhaps, but you are back in your body, even if through pain and blood. More present in your body is always less anxious.

The third thing that's blindingly obvious to me now, but I've only heard the opposite of, relates to avoiding attention. Many of us buy our sanctuary-like thing because we want to HIDE. That's quite the opposite to the standard enlightened story that those like my younger me or the girls on the train are doing it for the love and attention, for being seen and accepted.

No doubt some do. After all, there is a meaningful degree to which certain forms of love, attention and belonging come with artificial eyelashes and blemish-free skin and the right running gear, wine, car....But this misses the point for many of us.

No matter how flawed many of our ideas of love may be, I'll bet my head that most, if not all, of us seek a love that can last whatever happens to our bodies. We may want what we see as love available to the most beautiful amongst us, but we'll always want to be loved for far more than how we look.

No matter how many people want the attention of the world, I'll bet another head that enough, maybe most, of us don't want anything like it. Undivided person-to-person attention is one thing. We blossom under its light. Our soul dances and sings in it. We even see ourselves at all because of it. But being noticed by dozens, hundreds, thousands, millions at the same time? What a nightmare for the majority of us, or how exhausting beyond some brief moments.

Not having the redness and breakouts and blackheads and shiny oil on my skin was, for me, the way to be seen less of in the wrong way. Without them, with less of them, I could face others without being self-conscious of what they see and conclude about how I wash (obviously not enough, though truth was very responsibly); how I eat (obviously terribly, though truth was very healthily); what my hormone levels are (obviously messed up, but entirely within the expectations of a teenager's body and hardly my fault); or how I've been picking my face, which is BAD (and yes, this time you are judging me right, I did). But I'm fed up with being judged.

Often enough, we want to possess certain outward attributes to avoid attention of the wrong type rather than attract positive attention. We want those attributes to fit in. To blend. To trick people into not using the external that's wrong as a conduit towards the internal or broader life which is x times wronger.

WHAT ARE YOU SEEKING?
WHO ARE YOU HIDING FROM?

Do *you* have an overvalued type of possession or activity that, through the money, time and mental space it sucks, may be compromising other aspects of your life, even if it's also 'saving' you?

If so, what is its healthy core? What are you giving yourself through it which you are not giving yourself in other ways?

What does engaging with this 'thing' knock your mind away from? Is there something you'd better face there rather than persistently block, dial down the anxiety of, resolve in ways external to it?

Who are you hiding amongst by using the cover of this type of possession, even if most would say you want to be showing off through it?

How come you've lost the faith, or never grew it, that there are people you don't need to be hiding from?

How come you've lost the faith, or never grew it, that there is nothing so scary or lost or dark about you that light can't reach it? You are not that exceptional, honey, even in your extreme brokenness.

If you have such a thing or activity, hold on to it. It shows you where you are going.

NAKED MORE OFTEN

I obviously can't say or ask any of the above on a train journey where the false eyelash of a girl falls. Or, rather, I can but jaws will drop and that can be dangerous. Is there something else I can do, something better than disconnecting?

You never get on the same train twice. But if I get on a similar one, I can bend down and look for your fallen eyelash with you. Maybe I can find it.

Maybe, when I find it, I'll hesitate if the best thing to do is squash it with the heel of my shoe, let it stick on it and carry it away when I get off the train at the next station. Sometimes having to do without something we believed we MUST have is the best lesson in doing without it.

Maybe I'll see it, pick it up, blow the dust off it, ask you if cleaning it with a wet wipe is safe, and open my bag to find one for you.

But one way or another, I'll say that "I'm so sorry you've lost it, I know a bit about how you feel, I've never worn false eyelashes (how do you call them actually, 'false' sounds too negative!), but I hate going out without mascara. It's as if I'm half-naked.

Your eyes are beautiful though.

You should wear them 'naked' more often."

The train is now approaching Truro, or was it True-Raw.

Your final destination.

Please take all your belongings with you.

CHAPTER 19

BOOKS OF LIFE

You my love have quite literally saved me from dear [heart] [heart] [heart]. Death* xxxx

Eight minutes before this message flashed, I'd sent an email — of hope, determination, love — I had no intention to write. It was pestering me to be written. *Right NOW. You can't go out before you do.* I never learnt if I'd intercepted the turning on of the gas, a trip to the dam, or the completion of a thought, but I intercepted it with words. Not that it was *me* who saved that luminous man, regardless of what he wrote. It was his Higher Being, Inner Witness, Guardian Angel, God, Fate, Luck, Chance, whatever Higher Power co-opted my words in Its workings. But words they did co-opt.

Of all possession types I've needed to make decisions about, I cannot think of another more life-changing, potentially life-saving, than books and other 'word-things', such as letters or lyrics to music. I suspect you'll agree. After all, picking a book on house moving is akin to the tree-top request of a boy who could have been my stepbrother. He climbed up a tree, struggled to get down, hung in there thinking, then shouted out to his dad not for help, but for a book on climbing down from trees.

We know we would steal, starve, fight, burn, die for books and the freedom of what's in them if we are called to. Have starved for/ stolen a book at least are common book lover experiences. And even if it's only a theoretical 'would', because we've always been good, well-off and well socialised, we've never been that good, well-off and well-socialised not to need saving by books.

Yet I will be telling you that you can leave most of your books behind and that it's not a big deal. Well, it is not a big deal after it stops being a big deal.

No. NO, you argue. I can't. Not me, really. I am different. It will always be a big deal. The ultimate deal. Books are my true home. More, they are who I am, markers of my life path, the reason I'm alive. I can never leave them behind.

Sure, please carry on. My past self would have marched, fought and died by your side. But, if you would allow, I will rake a thought you've already thought. I'll get there but let me tell you how it began.

Once upon a time, books were my kingdom. My granddad had a personal library of over six thousand volumes (I know. I helped him catalogue them. I read out author, title, publisher, year. He typed them on his typewriter. I wrote a number on the front page and circled it. Next). My parents had around two thousand (I've always despised the mediocrity). It wasn't a surprise I grew up thinking that you can't live without reading. I went on to earn six university degrees of various calibre. I work at a university. The belief that living requires reading only grew stronger with time (though I also read far less than the above may suggest; I spend too much time floating, observing and thinking).

Books were, for decades, my most sacred possessions.

Markers of the words which have changed my world.

Suppliers of parts of me. Feel into, lift off the page and fill in the blanks left by genetic and environmental determinism. Have you ever wondered how many book characters and scripts you embody, even if in single features of them?

Water to the expectation that the grass is greener on the other side. Gosh, two thousand shades greener and two thousand other sides to check.

Flying carpets to The Great Mystery—the best and fastest after love.

Feathers tickling your emotions. Sometimes groins. Or not so much feathers as explosive devices.

Herbaria of splashes of tears—true emotions conjured by untrue events—pages glued in a kiss turned dry.

Home for every homelessness.

Path when I was pathless.

Shelter in the storm.

Hideaways for my shyness.

Glue in any heartbreak. Some of it first salt.

Bags of promises and solutions—you'll be happier, more beautiful, more loved, confident, successful, richer, wiser, younger by the end. If only you didn't give up by page twenty. If only you didn't expect it of just reading.

Grounds for confidence at displays of intellectual penises. Mine consistently reaches the end of the full edition.

Accusations of ignorance. Two in one with the acquittal: READ ME.

Proofs of love. Or while proofs were still too scary, a safe object to channel it into. *I loved this book too! Can we talk for the next two*

hours about it, and about us, while completely avoiding the latter topic?
Decoration.

My non-clothes, non-shoes, non-other (because it was, often
enough, 'either books or–'). Little daily restraints that have big-
bang-birthed grand books later.

Furniture, of the sacrilegious kind–a base for my laptop to
watch movies on; a step to reach higher from. Which reminds me:

Gym equipment–one book for a yoga block, four for a stepper.

My books, serving all of the above functions and many more, look
in two extreme ways. The ones for reading are distinguishable
from new only by the extra air between the pages. The ones
for studying look alive, mine-and-only-mine and *a-ha* ready to
speak to you–neat pencil underlining and my most beautiful
handwriting (still a shame according to my granddad, you mustn't
write in books, including your own, period). If any of my books
have a level of damage, 97% of the time it's because I'd lent them
to the wrong person (first and last time).

I would lend books with a tinge of fear. I didn't want the
dog ears. I didn't want to burden my emotional space with the
vague sense of something of mine being taken away. It took me
over fifteen years to let go of my favourite (and quite expensive)
dictionary–a Longman dictionary of phrasal verbs I'd lent to
my housemate's boyfriend in 2001. She'd married twice after
him. Longman had almost gone. At least 2,001 phrasal verbs
had entered and exited the English language. I still wanted my
dictionary back.

What happened? How come I could let go of my books if I used
to be (almost) like you, worse then you?

DUST AND MAGI'S GIFTS

Predictably, I moved too often. My piles of books were growing. 95% were never opened between one move and another. At least twice a year I was dusting them off, boxing them in, carrying back-straining boxes to the not-so-near-nearest post office, sending them from myself to myself, and paying money I didn't quite have. There comes a day when you ask yourself, *What's the point?*, and you can't answer.

Around the time when my answers were beginning to sound more and more emotionally hollow, even if beautiful, I also received gifts from three Magi. A man I loved (and spoke with about books rather than love) gave me the books he couldn't stuff in his suitcase on leaving the country. I couldn't believe a book lover could let *those books* go. I would never have done that.

Or wouldn't I? I was a good person to give those books to. He was the perfect person to give mine to in a similar situation. And it can't be just me, him and you. It must be most of those who'd love the books we've loved.

Not long after, my mum and my brother gave me another gift—a Kindle. Society was still debating the pros and cons of electronic books as if we could, and might, collectively choose against them. I didn't mind them. But I was on the "touching a book's body, turning her pages, falling asleep with her on your lap" side. I didn't want a Kindle. Then, within two minutes of receiving it, I've always had it.

THE INNER GAME

I also faced the rather pathetic fact that I didn't want to let go of my books as they are the Chanel bags and Christian Louboutin shoes of my circles—a status symbol and a sign of belonging.

My carefully curated library was partly there as evidence for you. Evidence that *I know. I think. A lot and deeply for some things. Please don't write me off when I come out with a spoken mess. I want perfect clarity and I used to be shy. And my thoughts are often newly glued, struggling to reach out to you, from the depths of my guts, little bones of the most difficult getting stuck in my throat.*

How boring, and how not an inner reality I wanted to nourish.

Perhaps most importantly, I was defeated by the impossibility of cataloguing two of my favourite subjects—my deepest beliefs and my life transformations. Most of us hold on to reminders of these. We feel a need to anchor the knowledge of who we've always been and shouldn't move too far away from; the appreciation of who we've become and the path we've walked. We do it with different levels of systematicity and different primary objects (photos, clothes, books, cars...). I am of the book club. If a book has had a paragraph, a sentence which made my thoughts take a sharp turn, I wanted to keep it.

That was almost every book. If the book wasn't mine, it would be notes from it. Copious.

Until one day I stopped. I believe it was after *Oscar and Lucinda* in 2011. I was defeated by the infinity. Too many books, too many new thoughts, too much and too fast a change. I couldn't keep up with myself. Plus, the cataloguing was beginning to feel dangerously biased. Nothing of the wordless, inarticulate, bodily. Nothing of the wild soul burning, life-changing friendships, brief random encounters.

And here's the thought I told you you've already thought, no matter how attached to your books you are.

We live the books that have truly changed our lives and thoughts. Their words are printed all over us, even if we can't remember where we copied them from.

They are in what we see, how we listen and what we say. In how we tie our hair and infer the beautiful teeth of the woman in the queue behind. It's in arriving dead on time, with the chiming of the town clock bell. It is in how we keep fighting, keep running when we can't even crawl. It's in how we speak to the man who's having a fit at Paradise Street. It's in the inner quote at peeled almonds. In how we hold a knife above a cake. In how we love the colour green. In how we love.

If they've mattered, your books are quoted, be it wordlessly, be it without a trace you can uncover, by the walking, living, breathing Book of Your Life. If not, they are dead wood. Up to you if you want to carry it.

DEALING WITH THE PHYSICAL CHAOS

I currently have four main criteria for keeping books:

1. I use them regularly in my work or, having digested them with their covers, I have a strong intention to use them in future work. This means major use, when I base a piece of writing or analysis on them, not just quote a sentence or two. For the latter, a library copy would do.

2. They have changed my life—there are too many pieces of Me I've lifted off their pages.

3. I loved them, and even if I may not open them ever again, I would be thrilled to give/ gift them to somebody who would appreciate the pure gold they are.

4. I haven't read them but feel like adding them to my bed-side table pile NOW. Note it's a very strong and current emotional intention rather than an 'in principle' to-read. Books that I've long intended to read but haven't done

so, move after move, I donate. I do it in the belief that if they were for me to read, we'll meet again when the time is right.

I don't keep books for the sole reason that they have a dedication to me on the front page. If a book has served its purpose and doesn't meet one of the preceding criteria, it goes. For once, I also tear the page to keep it. Don't cringe in horror, on all occasions it's been blank before the message! I still resent the person who'd torn a mid-book page in a charity shop copy of *The Time Traveller's Wife*. I've most likely failed to read the two most beautiful pages of this beautiful book.

When choosing what to keep, don't forget the practical books and books' cousins which, in many houses, inhabit spaces different to the main library—such as cookery books, DIY-manuals, and travel guides and maps.

How to sell the books you are not keeping (or why not to bother)

Expensive textbooks and professional books sell quickly and reliably (why wouldn't a student buy a philosophy of science textbook for £25 rather than £62, even if its final pages are bloated with dried raindrops?). Putting up books on Amazon is one of the quickest ways to create an ad, with books linked to a pre-existing record. You don't need a photo. It's automatically supplied from the formal book record. The data entry is minimal.

Every book I've offered on Amazon has sold (with one exception, they've been in excellent condition). Below a certain price threshold, however, selling is a negative investment. I spend too much time erasing underlining and notes (if too many, I only donate, though I still do my best to erase), wrapping, labelling and waiting at the post office. But I used to do it when every penny mattered. I used to do it when I wasn't thinking of the books I am not writing or reading while selling the ones I'm not keeping.

You can, of course, sell books to physical second-hand/ antique booksellers. I've tried this approach mostly in my home country, where there is no Amazon, for good or bad. Unfailingly, I've been asked for a bibliography first. I've always felt quietly offended. They should have looked me in the eyes and 'known' that all my books would be amongst the best on their stall. But since they never saw the obvious, I would typically choose to donate my books (obviously elsewhere).

Once, my mum and I had a bookseller come home instead of us compiling a bibliography. We were clearing our library (it's not a moving-out story but it's too relevant to ignore), as new books could only go on the floor. It ended up a two-week project of dramatic disagreement over book classifications and positioning. I remember slamming a door over the relocation of Shakespeare. Towards the end, the owner of a second-hand bookshop came over to see if there were any he could sell. He took over fifty. He was going to pay a percentage on every sale. He had clear blue, beautiful, honest eyes, and never paid a cent.

Most of our books had sold, but his business was struggling. After a few weeks of 'next week', we shrugged it off. Our books, as well as those beautiful honest-looking blue eyes, deserved better ethics. A bookseller too deserved an easier life.

Donating books

In Britain, almost every charity shop has a book section. If there isn't a similar donation default where you live, many village libraries, school libraries, community centres, even book cafés will bite your hand off for good books.

If I have more time, I choose projects and spaces where my books will feed the desperately book hungry. Once it was a project that was sending books to Africa. Once it was the newly opened Cultural Centre at our Embassy in London. Last summer it was a little bookshop in my hometown which sells foreign language books which can, otherwise, be prohibitively expensive for the locals or nowhere to be bought.

Letting go of most books' cousins– articles, lecture notes, notebooks....

In one house move which also involved an office move, I recycled 98% of the academic articles I'd kept, even if with sadness over the loss of my annotations. The attachment to my notes couldn't compete with the aversion to carrying 30-40 kilos of paper. I did, however, find electronic copies for the best of them. I've not opened a single one. What was read was read. I no longer print articles.

Photocopies of life-changing book pages I've also, little by little, recycled. I always made sure to read them first. It would show me that there was nothing more to keep. I lived what I'd kept. I'd moved beyond it. I could easily buy the book which I once couldn't.

My lecture notes were thrown out by members of the extended family when clearing a flat they'd inherited. I have the luxury to mourn the loss and bubble with indignation while, realistically, they did me a favour.

I keep (at home home) a collection of notebooks from high school. Conscientious, crystal clear, girly handwriting–a bridge to a younger me that's worth the space. The **next chapter** (on sentimental items) has more on paperwork with a stamp of emotions, personality and nostalgia.

An even more distant book cousin–stationery

Stationery can be a significant source of microprojects. Many years ago, I gathered in one place all my stationery, in whose nature it is to become scattered (pens, pencils, erasers, paper clips, adhesive tape, blue tack, document pockets, folders...), recycled or threw away what I knew I wouldn't use, sharpened all pencils, and stopped buying any new supplies until I used up what I had. It took me years with some item types.

I've donated folders to the above-mentioned project in Africa but, overall, I recycle the ones I won't be using any longer, even if well preserved. I've seen too many used folders in stationery cupboards at work, left by people who've left, lingering until thrown out long after. I've also stopped using folders. Most of my paperwork is in (colourful) cardboard boxes which can be repurposed for gift wrapping or house moving needs.

More recently, a community library welcomed my unused stationery as a resource for kids' activities they host.

...and if you want to save a life with words

Whatever you decide to do with your books, please do us a favour. Make a pile for the ones that have changed, maybe even saved, your life. Catalogue or photograph them. Post the outcome for us.

Most of us live lives that still need changing and saving.

Now before you begin to take me too seriously and consider letting go of most of your books, remember that there is always a book that tells you the opposite to what you've read in some other book. We, writers, simply relate powerful emotions to objects and experiences. One can always relate different, often opposite, emotions to the same objects and experiences. It's a matter of the lives we've lived and the vagaries of our creativity. When I buy my big bright airy house by the sea, I will be telling you how I re-created the library I've lost at house moving.

Remember that I have a back-up plan, too.

I still have my granddad's library for when I need the comfort
of a home of books.

Every book there carries a number I've written and circled.

I can summon an army of dead wood behind me.

Cos' I've read in an old book

that an army of dead wood

can win you

the kingdom.

CHAPTER 20

THE DARK BRONZE ENVELOPE

There is a dark bronze envelope at the back of my underbed drawer. I'd carried it through four house moves, over three and a half years, unable to either open or throw it away. It held unfinished emotional business. I knew I should and could address it. Gradually. Later.

There is a letter in the dark bronze envelope. It was to the then teenage daughter of a colleague who died in her early forties. I will call my colleague Laura. It will only work in Facebook-world to say that Laura was a friend. There wasn't time enough to decide for the real world, but more time would have probably decided the same. 'Colleague' is fair. Still, her death unravelled me more than the closeness of the relationship justified.

In the village hall after the funeral, I hugged and spoke to Laura's daughter. I let jumbled words flow, trusting the sincerity of the emotion was reaching across and holding her. I told her clearly though that I had a letter for her and a toy for her little sister. I said I'd leave them somewhere there on the tables, where candles flickered, petals shrivelled, and photos were beaming eternal smiles.

And then I didn't. Or, rather, I did, but picked them back again on leaving. I had decided I MUST re-pack the toy.

Of course, no matter how strongly I felt that the pattern of the gift bag was all wrong, that its structure was too stern and soft wrapping paper would have fitted the occasion better, this was not the real reason. I was scared what my letter might do. I was scared because my words can sometimes be more precise than you expect. I give those precise words to your pain too. I want to show you that I am trying to understand, that I truly want to understand and that I feel for you. I won't run away from you with your pain. And maybe I sharpen it rather than console you. How can I be certain what my words—of not quite a stranger, but almost one—will do to a teenage girl who's just lost her mum?

I had intended to give the condolence gifts to Laura's husband. He could read the letter and decide if it was to be given and if yes, when. But the man was a ghost: bones holding no flesh and autopilot deputising for life force. And, as becomes a ghost, he disappeared from the village hall. I really had to re-pack the toy.

In the weeks that followed, I wrote a letter to Laura's husband too (pinned to the desktop, waiting to be copied in handwriting), re-packed the toy, got a cardboard box and the address of the family. I never sent anything.

My laptop died and I stopped seeing the second letter. I was about to move. I gave away the toy. I put the dark bronze envelope in a 'to process' folder. I moved on.

UNFINISHED EMOTIONAL BUSINESS

The dark bronze envelope was, for years, the material expression of emotional baggage being worked through—in fits and starts, but determinedly—and a reminder to complete the process. The emotional baggage was of more than Laura's death and the dilemma of whether to give the letter and to whom.

It was about my aunt's death from the same tumour, three weeks after being diagnosed with it and at least thirty years before her time, as per the low range of the family standards. It was about the pain of my aunt's daughters, the cousins I've grown up with.

It was about 'my right' to feel pain in situations where 'the true rights' reside elsewhere (my cousins, my uncle, my mum, Laura's real friends). It was about my right, in a completely different context, to be centrifuged by emotion when I was never the wife, never the girlfriend, never the lover, never even a recognised friend, but somebody's best kept secret and invisible helpline.

It was about how I can offer help and compassion when my whole being rushes to, but it may be too much, I may be too much, relative to how distant a figure I am.

I completed the final piece of emotional processing—resolving the ethical dilemma of whether to give or not to give the letter—almost four years later, through a blog I wrote for work.[1] The business was finished.

The letter is, however, staying. I haven't got round to deciding on the ritual of its release. It's not avoidance. It's lack of urgency. When the emotional work has been done, the physical world can catch up in its own time, especially when two pages and an envelope light.

1 Petrova, M. "The words we never said". NIHR School for Primary Care Research blog, 21 Mar 2019. spcr.nihr.ac.uk/news/blog/the-words-we-never-said. Last accessed Aug 2022.

WHERE'S YOUR UNFINISHED BUSINESS SEALED?

Your unfinished emotional business is, obviously, sealed in your mind, body and soul, but it's in things too. It is your mum's jumper, gently folded and tightly wrapped in a vacuum bag to preserve her scent. The wedding day suit your husband left behind when he left. The envelope on which your name was followed by a heart, even if, realistically, that beautiful broken man wasn't declaring his love for you to every postman and the world but couldn't remember your foreign surname.

It's in possessions stamped with death and loss. Of love gone. Of a home we've lost the road back to. Of youth that was too brief. Of brilliant selves we never lived up to or let be bitten away, morsel by morsel to bare bones of memory, by hungry rolling years.

It's in objects of relationship ambivalence—things that came to us through relationships and friendships we were never quite certain about but stayed in/with, backwards and forwards in our responses to the question of "is it worth it?!", in our intentions to try harder, in our desire to be better people.

It's in creations, of others or our own, which speak our truth like we never do. The books, the music, the art that shine our essence; full on, wild, luminous, brave, impossible if it weren't real. Right as we do, before it all evaporates like August morning dew, and we are left again needing it from imaginary worlds.

Which objects is your unfinished business sealed in?

SENTIMENTAL ITEMS, GENUINE AND IMPOSTORS

Anything signalling of unfinished business is NOT, in my conceptualisation, a sentimental item. I keep the phrase for objects of the (often distant) past which contract time and space, catapult us back into forgotten worlds and light us up–youthful, curious and fairy-dust-sprinkled–even if they pinprick our heart. Much of what people call sentimental items at house moves are, I'd say, impostors. Our dark, ignorant, lazy fragments love taking a hint of sentimental value and blowing it out of proportion. Apart from avoiding dealing with unfinished emotional business, this process lets us avoid dealing with:

- Expensive possessions we never or hardly ever use and which our scarcity mentality finds hard to release into the world.
- Bad matches to who we are and how we live our lives, even if they match our good intentions and were given to us by people we love–such as gifts of sporting or cooking equipment.
- Old intentions which, no matter how admirable, won't become a priority until circumstances force us–such as to brush up your (my) French, meaning I carried high school notebooks (the sentimental items) from house to house for over a decade. It didn't help. What helped was spending two months in Geneva, the new books I bought on the way there, and women's magazines from Migros.
- Objects steeped in superstition. I cannot throw coins, even if they are Hungarian fillérs from the 80s, it may affect how I attract abundance! I don't really like this icon, but how do you bin a blessed image of the Divine?!
- Perhaps most of all, towering 'rocks' (piles of possessions of the same type) with some 'gold nuggets' (the sentimental items) trapped in them. Yes, it's normal, even healthy, to be attached to your childhood books

and toys; to your mum's jewellery; to the transformative work you did in your thirties, paperwork stored in dozens of thick folders. But only some items in those collections are true gold, while it takes endless hours-days-weeks of boring, sometimes emotionally intense work to extract them. There is a sloth's logic to being deeply sentimental.

WAYS OF THINKING THAT MAY SOFTEN ACUTE "KEEP—DO NOT KEEP" DILEMMAS

If I am forced to state my core principle for dealing with possess-ions during a house move (though if I thought it was of much use, why would I be writing 90,000 words on top of it?), it would be a version of "redistribute unless you love and/or use, aiming for both love and use". Yet with sentimental items and what presents as them, it will be "keep until you figure out why you keep, then keep what you love, regardless of whether you use". Here are the details.

What to do if it hits you in the stomach?

If an object brings up an emotion that is too heavy; if seeing it hits you in the stomach; if it bursts the dams of the here-and-now and the past begins to flood you; if you had it hidden because you didn't want any of that, you might be better off packing it and taking it with you. You read that right.

While states of chaos can be a fruitful time to invite even more chaos (although, typically, chaos invites itself irrespective of our desires), there are times you'd better 'box' old issues. House moving is intense enough, even without the poking of hairy old demons. But when the time comes, a ready bridge to an emotional territory you've been avoiding can be a force for good.

Most advice on recovering from a break-up asks you to throw away HIS/HER things and everything that reminds you of HIM/HER, or put them in a box, sealing it up and removing it from sight. I've read enough on break-ups to know. Similarly, most decluttering advice will ask you to let go of the past and bury your dead.

Always up to your better judgement, but allow me a tinge of scepticism. Your mind will find its prompts even if you change planet. Moving on emotionally by telling yourself that it's time to move on is about as efficient as winning a marathon by reading on how to win a marathon. In a few years' time, you'll also miss smiling at old love letters. More sadly but crucially, you'll have obliterated some of the best tests for the tumour of a painful love, which may be growing largely symptomless.

That said, of course it makes sense to let go of 'unfinished business' objects in response to the exigencies of a house move! Having a material reminder of what you need to work through is not a requirement for remembering to do it. The physical letting go can also be a powerful symbol of starting the work. Only don't mistake the letting go of objects with the letting go of the dark emotions around them.

You may also be surprised that what once hit you in the stomach is now just another thing. Somewhere along the way you've done the work. The shift may have also happened without you realising. It's now time for your material world to catch up with the emotional one. It's a non-issue.

Extract trapped people and relationships from the objects. Decide about each on its own terms

Don't conflate objects with the relationships that brought them in your possession. If you donate, sell or throw away something which a loved one gave to you, you *say nothing* about the relationship and *do nothing* to it. The thought and the gesture mattered. You appreciated them. The quality of the relationship matters. You have that. And you appreciated the former and have the latter with or without a fruit ball, an Ascot-style hat, or a ceramic mushroom with phallic undertones.

Do not repair/ justify a relationship through its objects. Many of us will find we've kept presents from people we can't embrace fully, no matter how earnestly we try. *I rarely use this serving plate, I wouldn't have chosen it myself, but it's perfect for such occasions! And it was so generous of her. Yes, she sucks life out of me after the first fifteen minutes, bless her, but she has some truly fine qualities. And it's a pretty plate, isn't it?*

Separate the object from the person. Decide about each on its own terms. Serving plate now, kind-of-friend later, whichever you need to decide about during this move. If you love the thing, love it full-heartedly and don't let that create an obligation to the person. If you are uncertain about the thing but feel guilty about wanting to disconnect from the person, don't try to evade the guilt or strengthen the relationship by keeping the object. It ain't gonna work. And don't make a poor plate, bowl, cushion, painting (can I add a dog, a cat, any pet, even if it's not their chapter) a hostage to your inability to be truthful to yourself and to choose, with honesty and an open heart, the people and objects in your life.

Respect the resistance

If you have objects of sentimental value you want to separate from but also can't, consider if finding a person who'll truly appreciate them can shift the balance. Sometimes finding a special home is all you need to do to release such possessions.

If you still can't feel fully that letting go of something is a good thing, respect the feeling. There is an inner calculation that's happened, and it carries a truth or a systematic error you can't yet access. Pack it again. Your brain has done some work. It will work it out sooner or later.

DEALING WITH THE PHYSICAL CHAOS

Sentimental or unfinished-emotional-business paperwork– letters, cards and photos

Whether separating the chaff from the wheat makes your collection of letters, cards and photos straightforward to move around, depends on your thresholds for 'sentimental'. Such thresholds are highly personal. They also fluctuate a lot within the same person depending on the demands of a move (or a series of moves).

I keep all **handwritten letters** I've received, including love letters from ex-boyfriends. I'm not making a recommendation. I am asserting that moving on from loss, hard or intensely emotional times does not demand a particular type of attitude to the possessions of those times. It can go either way, any way.

I keep **cards** whose messages continue to move me. I recycle the rest, no matter how pretty the card or dear the person who gave it to me.

Being of a generation who needed to have **photos** developed in a studio so as to see them at all, I used to have plenty of printed images. I've whittled them down to the very best.

Sifting through sentimental paperwork may take you several moves if you've never addressed the task seriously. It starts as intensely moving and heart-opening. It soon progresses to just as intensely boring and tiring. I can't even remember how many moves it took to complete mine ('complete' for old stuff, there is always new to go through at each move).

Burn after reading!
Notes from finished emotional business

If you are somebody who takes notes, if you were born in paper times, and if you've not moved recently, prepare for the paper storm. My emotional business externalised on paper used to be mostly of ideas, quotes, intentions, self-explorations, streams of consciousness processing bad days....They would be invariably mixed with notes of the professional and the mundane — presentation notes, book references, addresses, task lists....I would find them in diaries, folders, cute boxes, writing pads, post-its, fleeting sheets of paper....Most were chaff to be recycled. A small number, I transferred into electronic format. I followed up on the active intentions. But the most precious of my notes—pieces of paper that carried insight, clarity and visions—I burnt.

Whenever the notes were of hard times, a way of processing them, I would burn the pages so as to turn the past into ashes. Whenever I'd written positive visions, good luck charms, affirmations, etc., I would burn them so as to have a wildfire's energy feed into their execution. There is practical convenience in the duality of symbols.

It requires safety precautions. It STINKS. But it's liberating. Intoxicating. Strike a match. Touch a sheet. Tongues of fire blacken and shrivel your life's drama. Add sparkle to your dreams. Ashes in the sink.

Don't let jewellery and watches darken unworn

Speaking of witchcraft, I usually wear jewellery I've loved on receiving (or buying) as if it wields magic powers. I don't take it off, even if sleeping. Then, as if out of nowhere, I stop wearing it. Never again. I kept such old loves for long, until I decided they were suffering unworn.

I donated the costume jewellery (many charity shops take it), sold the gold and silver, and kept a tiny collection of favourites. In parting with an item, I found myself led by the lack of a story— not being able to remember who gave me a piece of jewellery or how I bought it, and not having any distinct memory of wearing it. The remaining old favourites are mostly to smile at, though they can get some airtime. I recently wore a wristwatch from teenage times, a present from my granddad. I wanted to go out without a mobile. I wanted to be infused with the peace of times when watches needed winding and the family I grew up with were all alive.

Honour your superstitions with one hand while dismantling them with the other

If you have superstitions around what you can and cannot throw away, you may try honouring them with one hand while taking them apart with the other. I cannot throw away coins. They may be the smallest coin of a foreign currency out of circulation, yet I can't. It's ok. I'll spend far less energy if I find a charity box for foreign and/or old coins (most recently in my local hospital) than if I stage an inner debate on the energetic impact of throwing money in a bin. I make a trip to a charity box. I drop my coin(s). I waste hours. But, in parallel, I also do the far more constructive work of learning about true wealth from those who've mastered its energy.

If you are one for thoughtful gestures
and small acts of kindness

....you may have a reserve stock of cards, presents and wrapping paper at home (jump to the next subsection if that's the last thing you'd keep). You'll carry less, re-connect with people you've lost touch with, get a high out of the randomness and, of course, relish in starting afresh in your new home.

I sometimes send more cards during house moves than I do at Christmas. There is no social obligation. No expectations or need for expectations management. I don't struggle to write a smart deeply felt message, as I sometimes do with occasion cards. I don't feel constrained by pre-printed messages. As per a creative solution I stole from our team administrator and dear friend, one can always cross out the 'birth' in a 'Happy Birthday' card and send a Happy Day instead.

In one of my moves, I sent a bunch of cards and little presents right before I left a home and a city. I was lightening my luggage. Unintentionally, I had weaved a protective web. As is often the case in a new city, I felt like a rag doll: "Here hang pieces stitched together with a thin symmetrical smile." I was heart-broken too. Until the thank-you notes started arriving. I was real. And I was loved.

Don't die before you've sorted it

Even if you can't do it during this move, please commit to going through your sentimental collections, singling out what's truly sentimental and dealing with the rest. Don't leave it for those of us who'll outlive you. It's too much work. Ours is enough.

There are only three regrets I have from nineteen years of donating, selling or throwing out 'things', which must have been in their thousands.

The biggest of them is having sold a pair of heart-shaped pendant gold earrings from when I was about fifteen, to a gold buyer who didn't look me in the eye during the whole exchange.

I would never have put them on again. So childish. So old-fashioned.

I should have kept you though. Once you made me indescribably happy. I made you happy too.

I hope you've found new ears to be your home.

Mine is still where the heart is.

Pendant.

PART V
FINAL THINGS

CHAPTER 21

BOXING IT

Is there a law, of the well-balanced life, that what keeps us moving keeps us anchored and vice versa?

The suitcase you jet around with is 'storage solution' for when you don't.

The passport you cross boundaries with confirms you have a right to be HERE.

You are grounded in who you are and so you glide – from one house, city, job, relationship, social interaction, mess, victory to the next, unpunctured by doubts about who you REALLY are.

If there's such a law, do we recognise we've broken it when we can no longer convert movement into stillness and stillness into movement?

If you must keep moving, after having done it so many times, is this always escapism, wild goose chasing and inner fragmentation?

If you can't raise your anchor, after so many winds have touched you and gone forth without you, are you necessarily a

Prisoner of Dangerous Safety and Perfidious Goodness?

Maybe yes, maybe no, maybe both. The thinking's not for now. The clock is ticking. There is always something, whether of the soulful or practical kind, which remains incomplete or undone in preparing for a move. There comes a time when intentions are to be abandoned and task lists to be dropped. There comes a time when the doors to the soul turn narrow.

It's over.

It may be feeling sad but it's also liberating. Just right. Perfect. The work that had to be done is done even if The Work is never finished.

It's time to box and seal. Hence this chapter—about suitcases, rucksacks, boxes, bags and suchlike containers for our luggage— will remain practical. (We'll take a flight of the soul again in the next and final chapter, in the space between the home we are leaving and the one we are entering.)

Imagine your transportation solutions in your new home, not only on the way there

Remember that durable packaging/ transportation solutions now are a storage task later. I, for one, don't want to see boxes stacked up, threatening to uproot me again, from the moment I've moved in. Whatever I can't fit into the suitcases, rucksacks and big bags I already have, I pack in cardboard boxes, easy to recycle or flatten out of sight on the other side. It helps my stillness after a move. Yours may be the opposite logic—of finally buying durable plastic boxes because you know you'll need them again. Equally valid.

Variety of box sizes matters. I try to have one category of items per box so as to be able to find immediately what I need in my new place (of course, sometimes only I/you know how a category is defined). You can optimise weight better too. Think of a king size duvet box filled with books. Now think of your back, or the porter's one. Now define 'compassion'.

Give a chance to low-value storage and/or transportation solution – battered suitcases, plastic bags and hangers

If you have travel-hardened, wheel-missing, zip-broken suitcases you want to throw out, first check if it's not *you* being battered by the lifestyle which a veteran suitcase has enabled rather than them being beyond repair. Then consider offering them for storage needs or pet beds (a standard use, as I found out).

If you have an excess of plastic bags, try giving them a function instead of recycling them. If I have a collection, I'm 'not allowed' to use bin liners before I've cleared it. I then get a high out of using black bin bags. Never underestimate the happiness potential of post-minor-deprivation states.

In recent moves, I'm usually short on plastic bags. I use compostable bin bags to pack what needs protection or separation, not least because I find them smelling less (and yes, I am only talking of new ones!). The smell of normal black bin liners tends to stick onto clothes. Compostable or not, bin bags simply return to their rubbish purpose when I arrive.

As I've found hangers hard to redistribute, I've committed to only buying ones I'll take forward (wooden or velvet). If I know I am in a place briefly and will move on lightly, I buy cardboard 'eco hangers'. They are sturdy enough to hold a coat, yet readily recyclable as cardboard.

Measure, weigh and label only once

Unless you are booking a van, where rough estimates will do, you'll typically need to provide specific measurements of the items you want picked and shipped (length, width, height and weight).

When you take them, write them on the boxes. You may not reuse the latter, but you'll be checking shipping offers on different websites, perhaps on different days. Most of us won't remember the length, width and height of a box for more than thirty seconds (not sure why weight sticks better). Most of us won't find that scrap of paper. If you already know the hack, I wish I could think like you more often. It took me seventeen years to come up with it and stop re-re-re-measuring while cursing my memory for numbers.

If I don't have scales at home (and I never do, unless the home has them), I guess and add 10%-20% on top. I've trained the inner scales through years of posting parcels and checking in at airports. I also prefer to pay marginally more than stress that the courier may refuse the consignment.

Consider buying transparent pockets for surfaces on which you can't stick a label easily (such as the fabric of a suitcase or the handlebars of a bike). I use A5 in size, thread a cord through one of the holes, and tie the pocket to the handles of whatever is to be carried. The address is visible. You can also slip in a page describing the contents of your consignment. Address or gift tags can also work, but they are often small and/or require extra effort to reveal the address.

If you are moving abroad, you need an inventory.
If you need an inventory, you need a classification theory

If you are moving abroad, you'll need an inventory of your

luggage. It needs to accompany your physical luggage. I once had to unpack, itemise and repack the whole of my luggage because I'd thought that a) proper customs forms are only required of commercial companies; and b) the company I was shipping with will generate a collective form for all its customers. Wrong. Thinking too much again.

Compiling an inventory calls for a personal classification theory. Is a cable a part of a charger if you've removed it from the charger? If you combine knickers, bras and socks into 'underwear', do you count socks per pair or per sock? Do I really have to list make-up brushes, cuticle removal sticks, nail files, etc. item type by item type? Of course it doesn't matter, but you need a consistent approach to be able to count at all. You need a simple approach too if inventorying the mundane turns you into a tangled ball of nerves.

I make good use of words like 'sets', 'accessories' and 'utensils'. Then I don't have ten cuticle removal sticks, nine hairbands (none in nine weeks' time), seven make-up brushes and four bottles of nail polish, but four sets of beauty accessories (hairbands, make-up brushes, nailcare). I don't quantify at the lower levels. One day I'll read the official customs documents. Or not. I've not had issues when transporting luggage across borders.

Learn from the diaspora

If you are sending luggage to a lower income country and if you care about the cost, find the webpages/ forums of its diaspora in your country and use its transportation services. It has cost me, for instance, between £15 and £34 to have my bike shipped this way as opposed to the 'normal' £115 - £200.

Fighting against posting and shipping restrictions is a losing game

Some companies do not take art or musical instruments, even if you are prepared to accept full responsibility for the risk. Cosmetics with no size restrictions is accepted towards some destinations, while no cosmetics at all is permitted towards others. There are rules for the packaging of certain item types, such as devices with batteries or liquids. Do read the instructions and restrictions of postal services, couriers, shipping companies, etc. Expect you won't notice something nonetheless.

I've been fuming, numerous times, because of 'stupid (new) rules'. I've tried to negotiate exceptions while accepting responsibility for damage. Overall, it's been a losing game. I now expect to be repacking non-compliant consignments and to be seeking alternatives for difficult items. Then I'm often ecstatic if it turns out simple and straightforward.

Storing luggage is a bad idea 95% of the time

There is a scene in *Eat Pray Love* (2010)[1] where Elizabeth, standing in front of a self-storage unit, exclaims that her whole life is held in there. The guy pottering around barks back that that's something he hears every day, then nobody comes back to collect said life.

I am still to hear of a positive experience of self-storage, other than as a long-term static life solution (namely, an extension of a small house where one stores business inventory or sports and adventure kit, all used regularly). A mostly positive experience was a one-month stint of my own, when I stored a suitcase in a space that could have accommodated forty (and paid accordingly).

---

1 Directed by Ryan Murphy, starring Julia Roberts, Javier Bardem, Richard Jenkins.

Earlier this year, I vacated a unit thirteen months after I'd booked it for 'a couple of months'. A pink woollen coat and my bike were the only possessions I would have regretted losing. I'd paid them several times over. I'm not an extreme case though. I know of people having items in self-storage for almost four years, and rising, in an inaction inertia manner.

Overall, what you'll pay for self-storage will far exceed the value of what you store. Alternatively, or also, you'll find it damp-damaged (the other default story I hear).

The business of self-storage is almost as perfect as that of insurance. The latter feeds on fears. The former on attachments. In a small number of cases, they serve you brilliantly. In most, you lose money, as regularly as it is unnoticeably.

I've stored luggage at friends' houses, of course, sometimes for years, even if the intention has always been for two-three months. On picking it up, I've had the same experience as with paid storage: I am willing to let go of 95% of what I've held onto.

I'll do my best not to store luggage ever again.

And I'll keep wearing my pink woollen coat.

So when you are ready:
neat
messy
BIG
SMALL
suitcases, boxes, rucksacks, all
weigh them.

Excess baggage can cost a fortune.

Though at the Airport of the Soul
you can keep it all.
The only price you pay
is indefinite Life delay.

CHAPTER 22

WHAT MAKES A TRUE HOME

When you leave the home you are now leaving:
looked around it one last time,
lingering in some of its clean empty rooms (or not),
saying thank you to them (or not),
delaying your final step over the threshold or speeding it up—
it has to happen, make it fast;
when you've locked its front door,
passed on the key,
would you say you've lost a true home?

No?
What wasn't enough to make it true?

Yes?
If you could lose it, how do you want me to believe it was true?
The Truest of True Things cannot be lost. They may appear to
break—regularly even—struck down, blown away, demolished,

sharp-edged pieces of the sublime glistening against the sun in the collapse. But then—nothing happens. They don't scatter shards to lie prostrate, cut wrists with, lose their edge to the sea water. They vanish. They wait.

Until one day they shoot out, bamboo saplings of a True Truth. You can't break them. You can't uproot them. You can't slow them down. And if you don't make space, if you don't climb on their stems to be lifted up as they progress, they'll grow-rip through you.

SEVEN FOUNDATIONS

If I look back at what I've written (and unique as it is in its details and entirety, any thought I've thought is first and foremost a social accomplishment, so I must have thought some normal social thoughts, including yours), we think of a true home in clusters of ideas shooting out of seven foundations:

1. The feelings, emotions and experiences
a perfect home evokes and nurtures

Home is a space, a relationship, an activity, a moment, words spoken, a dream even....where you feel:

safe, protected, nourished, warm—
   both physically and emotionally;
LOVED and accepted—no matter how difficult, different,
   noisy, messed up, silly, frightened, weak, hurt,
   disappointing, enviably brilliant...you are;
supported, encouraged, prided on—in your achievements
   and (failed brave) experiments; in your dealings
   with the spillage of dark emotions and subpersonalities;
true, authentic, naked—nothing to hide, nothing to defend,
   nothing to protect;

sovereign, powerful, free—a castle's king or queen;
replenished and restored;
eyes-closed certain, trusting, knowing;
stable, grounded, peaceful, solid....

While those and similar feelings are, ideally, intensely and unfailingly present at the address we put in home address boxes, they are in no way its prerogative. If anything, key aspects of 'home' as an emotional experience are found, for many of us, more strongly, even at all, away from the primary place where we rest our heads at night.

2. Special relationships
We find home in the arms of a great man/woman; where the heart is; amongst those we love, whether or not we have the chance to share our physical spaces with them.

3. Particular possessions and their qualities
We touch home via a golden spoon from the family set; a bottle of face wash (even the smell will do); our softest bedsheets; our books. Home is in the magical possessions which hide a home genie or can flying-carpet us to its lands.

4. Physical-social spaces
These are spaces where we can't rest our heads at night or put slippers on, but which evoke emotions of the home-like kind. For me, it's every nice café where they make good coffee; by the sea; on the South West Coast Path; in some old libraries....For you, it may be the pub, the mountains, open road, temple, gym, stadium, the highest hill above the seven-hill city....

5. What is uniquely, essentially ours,
the beginning and end of us

This is the home within, in our body, heart and soul. It's the home most of us begin to search for frantically in the middle or following a crisis; where we discover nooks and crannies of strength, love and shelter we could never have imagined existed; and which we, typically, forget about when outside life is good again.

6. What is 'always there'
(or nowhere to be seen, or on the brink of extinction)

This is our home "in the world and with its people", our home in God, the Universe, humanity, nature, planet Earth, whatever represents for you the miracle of life, meaning, beauty, certainty, mystery....

Sadly, until we've found our personal and unshakeable way of feeling and trusting the eternal, the oneness, that which is bigger than ourselves, this is either a very precarious, unreliable home or a Big Nothing, one of the most irritating, disappointing and deluded human ideas ever.

And, of course, we think of a true home in terms of:

7. Exceptional physical spaces

They hold, protect, reflect, enhance and, ultimately, co-create all of the above.

Does the variety of (sort-of-)definitions and referents make 'home' a complex and elusive concept? Perhaps. I would rather say it is one of those concepts we can never define in a way that does it justice yet we recognise unmistakeably what it stands for. We can feel a home in the first few seconds of entering it.

Importantly, we don't lose our ability to recognise a true home even if we've only inhabited surrogates or lost our one sweet home decades, as if lifetimes, ago. The blueprint of a true home cannot be destroyed. It's knowledge that cannot be obliterated by the pain and suffering brought about by metred love, rejection, abuse, fear, loss; by getting used to mould, cold, dirty mattresses or concrete floors; by thousand-mile walking, all our former life hanging in a rucksack from our shoulders. Such experiences may damage severely our capacity to create, expand, keep or trust in the reality of a home, but not our capacity to recognise it immediately.

This indelible, yet often suppressed, knowledge is also why we feel so unsettled when we are making apparently sensible, normal, even decisively positive choices around settling down which, however, don't align with the wholeness of our idea of Home. (By 'wholeness' I mean that which emerges from the seven foundations above; or more, if I've missed something. If only some of the seven resonate with you, it is usually because, with time, many of us try to strike a deal with Mean Life: "Life, give me what's most precious to me and I'll give up on asking for anything else! I'll even forget I've ever wanted it.")

The original of your vision of a Home — a vision which is always uniquely personal — is immodestly magnificent. Because, let's not skirt around it any longer, if we go into those deeper, more symbolic meanings of a home, there, where we want more than a roof above our heads and an address for our bank, local electoral commission or country authorities, our idea of a True Home overlaps with our idea of the Good Life.

Most of us will prune this vision beyond recognition. Often, it is because we want to be home as soon as possible—relative to an unforgiving inner timeline, which is our personal translation of the socially sanctioned life landmarks, and a shapeless anxiety from what is there in the void. We must have a stable home as soon as we leave our parents' home, or even as a way of leaving our parents' home; before we turn thirty; not long after our friends; as quick as possible after we've divorced; right after we've raised enough for a decent deposit.

And so we seek, more or less frantically, an intersection between relationships, spaces and expressions of our identity and service to the world (each of them with their financial dimensions), which generate *enough* of the emotions of a good home—safety, love, authenticity, replenishment, empowerment, comfort, intuitiveness, peace....We either pick one such intersection at about the right time and nail it, both the home and broader social success, or we keep floating. If we keep floating, we are, usually, either feeling on the path to our True Home and enchanted life, ecstatic of what awaits, proud we haven't sold out to false safety and comforts, or complete failures. It often depends in what weather, after how many hours of sleep, or in what state of our skin you ask us.

The problem with the former choice (of nailing your home when it's time to do so) is that most people let a temporary intersection of the foundations cut short the foundations rather than make space for each individual foundation to grow and shift the point of the intersection. Said less metaphorically, too many of us will make significant compromises with what they've dreamt of in terms of their love/ family life; their job (which was once supposed to be an expression of Self, service to the world, soul work, etc. AND a source of financial abundance); their beautiful house; and their prevailing emotional environment so that they fit together around the time they were supposed to fit together. The interdependencies then become so strong that any attempt to wriggle out of one compromise means that the whole structure (of our life) falls apart.

Too many of us will entangle loves and houses and decorate the love to secure the houses. We will resign ourselves to jobs that do not sing the songs of our soul while building the nest to sing from without a voice. We will choose to travel less, study less, delight in our senses less, venture less, help others less and many other 'lesses' so as to own a home.

And in that beautiful home we are allowed to call 'ours',
we will live
a shadow life
of a shadow self
with shadow significant others.

Yet a True Home to belong to us and we to it, to stand the tests of time and adversity, to be rebuilt from its ashes if burnt, can only be built if we respect all of the above foundations and all of them in their ultimate brilliance – of the pure, be it humanly imperfect, expression of home-like emotions; of deep, soulful relationships and connection; of showing up for the truth of our soul; of belonging to that which is bigger than us; of as-in-my-dreams physical spaces; of possessions infused with magic.

This takes learning, trial and error.

What is more, the more we've dreamt of as young souls, the lower the baseline of our childhood, and the more volatile the times we live in, the more lives we'll be building and destroying, moving in and out of homes and starting again.

FOUR WALLS

So what can we do to make creating our True Home easier, possible even?! My suggestions are four (and you need all four).

1. Ask for it all and follow
the path wherever it takes you

You create the homes—of love and safety, of rooms and bedsheets— you decide to create. The past doesn't matter. The trade-offs of others don't matter. The normal ways don't matter.

There is no limit to the magnificence of what makes your home a home, whether that's your love or dining room curtains.

There is no price to pay for the brilliance of your physical home through the squalor of your relationships or vice versa.

There is no need to live in a cave to reach the depths of being at home with yourself, others, in our world, God or the universe.

Unless you choose to.

And while you can choose differently right now, as simple as that, it's often the case that to choose from your grandeur rather than your smallness, from your true desires rather than self-defeating beliefs, you may need to exorcise a crew of old ghosts first. Here's why and how.

2. Identify the pattern from your personal history
which can be blocking you from asking for more

Most of us are hostages to our childhood in terms of the homes we create. We improve the lives we knew only a few notches up, orbiting in a familiar parameter, whether we live 10 or 10,000 kilometres away from our childhood home.

Imagine the opportunities of life—let's say, around vibrancy of Self; creativity and service to the world; love and relationships;

material abundance – as laid out on a coordinate system. As adults, we locate ourselves at points which are almost identical to the ones we knew from childhood. We believe we've moved far away, so much higher than our parents, yet it's largely the coordinate system of our times that's moved. Alternatively, we've moved to a place with higher baseline values. Our relative location is typically intact.

More subversively, we are controlled by our childhood homes even when we live in a way that's polar opposite to what was back then. 'Polar opposite', as we discussed more than once over the preceding pages, tends to be psychologically equivalent to 'the same'. It is an extreme reaction cut, sewn and thrown upon us by our past rather than a genuine choice.

One of the greatest sources of self-sabotage around the homes we'll create as adults is what we believe about the relationship between a physical and an emotional home – about how they determine, arise from or put boundaries to one another. If you've read *Chapter 13* (on bedsheets and dangerous associations), you may remember that it argued against a necessary relationship between the two, even if it's easy to think that they come in pre-specified combinations, more or less available to us.

The reasons why it's easy to see a necessary relationship between a physical and an emotional home are many, but it certainly helps that we are sold homes and possessions for those homes through images of beautiful relationships and inner bliss. Yet the physical and emotional aspects of a home (or, if they've spoken to you, the seven foundations of a True Home I suggested above) are, ultimately, each for itself. We need to ask for, desire, choose, commit to each and every one of them so as to bring all of them into our life. They are not in a bundle by design, with the bundle revolving around a brick-and-mortar home, although some may co-occur, as if naturally, in our lives. It's not that natural. And it's you who needs to ask for the whole bundle.

To complicate matters further, most of us live the consequences of a childhood where either our physical or our emotional home, or both, were a compromise, at least for a period in our lives. This feeds into a (semi-)unconscious lack of faith that we can have it all. Our mixed or negative childhood pattern will then either overpower or enter a tug of war with the socially supported ideal. The result is that most of us are running various, often contradictory, scripts which undermine our ability to create a True Home. We need to unravel those scripts and exorcise many a Ghosts of Homes Past if we are to create our True Homes. See if you'll find your ghosts in *Box 13.*

No matter where we are and where we've been, there is no law, no curse to repeat the fortunes of the homes we grew up in. Yes, we are compelled by familiarity and habit. Yes, we fail to imagine alternatives and grasp how we can un-choose anything that doesn't feel like home. Yes, we mistrust opportunity even when we have its messenger bird perched on our shoulder. Yes again, if we refuse to be victims of the above, we may be challenged into an epic battle for Home and for Freedom.

The comic, tragic or tragicomic thing is that we don't need a battle. We can just step out. 99% of the time, we'll find the door unlocked. We'll also find that the guards trying to stop us have no real power over us and no weapons other than words of doubt and fear. They are not even real guards but, rather, other prisoners of a small past and lack of imagination. The latter is especially hard to accept if (and it will happen often) those are people whom we love dearly or whom we've always trusted to know better because there are some things *they know better.*

BOX 13

GHOSTS OF HOMES PAST

*P stands for **'physical home'**–the house, flat or any other space we live in, its possessions and its surroundings.*

*E stands for **'emotional home'**–the emotional, psychological, social, soulful, spiritual, etc. home we inhabit and which also inhabits us, as our inner landscape.*

When we were kids, our emotional home was created by the prevalent emotions, beliefs and experiences within the home space. These were determined most strongly by the personalities of, relationships between, and events in the lives of our parents, as well as the ways in which they 'filtered in' the external environment. An emotional home is also independently affected by features of our physical home. The emotional home of our childhood determines much, for many of us most, of our inner emotional environment throughout the years.

As we grow up, we increase our capacity to have and nurture an inner emotional home that is separate from the emotional environment of our physical home. The stronger our inner emotional home is and the healthier its boundaries, the easier it is for us to feel at home anywhere, whatever comes our way.

+ or–represents anything above or below average, respectively.

~ stands for the quintessential average.

You are likely to belong to more than one type if, when you were a kid, the fortunes of your home were dynamic or contextually relative (for instance, abundance looks very differently in the context of a poor and a rich country). Also, if your childhood experiences place you in one of the mixed (+/-) categories but you made a conscious, determined effort to create as good a home as you can, you may be up against the

*risks of the 'lucky ones' (Type 1), even if you were anything
but lucky.*

*Remember that those are all potential risks, not a fate or a
sentence. Sometimes as little as basic awareness of them can
immunise you against their powers.*

Type 1: P+ E+ Lucky but unprepared (or determined but unwise)

If you've grown up at the positive ends of the spectrum,
both in terms of your physical and emotional home, you are
often seen as one of 'the lucky ones'. And you are! The down-
side is that you are particularly unprepared for a long and
bumpy road Home, if you find yourself on one. People whose
childhood home was far less enviable but who committed
to do all that's necessary to create a dream home may face
similar challenges:

- **Expecting natural progression, P+ to E+**

  You may create (buy, do up, furnish) a beautiful home
  and expect the love, relationships and home-like feel-
  ings to follow as a matter of course. Then they don't.
  Years pass of you searching or patiently waiting for
  them, opening the space, time and your heart, and they
  still fail to enter. Gradually, your lovely house may begin
  to feel like a golden cage or an empty shell. It wasn't sup-
  posed to be for you alone. You weren't supposed to be
  living such a flat life either.

- **Expecting natural progression, E+ to P+**

  You commit to a beautiful relationship and a vocation
  that feel like home, expecting to work out the (almost)
  ideal physical home as you go along. And when it

doesn't, and doesn't, and doesn't work out, and buying, or even renting, something much more home-like is so so so difficult and requires so much sacrifice, the struggles unsettle the relationship of your heart and/or the quests of your soul.

- **Building from weak foundations, or the 'prefab home'**

  As a young adult, you may try to mirror what you've seen in your childhood as soon as possible. Unwittingly, you may follow appearances that do not represent the depth of what your parents had created or models that simply don't fit you. When the novelty wears off or Life black-eyes you with some of its unavoidable uppercuts, the flimsy configuration of your primary relationship, job, home space, lifestyle, etc. begins to unravel. Your home is now a small boat in a rough hostile sea.

- **Taking the love for granted**

  You trust deeply in the home of your heart—you've found your One for this life and perhaps have a lovely growing family too. You turn most of your attention towards what doesn't stand so strong, such as the needs of the brick-and-mortar house or your service to the world. Then, one day, as if out of nowhere but with the erosion of love lasting for years, you find you've lost the home where the heart is.

- **Perfect home with a shadow You**

  The love, warmth and abundance in your household and the lifestyle you've created feel so sweet and beautiful, even heart-breakingly so at times (life's normal irritations and imperfections wisely accepted!) that you fail to notice it's at the growing expense of your soul's home.

Your personal passions, dreams, creativity and quests have slowly been checking out. Then, one day, you look around and see an amazing home, a love-filled household and hardly anything of what was once You.

- **Forgetting the Grace**

  You may have long been graced with a lovely home and also worked hard to create it, so much so that you forget that nothing's been promised to you for eternity, that nothing humanly created can withstand all life's turbulences. Then, if your home is struck by a heavy blow – a serious illness, natural disaster, untimely death – you find it impossible to cross over to the other side. Life is never meaningful, beautiful and happy enough again.

  Alternatively, you may be acutely aware how lucky you are and to be turning increasingly, pathologically protective of your home, family and lifestyle. Yet no walls, alarm systems, insurances or precautions will keep you safe against all of life's eventualities. Unless you find your transcendental Home of feeling safe, cared for and supported, trusting you can rebuild it all from rubble and ashes if need be, you will never be fully Home.

Type 2: P+ E- Shell without a pearl

If you'd spent your childhood in an aesthetically pleasing, abundant home yet in a negative, impoverished emotional environment, as an adult you may:

- Replicate the **appearance-substance mismatch**. People may be looking at you and seeing a good, solid – quite lovely really! – domestic life. It may even be one of an enviably high-flying lifestyle. You too may be telling yourself the same, ticking along through daily life in an 'all fine' inner fog and perfect outward adaptation. The trouble is that sometimes the fog lifts. You face the abyss. Foggily fine or confronted by the abyss, you are frozen. You don't know what to do, maybe because you've already tried so many little adjustments or even tried to be brave, once or twice, and failed. And so you do nothing. You stay in your pretty and safe home, making it even prettier and safer and yourself even better adapted, patching wall and soul cracks rather than questioning the foundations you are living from.

- You **dream of so much more**, of what feels like love, truth, depth, living. You dream of it daily, nightly, every hour, sometimes every minute, but you don't dare lose the safety, security, normalcy, stability, beauty, comforts of your home and current life. I want to, I must, it's finally time BUT how?! If all goes horribly wrong, how do I return to peace and safety? Even when you decide, even when you've packed your bags, safe home gravity will pull you back.

- Alternatively, you may choose to escape the beautiful places, home comforts and stylish objects you once knew. You create an **overly simple life**, as if the failures of love, warmth, connection, truthfulness...were the fault of spaces and objects, not of humans who used them as shields against emotions and as flags to prove success.

Type 3. P- E+ The rich in love

If you've lived simply, maybe even poorly as a kid, but in a household of immense love and warmth, you may be controlled by your past if you:

- Glorify the overly simple, basic life. You uphold the logic of **'poor but happy'**, as if the latter is a necessary consequence of the former rather than a chance combination amongst several.

- You fail to appreciate, dismiss or even attack the nourishing potential of extraordinary spaces and the creativity, love and spirit that may infuse objects.

- You make decisions out of the (unconscious) fear that if you choose to live in a much more amazing place than what you are used to, you'll be **made to pay with the love, safety, human warmth and connection** that mean everything to you.

- You inhabit mediocre physical spaces which don't reflect your dreams, current means or inner home, because anything better feels foreign, unfitting and **about to be snapped away** the moment you become used to it.

Type 4: P- E- The short straw
(yet potential for greatest achievement)

If, in your childhood, you had a short straw drawn for you, in creating your home as an adult you may:

- Have no vision of what a good home feels like, let alone a True Home, and undervalue its potential goodness. Somewhere in the mix you also mistrust your ability to play your part in creating it. **Not knowing what to look for and not believing you can create it,** you persistently end up in both uninspiring places and negative emotional environments.

- You long for a home with the whole of your heart but put it **on a pedestal**, which stops you from taking the meaningful steps to creating it.

- You make **rash decisions** towards anything that helps you stay away from the negative physical and emotional environments you've escaped (and fear you may find yourself back in) but, in so doing, you **fall for appearances** without substance. After a while, you are either back at ground zero or resigned to a mediocrity which is way below the glory of your inner home.

- You improve dramatically on one of the dimensions (physical/ emotional home) but **never on both**. Some can have it all. Not you.

- You have your demons resurfacing and sabotaging you whenever a good home, which feels **too good to be true**, becomes a realistic possibility.

Type 5: P~ E~ The quintessential mediocrity

- If the home you grew up in was lack-lustre average, never too bad to cry to the skies for change or never too good to imprint the standards of the Good, you run the risk of replicating its total mediocrity. Please, run. Even if it's into trouble for a start.

I used to hate the phrase "Go and sin no more". Jesus should have known it's FAR MORE COMPLEX! It can be. But it can also be as simple as that. You choose to leave the past behind and you don't look back, even if walking the distance that will distance you from it may take time.

You commit to the ALL of your True Home and turn into a bird building its nest. A straw and a mud clump at a time, from whatever's around.

3. Start from whatever is available

I won't argue: the archetypal way to feel at home is to have a safe and beautiful place you (and the law) can call your own; in surroundings that lift your spirit; shared with people you love with the whole of your heart (or with nobody at all, sometimes 'blissful solitude' is called for); *clickety-click* clicking in with your needs, tastes and daily routines; furnished, decorated and fitted, if you wish even cluttered, with things that bring you joy.

But such a place is just that, one pathway out of many towards a rich, multi-layered, composite and, in its sublimeness, rare experience. And this pathway is neither a royal road, nor as certain and as direct as we are encouraged to believe.

Sometimes it's blocked.

Then you can wait. You can weep. Cover yourself in self-pity oil and massage it gently, firmly; have others help. Work harder. Strike a deal, compromise after compromise with your life so that you approximate the picture above as close as possible. Moving in with your ex is a good start. Set up your savings goals for a deposit. Accumulate an interest of £1.63 per month. Cut out your daily barista-made coffee (f*** off; where I live, this will come to a meaningful deposit after 150 years, and then you'll want me to cut

it out for the mortgage too!). Start a social movement? You have
every right. The inequality and unfairness around housing and
home ownership are outrageous.

Or you can start from what's around.

The feeling of home can come in 10,000 ways.

The spaces and objects to wake up that feeling can
come in 10,000 ways.

So can the love of people.

If one way of feeling at home is in ruins,

the others stand,

take strength from what stands.

If all are in ruins,

start building, from whatever's easiest.

You can feel more at home in the next three minutes. Incompar-
ably more in a week's time. You can have a new life, as far as home
goes, in a month.

There is only one thing to do: REFOCUS on what is available
and accessible AND FEELS LIKE HOME as opposed to what's missing.
Then take the path—of acting, feeling, planning, whatever's shown.

There are two warnings and one rule.

The first warning is that it can be exceptionally easy and
exceptionally difficult to refocus.

It's easy because there are so many feelings that are part of
the home feeling, which can be called forth in many ways if you
decide to.

It's easy because even if you can't buy the dream bed of your
dream home this year (not to mention the home itself and add
salt to the wound with a timeline), you can buy the bedsheets to
belong to it. Or at least a mug for the bedside table. The direction

is not all for your home after you have a home. It's one by one for your home so that you have a home on the way Home.

It's difficult because so many of us have surrendered control of our attention to pings, notifications and our favourite chronophages. You can't refocus your attention reliably if you've lost meaningful control of it.

It is difficult if you've squashed and socialised your feelings so thoroughly that you no longer know what you feel, including whether something feels like home or not. But then it's good practice. Plus, something in you, usually in your body, always knows even if your mind can't make itself up.

The second warning is not to fall into the trap of 'gratitude porn'[1] and 'life wisdom'[2] by accepting what is available and accessible—part of your current home—without *feeling like home.* You won't be able to replace or leave behind immediately many of the things you've acknowledged as 'not home'. But you can—and need to—start searching, scanning, planning for their home-like versions.

Finally, the one rule is that each element of a home is free. It stands by itself and is free to come home with you or not.

No element, whether it's a feeling, a bed, a soap dish or a person, which, for you, contributes to the feeling of home, can be made obligatory. It cannot be made conditional on having any other element either. Nothing hangs entirely on anything else. To think in the form "*if* only this person or only this thing, *then*

---

1 'Gratitude porn' is again something I borrow from James Altucher. See, for instance: Altucher, J. "The sick truth about gratitude porn". *jamesaltucher.com/blog/gratitude-porn/* Undated. Last accessed Aug 2022.

2 'Life wisdom' (in quotation marks) is something I use for those claims made with the gravitas of "Something important and certain I've learnt about life and about not expecting too much of it" which sound very wise but have an undercurrent of sadness and defeat rather than lightness and liberation, which are marks of true wisdom.

and only then this feeling" is a cosmic fallacy.

Any home-part can come through some other source or in some other combination than the one you wanted it to come from. Remember this when you feel like squeezing things in spaces or squeezing love out of people.

Some other source, some other way doesn't mean less. Less, equal or more is entirely up to you. My personal rule (or, rather, a reflex which emerged out of chaos) is to always find something better than what I couldn't have or create the conditions to have it. There are countless unusual, free-floating ways through which things, emotions, people can come your way, as long as you stop stomping your feet about them coming the 'normal way', the 'fabric softener ad way', 'your way' or NOW.

You don't need bedsheets of four hundred threads of cotton and percale weave or a memory foam mattress to fall asleep in deep peace. Oftentimes, you only need night to follow the day when you've been the person you've always wanted to be. How about trying that. It costs only your fears and excuses.

You don't need to have the person you love love you back, let alone live with you, to have a home overflowing with love. If your love deserves its name, it can also just BE, disconnected from the presence or absence, actions or inactions, willingness to commit or float free, love or is-this-love of another. It will fill up not only your heart, room and house, but at least a dozen other unlikely containers, pinching noses, ruffling hairs and awakening whoever meets your loving eyes today.

You don't need a four-wing mahogany and mirrors wardrobe to feel better in your bedroom. By all means, consult *Elle Home* to discover what you really want and then ask for it for Christmas, but if you don't get it, you may work for bedroom improvements in the gym, for instance. I guarantee your bedroom (experiences) will feel of a different dimension.

You don't need to own a palace to feel like a king or a queen. Don't make me give you boring suggestions of where in Europe (or Disneyland) you can find them. Or tell you again how I once responded to a most normal looking ad and ended up living in an eighteen-room manor house, with a seventeenth-century door, with a nineteen-year-old housemate, and couldn't decide whether I loved the most the drawing room with the piano, the yoga studio under the crossed beams of the loft, or the dining room with original Dutch tiles. It sounds more bitch-like than queen-like. Let alone that a true queen is one with or without a palace.

You don't need to own a home to feel at home. There is something more independent, lighter, quieter, warmer, cleaner, fresher, more home-like at any price range at which you are renting. Yes, you may need to walk more, cycle more, move more, but sometimes you only need to move your decision-support muscles more (brain, fingers, eyes, ass).

Ultimately, you don't even have to be at home to feel the feelings of a home—safety, love, acceptance, authenticity, peace, slow time....There are many circumstances in life when you must walk out of what's supposedly home and go elsewhere to feel such feelings at their best, or at all.

Call up the feelings of a Home.
No matter how, no matter where:
in a book, in a movie, in a café, on the Coast Path;
on your mission to save the planet and its people, its wild life;
through baking gingerbread men,
    writing a love letter,

ironing your nightdress,
fighting a lightsabre battle with your unborn son,
staying in a hug for a ten-second longer eternity;
through replaying a memory, assembling a vision;
through connecting with your soul–the beginning and end of all.

Let the feelings infiltrate you, let them
stay, put up their tents, grow roots and beards in your heart.
And when they do,
they will guide you to the
Spaces
Objects
People
that you need to bring home –
or walk away from.

4. Regularly step out to see the Whole

The trick in choosing your physical home (and how much you pay
for it) is having it enhance, rather than compromise, your broader
life, expression of truest self, relationships, your long-held dreams
and wicked new plans, your optimal emotional environment....
The right physical home grows out of, through and relative to
these, not at their cost.

Sometimes we open the space to become more of ourselves
and bring dreams to life when we move, temporarily, to the
smallest and simplest of places. At other times, the best thing we
can do for ourselves is to let a physical place–the space, beauty,
luxury, views and peace of a magnificent house in a magnificent
environment–infuse and restructure our inner landscape, even if
it means taking a financial leap we'll have to learn to repeat.

Whatever you've chosen for the home
you are moving to, step out of it, often.
Walk away, far away.
Turn back.
Look straight.
Is this the Life you came here to create?

I'll miss you when you've moved.
But I'll know
you are going Home.

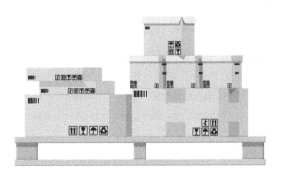

ACKNOWLEDGEMENTS

My first thank you is to the houses, flats, rooms, spaces which have been my home throughout the years and to the landlords and landladies who have welcomed me there.

My biggest thank you for the contents and nature of this book is to the man I'll here call Arthur. I would never have asked myself the question of "what makes a true home" as often as I did if it weren't for you. Thank you for teaching me so much about the material groundedness of a home. I might have never descended from the clouds without you, and I love being solidly grounded in addition to floating amongst clouds! I wish I was able to show you "the whole of the Moon"–the whole of a Home–where you only "saw the crescent". I wish we were able to create a home together but I've probably built a home I'll never lose because we didn't.

My parents and my brother–Krastina Manolova, Petar Petrov and Borislav Petrov–are 'responsible' for most of the high expectations I have around what a home feels like. I am infinitely grateful for having this reference point. Less gloriously, my parents have shown me how a home can fall apart and stand as an empty, dangerous, anything-but-a-home shell, but that too is an experience I would not want taken away. It forced me to seek my True Home with an urgency and relentlessness I wouldn't have had otherwise. My mum is also the person who has supported me the most in writing this book with her enthusiasm, faith in me, and pragmatic interventions. She's given me both a roof above my head and funding injections at times when I'd reduced my working hours to have more time to write. If there is a regret I have about the book, it's that my mum won't be able to read it in the original.

My cousin Konstantina Stoyanova-Poix was the person who, perhaps as long as a decade ago, said that one day I'd write a book about house moving. I was certain it would never happen. It wasn't until hundreds of pages had been written and re-re-re-written that I remembered her words. Both she and Yolina Stoyanova-Brunner, the other cousin I've grown up with, continue to be part of my sense of certainty that I'll always have a home to return to, no matter what.

Apart from my family, numerous friends and colleagues have supported and encouraged me in the process of writing. Sometimes a word or two of what they've said have given me the confidence that my work is truly needed and meaningful. These are, in no particular order, Iliyana Hristova, Dennitza Ivanova, Georgi Iliev, Gloria Ayob-Sibson, Michael Carhart, Daniele Carrieri, Katya Ilcheva, Ani Vassileva, Ani Kircheva, Tanya Marincheva, Sarah Hoare, Pia Thiemann, Lauren Milden, Sarah Hopkins, Rachel Coghlan, Sara Bosley, Sandra Whitlock, Victoria Dinh, Emma Linford, Hristina Kuseva, Petko Kusev, Ruth Abrams.... Maya Manolova, Merike van der Vijver and Konstantin Manolov (Gandhi) also guided me down the road of deciding how I want this book to look apart from how I want it to read. I'm sorry for forgetting the encouraging words of many others I should have thanked!

I also want to thank my boss at Cambridge, Professor Stephen Barclay, who accommodated several requests for flexible and long-distance working, to enable my writing, before it had become the COVID norm. He also often made me laugh by asking about the progress of my bestselling porn book. Perhaps one day!

James Altucher and Katrina Ruth are the from-a-distance, I-hang-on-your-every-word (well, almost!) mentors to whom I owe so much of the courage to write a book and the ways in which I've gone about it.

The writing and publishing advice James has crystallised and which his work also embodies, as well as his encouragement of and guidance for people who write, have made the difference between me not writing and not publishing this book and writing and publishing it. He's also taught me that if you are not scared to publish something, it's probably not worth publishing.

Kat has been a regular reminder not to stand in the way of 'the message' which wants to come out, no matter the ways in which you may see it as wrong, weird, unpolished, repetitive, uncool, whatever. She's also kept me company in showing up for my work day after day after day after day, when the world is too good at dishing out encouragement to 'take a break'.

I've never met either James or Kat, never spoken to them directly and can't be certain whether they'll like what I've written, but I'm 100% confident they'll be thrilled that I've 'chosen myself' (James) and 'pressed play' (Kat) in the ways they've been teaching me/us. Not only this book, but my life wouldn't have been the same without them.

I cannot but thank from the depth of my heart (or the tips of my taste buds) the cafés where I've written and edited numerous paragraphs, and, of course, the staff who make those cafés and their coffee what they are. There are many a dozen I've sat writing and editing in, but the ones I've felt were also a home-away-from-home are: Hot Numbers (both the Gwydir Street and Trumpington Street ones) and the Espresso Library in Cambridge, Bula and Woodroast in Dartmouth, Society Café in Bath, 108 in Truro, and Costa in Varna.

Much to my surprise, I want to thank John Osborn, Hannah Brigham, Lisa Schwartz, Victoria Smyth and Chris Clayton-Jones for transforming my deep resistance to shared houses during the last year and a half of working on the book (my surprise is at the reason I want to thank them, not them deserving to be thanked for many reasons!). I'll still insist that my time for house sharing has come to an end, but if I need to do it again, I'll be confident that a shared house can be a home, and one of the best at that.

I am indebted to my editors—Ameesha Smith-Green and Jessica Powers. Ameesha was instrumental in taming 'the muchness' of the first complete manuscript, reducing redundancies and improving clarity. Even if I disagreed with half of her suggestions when I first saw them, I ultimately incorporated about 95% of them. With the distance of time and borrowing her sharp editor's vision, I saw she was right. Jessica not only polished rough edges and banished away inconsistencies, but also connected me with people on her—now also my—book design team. She also generously advised on details and practicalities of the publishing process I was ignorant of. Both Ameesha and Jessica gave me confidence that there was a book there, and that it had a heart.

Karen Vermeulen, who drew a cover design people were

consistently drawn to, even when I was asking them to look at something else, and Kathy McInnis, who did the interiors of the book, not only made me appreciate how much the visuals of a book create a book, but have been most patient with all the tweaks I've been requesting. Thank you for the beauty, its subtlety and for the many subliminal details. Thank you for making the book 'sing' rather than only read.

Karen Hamilton, who proofread the final version, caught some bloody irritating errors and typos, which might have made me run a second edition days after the first has been published! I dread to think that I hesitated whether to ask for a final proofreading and I'm most grateful it was hers.

Last but not least, thank you to my muses, who reliably showed up whenever I'd cleared the space for them by sitting down writing and first writing a lot of rubbish, and to my imaginary readers, some of whom I hope will become real readers too. If I didn't trust that you who would need and love this book, no matter how crazy and uncomfortable it is, are out there, I would not have written it. And since writing about home has been part of my journey of finding Home, I thank you most sincerely and humbly for the latter. I hope I am returning the favour.

LIST OF BOXES

DISCLAIMER

This book is partly a memoir. As such, it shares stories which involve other people. I've dug for the truth repeatedly and, typically, it has not been a self-serving truth (other than in the sense that, in the final analysis, truth always serves us better than any other representation of reality). I've also done my best to protect identities, other than those of my immediate family. It felt impossible to talk of them as of 'somebody I know'.

If I've hurt, offended or disturbed anyone, I am deeply sorry. Even the most unflattering paragraphs I've written are anchored in compassion and understanding. I also believe firmly that every story can be told from multiple perspectives and that nobody has monopoly over the truth, yet we all have a right to express ours, preferably kindly. This includes you who disagree with my side of stories and versions of truth. Finally, if I've not attributed an experience, behaviour, feature, etc. to a particular person, no matter how loosely (e.g. an aunt, a friend), I've created an abstraction. I may have had a seed of an idea because of observing a particular person, but I've never described them alone.

This book is also partly a manual of tools, suggestions and recommendations. I don't give advice and I don't make promises. Neither I, nor any person or company who've enabled me to share this book with you, accept any responsibility for how you decide to deal with your physical or psychological chaos and for the consequences of your actions. Personally, I want to, but it doesn't work. I've tried and failed too many times. Your chaos is your responsibility. Remember though that wherever there is chaos, there is creation; wherever there is responsibility, there is power. I hope you'll own yours.

For supplementary material,
go to *milapetrova.com*

Free contents will include:

a calculator to help you estimate
the time you need to prepare your move;

the complete set of
28 eating personality types;

links to further organisations
and resources supporting sustainable
decluttering and recycling;

blogs to help you in sorting through
both physical and emotional baggage;

and more, *there is always
more* in a house move!

Lightning Source UK Ltd.
Milton Keynes UK
UKHW041048081222
413530UK00004B/86

9 781739 137755